HOW TO NAVIGATE LIFE

THE NEW SCIENCE OF FINDING YOUR WAY IN SCHOOL, CAREER, AND BEYOND

BELLE LIANG, PH.D.

TIMOTHY KLEIN, LCSW

ST. MARTIN'S PRESS

NEW YORK

First published in the United States by St. Martin's Press, an imprint of St. Martin's Publishing Group

www.stmartins.com

Design by Ralph Fowler

Library of Congress Cataloging-in-Publication Data

Names: Liang, Belle, author. | Klein, Timothy, author.
Title: How to Navigate Life: The New Science of Finding Your Way in
    School, Career, and Beyond / Belle Liang, Ph.D., Timothy Klein, LCSW.
Description: First edition. | New York: St. Martin's Press, [2022] |
    Includes bibliographical references and index.
Identifiers: LCCN 2022005287 | ISBN 9781250273147 (hardcover) |
    ISBN 9781250273154 (ebook)
Subjects: LCSH: Educational psychology. | High school students—Mental
    health. | College students—Mental health. | College student orientation. |
    Academic achievement. | School-to-work transition.
Classification: LCC LB1051 .L652 2022 | DDC 370.15—dc23/eng/20220217
LC record available at https://lccn.loc.gov/2022005287

Our books may be purchased in bulk for promotional, educational, or business use. Please contact your local bookseller or the Macmillan Corporate and Premium Sales Department at 1-800-221-7945, extension 5442, or by email at MacmillanSpecialMarkets@macmillan.com.

First Edition: 2022

10 9 8 7 6 5 4 3 2 1

To our parents, who trusted us to figure things out,
and to our kids, whom we trust to do the same

CONTENTS

HOW TO NAVIGATE LIFE

Introduction

This is a book about how to equip young people to navigate school, career, and life with joy and excellence. The first step to doing this job well as parents, educators, or life mentors is to *know ourselves*. We have to be students of ourselves—by learning who *we* are, where we came from, what we believe, and where these beliefs came from. How we raise and guide our people is deeply influenced by our own stories. If we're aware of the core values and scripts that were passed on to us from our families of origin, we can be compassionate toward ourselves—understanding our knee-jerk reactions to our students and their life choices. We can be intentional about what we choose to pass on to the next generation. This has been true for us, as you'll see from our stories.

Belle's story: I am the middle daughter of first-generation Chinese immigrants who, like their compatriots, sacrificed heroically so that my brothers and I could get an education in the United States. My father borrowed the little money his sister had to come to the United States to pursue his graduate degree on a student visa. This decision came with another, more significant cost: leaving behind his wife and six-week-old firstborn child, my brother. It was two years before they were reunited on American soil. My mother abandoned her career aspirations when she arrived in the United States, leaving her family and home to live in a country where she struggled to work, communicate, and feel a sense of belonging.

She pushed through language barriers to befriend neighbors so I would have neighborhood playdates. She clipped coupons so I could buy trendy clothes. All of this probably helped me fit in with the popular kids at my affluent suburban high school. My parents relished the thought that I was a teacher's pet, two-time homecoming princess, student leader in clubs, class government officer, and a graduation speaker at the John F. Kennedy Center. These "achievements" were shamelessly evoked at afternoon tea with the aunties, because they satisfied everyone's expectations for me. They were proud that I "fit in" so well.

All their dreams and efforts to make ends meet were fueled by hopes that my brothers and I could achieve more. They expected that we would. It was never a question of "whether I would go to college," it was a matter of where I went and what I did there to become "successful." I internalized the cultural value that the point of education was to achieve financial security and respect in society. Like other "first-gen" people, we bought into Horatio Alger's myth that if you worked hard, you could achieve the American dream, not only for yourself, but to validate your parents' sacrifices. All of this prepared me to be the most successful student I could be. A rule-following, risk-averse, people-pleasing success. I was the opposite of Cheryl Strayed in the wild, driven by a free spirit to conquer the dangers of the Pacific Crest Trail. My ambition was to take the safest path to financial security and prestige.

I had gleaned from my upbringing that there were certain careers that were especially acceptable. Doctor, lawyer, engineer. I later realized that these were actually the acceptable choices for boys, but that there were alternatives for girls.

Up to this point, whenever faced with a big decision about school, work, and life at large, I asked myself: "What *should* I do?" Often, the answer that felt right to me was the one that matched the expectations of those around me. After two years of bouncing around multiple majors in the hard sciences and internships in health fields, a well-meaning auntie offered me this career guidance: "Don't work so hard, you'll prematurely age and lose your beauty. Just take good care of your hair and skin (your best assets), marry a doctor, and you'll be fine."

Imagine how those words landed on an American college woman. Yep, just the nudge I needed to begin listening more closely to my own heart. And trusting the wisdom and direction that could be found there. The women in my life were smart and competent, while content to sit in the back seat. Few were trailblazers, civic leaders, public speakers. With the most honorable intentions, they sacrificed personal goals and derived their identities from others. I realized that the standard-bearers I had followed were no longer a perfect match with my own journey. My spiritual-faith adventure provided fresh insight and courage for rewriting the script, following my call.

When I announced to the family that I planned to pursue a career as a psychologist, it was as if I had announced that I was dropping out of college. Had I thought this through? Could I get a job doing such a thing? They saw a huge distinction between doctors who focused on people's mental health and those who treated their physical health. But they comforted themselves by thinking girls shouldn't work too hard and that I would be fine as long as I married a real doctor, who could take care of me.

My transformation continued during graduate school, where I met a mentor and role model who believed in me and nurtured my creativity and confidence. She introduced me to community psychology, a field focused on addressing systemic injustices and partnering with disadvantaged and marginalized people. I felt such a sense of mission . . . Here was a way that my values, strengths, and skills aligned with meaningful work that could make a difference in the world.

I need to say that as I write this, I am so genuinely grateful to my cultural roots, family, and mentors for watering the seeds of my purpose today. At the same time that there are cultural and moral virtues to my story that I deeply cherish (like respect for your elders and sacrifice for others), there are imperfections. And all of it inspires my current work. I see that while the world is progressing, stories like mine reflect an ongoing ethos that reaches beyond the immigrant experience. In hundreds of our research interviews and surveys, adolescents (and their parents) lamented: "I'm living someone else's life. I don't know who I really am and what I'm really living for, apart from others' expectations of me." Similarly, I'd been basing my identity on what others told me about myself when I was a child. Trying to mold myself into someone's stereotype of me left me exhausted and confused. But as my understanding of who I am came into sharper focus during my later college and adult years, this understanding became my guide. It continues to shape what I value and believe, and how I feel, act, and connect. Brené Brown calls this embracing of who you really are *true belonging:*

> *True belonging is the spiritual practice of believing in and belonging to yourself so deeply that you can share your most authentic self with the world and find sacredness in both being a part of something and standing alone in the wilderness. True belonging doesn't require you to change who you are; it requires you to be who you are.*

She goes on to say: "True belonging is not something that you need to negotiate externally, it's what you carry in your heart."* This internal belonging, this sense of understanding who I was—what I stood for, what I had to offer in the world—began to free me from the need for external approval. It's been a glorious adventure to discover my innermost being, and to realize that what I've turned up there can meet a great need in the world.

Tim's story: I am the son of two Jewish/Anglo-Saxon parents who grew up in New York City. They were the quintessential hippies. Both were the youngest of three children, and both came from families with high expectations for academic success. Seeing their siblings achieve the heights of education, both parents, separately, eschewed these values. They each vowed to make their own way in the world. Growing up in the '60s and '70s, my mom backpacked across Europe barefoot. My dad, sporting a foot-long beard, made his living driving a taxi in New York City. Their

---

*Brené Brown, *Braving the Wilderness: The Quest for True Belonging and the Courage to Stand Alone* (New York: Random House, 2017), 40.

love was founded on their shared dream of adopting a yeoman farmer's lifestyle in the rural Green Mountains of Vermont.

Both my parents found success in life, but not by traditional definitions, and not by traditional paths. They passed this ethos of fierce independence on to me (so, interestingly, whereas Belle felt a pressure to meet family and cultural expectations for success, I couldn't even begin to tell you what those expectations were for me). My parents never pushed me in any one direction; instead, their constant message seemed to be: "Just do what you want, follow your bliss." And so I did just that, drifting through college without clear direction. I studied sports media and marketing because I "liked sports." In college, the one extracurricular activity I engaged in wholeheartedly (outside of heavy partying) was becoming the president of the student government association. I strategically positioned myself in the election as the candidate you would most want to drink a beer with. My campaign, called T.H.E. Party: Tim Helps Everyone Party, won me the presidency in a landslide. Upon graduation, I continued to drift, first landing a job as an ice cream truck driver. "Mr. Ding-A-Ling Driver" would be the first item on my résumé after SGA president (if I had thought to write a résumé). I then moved to Chicago and became a waiter at ESPN Zone, a chain restaurant based on the sports channel. Given my sports background, family friends mistook this job as working for the actual ESPN (my parents weren't quick to correct them).

I had the privilege of doing what I wanted when I wanted, and so I lived it up, prioritizing the here and now over sacrificing for the long-term. Where Belle's energies were directed toward family and community responsibility, I focused on *myself*. I came first, and I concerned myself very little with the world beyond that. This worked for me . . . until it didn't. As time passed, I found my existence hollow and unfulfilling. It was harder and harder to get the same high from this self-indulgent lifestyle. Something was missing.

The turning point was getting a job at a Boys and Girls Club at the Julia C. Lathrop Homes, the oldest public housing development in Chicago. There I worked every day with young people growing up in circumstances drastically different from my own rural Vermont roots. Vermont is the least diverse state in the country, and I often joke that as a result I am "glow-in-the-dark white." The Cotter Club was my first experience with people who didn't look like me. However, the more I got to know my students, the more they reminded me of my friends back home. Their humor, their passions, their dreams . . . I felt a kindredness with them in so many ways. Except one big way. They had not been born with the silver spoon. These kids struggled with immense barriers to success completely foreign to me—food insecurity, lack of access to stable housing, exposure to violence. In that first year at the club, 185 high school students in Chicago were victims of gun violence. I was humbled by their strengths and resilience, but the challenges and injustices they faced ate away at me. For the first time in my life, my attention shifted beyond myself. It was as if a light switch turned on. I was hungry to contribute to lives other than my own. And as my efforts to do so gained momentum, so did my sense of meaning, fulfillment, and joy.

I graduated from the University of Chicago and became a clinical social worker. I counseled noncustodial fathers trying to get custody of their kids. I worked as a community organizer, leading advocacy campaigns to fight extreme poverty. I have served as an outreach director for a national nonprofit. I've been a therapist, school counselor, and mentor. Most important, for the last fifteen years I've worked with low-income, first-generation students to support their purpose discovery, the same purpose I found in that Boys and Girls Club.

As we reflect on our drastically different stories, we laugh that our paths ever crossed. Not sure we would've liked each other in college, much less that we would find ourselves coauthoring a book, sharing a common goal. But while our routes here may be different, our stories illustrate a universal truth: that contexts shape our identities and values. We're sculpted by people who raise and mentor us. And those people are sculpted by their cultural and societal surroundings. Belle mirrored a generational and cultural belief in education meritocracy, whereas Tim is a product of the self-empowerment, countercultural era of the 1960s.

We're sure you have your own story to tell about history's hand in who you are, and how you parent and mentor your people. We'll shed light on how personal narratives—and societal narratives—animate our life choices. Some deep influences are painful to acknowledge. But facing them squarely is critical to rethinking and sometimes undoing them.

We'll start by naming societal strongholds: fear, uncertainty, and anxiety.

Parenting in the Age of Anxiety

We see a generation of young people who are *pressure cookers*. Man, are they hard on themselves. They mirror how we—as adults and parents—treat ourselves. Our common ethos: "Do more, be more, work more, build more, grind more, hashtag #more!" And rarely do we know what or who we're doing all this for. Where's this all headed? We can be blindly driven by someone else's definition of "success" or "happiness," only to find that the road we're on does not lead there.

We've struggled to find our way and to belong. We push our students hard, hoping they'll belong, too. The self-anxious parent becomes anxious for their student. We drive ourselves—and all those around us—to exhaustion. What are we so scared of? Why do we impose our fear—and solutions for it—on our people?

When we place overwhelming expectations on ourselves, it's natural for our expectations to affect those closest to us. If we're feeling insecure, like we might fail, we become fearful they will fail. Problem is, when we expect our kids to fail, good results don't follow. No surprise here. And then we feel all the more insecure, and put more fearful expectations onto our students. It's a vicious cycle.

Identity formation is a key task during the adolescent years. But even as we struggle to answer the question "Who am I?" we're being defined by others. Sometimes people attach labels to us that differ from those we would choose for ourselves. In the book *The Bear That Wasn't,* Frank Tashlin shares the tale of a bear who is told repeatedly that he's a "silly man who needs a shave and wears a fur coat." He's labeled this way so often that he eventually becomes confused about whether he is a bear or a man. In the same way, the process of forming our identities is highly influenced by others. Our perceptions of ourselves can be largely shaped by how others define us. Before the modern era, many cultures placed labels on people that were determined at birth—merchant, farmer, prince, or slave. Although the histories and cultures of these people may seem unfamiliar and distant, the reality is that our identities are shaped by larger society even today.

In this book, we explain why we feel compelled to keep the cycle going, even though it's not working. But we also bring good news—*there's a different way within reach.* Our research points in this new direction that'll lead to far more gratification, richness, and peace. We can provide parents, teachers, and other caring adults actionable advice—based on science—for guiding students on this journey. All you need to know is what and *who* to bring along—as well as what *not* to bring. One of the bags you must leave at home is an over-preoccupation with self-protection. And an essential bag you have to bring is a true intention to seek a purpose in this life—one in which the people who gain the most may not be you. As fate would have it, that's exactly how we end up helping ourselves the most.

Fear and self-preoccupation cause people to lose themselves. We think we're being self-protective, but ironically we do ourselves harm. Here's our intention for this book—we hope that when you turn the last page, you breathe a huge sigh of relief because you just got *free.* Then we hope that you look with fresh eyes at all your people—your kids, your parents, your significant others, your coworkers, your friends—who you are released to love and care for in a fresh, new life-giving way.

This is about cutting loose from our performance anxiety and fear of failure and rejection, self-directed and otherwise. When we ease up on ourselves, we can ease up on our students.

Spoiler alert: You belong. You are enough. You have everything you need to live a purposeful life. So do your students. Instead of constantly being on our A game, constantly jumping through senseless hoops, we can get centered in who we really are. This isn't just our opinion, it's based on scientific evidence.

So, we are extending a hand to you, good reader. We will be sharing with you how you can shake free from the endless rat race to measure up, the constant checking of your cell phone for fear of falling behind, the tightness in your chest. We hope to disentangle you from the various weights holding you down, the ones that others put there, and the ones you collected for yourself. We are going to let ourselves off the hook from fixing and figuring out everything for our students. And in the end, we will be free to live and mentor them well; to experience open, generous days; and to practice the centered and purpose-full living we were made for.

The first half of the book will teach you *The Five Purpose Principles*, which can be used as a decision-making framework to navigate every domain of life. The principles are:

1. Commit to a *purpose mindset.*

2. Play *growth games* even when competing in *fixed games.*

3. Future-proof your skills as a *creator, facilitator,* or *driver.*

4. Add your value as a *Trailblazer, Builder, Champion,* or *Guardian.*

5. Meet the *big five needs* in the world (physical, personal, community, societal, environmental).

The second half of the book is about how to *apply* the five principles in five key contexts: in our relationships, in high school, in college, in the workplace, and in the larger world. We will teach you how to:

1. Create moments that matter.

2. Listen for your call, not someone else's.

3. Diversify your brand, social, and human capital.

4. Cultivate an inner world that ripples into the outer world.

Each chapter will present a principle and how to use it. Our goal is to equip you and your students with the tools needed to navigate life. Ultimately, this book doesn't tell you which direction you should go to succeed in life. We provide you with the principles so you can decide, based on your best, most authentic, and purposeful self.

Oh! We will also be discussing cultural insights from Twitter to Tik-Tok, and life lessons inspired by LEGOs and superstar chickens.

This is going to be fun.

PART ONE

THE FIVE PURPOSE PRINCIPLES

1

Mindset

Commit to a purpose mindset.

The purpose of life is not to be happy. It is to be useful,
to be honorable, to be compassionate, to have it make
some difference that you have lived and lived well.

—RALPH WALDO EMERSON

Dream Chasers

Matteo Sloane was home on spring break when FBI agents showed up at his family's home in Bel-Air at 6:15 a.m. to take his father to jail. When his father, Devin Sloane, returned home that evening after posting bail, Matteo, then a freshman at the University of Southern California, confronted him with a heart-wrenching question, "Why didn't you believe in me?" Devin replied, "I never stopped believing in you, not even for one second . . . I lost sight of what was right, and I lost belief in myself."

Devin is one of thirty-six parents who were criminally charged with cheating the college admissions system in order to ensure their children's entry into top universities. Many of them have received prison time for using William "Rick" Singer's services as a college admissions consultant to rig their children's ACT/SAT scores or to disguise them as athletic recruits to ensure their entrance into elite universities.

In separate interviews by the *Wall Street Journal*'s Jennifer Levitz and Melissa Korn, each Sloane described intense anxieties about college that contributed to a pressure-cooker environment at home and school. This mirrored the accounts of other families drawn into the scheme. Here was a son who had an impressive academic record on his own merit. He spoke three languages fluently, was taking Advanced Placement classes, and was making the honor roll. Not the picture of a struggling student who needed to cheat to win. And yet we have a father sentenced to four months in prison and a son disillusioned by his family's pursuit of success.

Varsity Blues is one of the most newsworthy academic scandals of the decade. It was a lightning rod for public outcry because it symbolized what so many families have come to resent about higher education—the power of privilege shrouded in the veneer of meritocracy. The families involved in the scandal were ridiculed across the internet for their lack of morals and brazen disregard of norms and laws. Throngs of people were quick to take to social media to deride the audacity of these horrible people using their privilege to tip scales already weighted in their favor. Criticizing these "bad" people is cathartic for parents because it validates feelings that the education system is rigged, and that the rich will cheat to maintain their power. The Varsity Blues scandal proved to many, once and for all, that "pulling yourself up by your bootstraps" is a farce.

However valid these sentiments might be, this scandal reveals a deeper, more insidious problem impacting families across the country. Consider those involved in the admissions scandal: celebrities, high-powered lawyers, venture capitalists, and investment bankers. Arguably some of the world's most successful individuals, with all the financial, political, and social capital needed to lock up their children's futures. Their kids were headed to material success on their own merits. Olivia Jade Giannulli, daughter of actress Lori Loughlin and fashion designer Mossimo Giannulli, had already built a business and solid social media following as a beauty blogger. She had amassed 1.9 million YouTube subscribers and 1.3 million followers on Instagram. She had sponsorship deals with the biggest fashion businesses in the world, including Sephora and Dolce & Gabbana. These families had every advantage, yet acted deeply insecure about their kids' futures.

To truly get the nature of this problem, we have to be willing to take a deeper look into our own hearts. We have to ask ourselves: Why in the world families who had it all would break the law and risk facing jail time? It's tempting to cast stones and think of them as bad people with no moral compass. But is there *a part* of their story that resonates in us, though we hate to admit it? This is the part we can relate to—being scared about our children's futures. Can't we understand being so gripped by fear that we take matters into our own hands to ensure their success and happiness?

Varsity Blues isn't just a story about other people. It's a cautionary tale that can help us see ourselves more clearly. It's a way to understand the precarious world our students live in. It's a story that reveals how seeds of *fear* cause us to make the worst decisions. Our goal is to help parents and students break free of this fear. To do so, we have to first understand where it's coming from.

- - - - - - - - - - - - - - - - -

When We Are All Afraid at Once

As we write this book, the whole world's attention has been consumed by the novel coronavirus. What started as a small outbreak at the end of 2019 exponentially exploded into a global pandemic. COVID-19 is one of the few historical events that has affected every living human. People have gotten sick and died, the global supply chain was disrupted, and economies collapsed. As the first global virus to strike in the digital age, we could track, in real time, the terrifying speed and mobility of its spread. Watching it was like standing on a beach, bracing against the impending approach of a tsunami.

And as we observed how people responded to the pandemic, especially in its early days, we gained insight into the way the human psyche works. In the spring of 2020, fears about a worsening outbreak led citizens around the world to stockpile their "pandemic pantries" with canned goods, hand sanitizer, and bottled water. Tech billionaires in Silicon Valley spent tens of thousands of dollars to keep chartered jets on "standby" in case they needed to suddenly flee the virus. The high-end real estate market in safe and livable places like Boise, Idaho, skyrocketed, as the country's richest residents made their escape plans, buying houses sight unseen. Against the pleas of the CDC, people hoarded masks, bottled water, and toilet paper.[1]

Why, despite experts' pleas, did people continue their stockpiling? If we can learn from this scarcity mentality, then we can gain insight into how we react to our fears for our kids' safety and future. Research suggests that when people feel unsafe and insecure, they respond in predictable ways.

We Seek Safety

The more unsafe and insecure we feel, the more we search for security in the form of material resources.[2] We seek safety and comfort in *physical things*.

This makes sense from an evolutionary standpoint: when we are hungry, our stomachs growl and all we can think of is food. When we're cold, we seek warmth. When we feel unsafe, we look for physical sources of relief. We focus like a laser beam on getting the material things that will make us safe. It wasn't an actual shortage of toilet paper that made us run to Costco and clear the shelves—it was our *perception* of scarcity that did it. Our survival instincts kicked in and we fixated on stockpiling goods. The worry over not having enough supplies, not being able to maintain our lifestyle, being left behind if we weren't proactively preparing for survival—these fears sometimes upstaged fears of the virus itself.

- - - - - - - - - - - - - - -

Fear of the Future

"Unprecedented" and "uncertain" were two of the most used adjectives describing COVID-19 times. But uncertainty—and the insecurity that comes with it—isn't new to us. Americans have been plagued by a gnawing fear over their children's future economic and emotional well-being since long before the pandemic. We fear that students won't be able to find a job that earns them an honest living—especially when countless others are vying for the same positions in an increasingly volatile economy. But that's not all. We fear for our kids' mental health. Prior to the lockdowns, we were already navigating a world where youth in alarming numbers suffered from depression, anxiety, and near mental breakdown. The majority of parents fear that their students will struggle with anxiety and depression at some point in life.[3] The world our kids inhabit feels dangerous. Seventy percent of adults feel that the world is "less safe" than it was during their childhoods.[4] Even before COVID-19, rising social unrest, racial injustice, depression, and stress overwhelmed the resources available to overcome them.

In addition to this generalized fear, we worry for our students' livelihood. Insecurity guides the values, motivations, and choices of young people, and the adults in their lives. This fear is as contagious as COVID-19. Not even the most privileged escape its grip. People share universal fears about their students' future success and happiness.

In the next section, we expose two overarching threats responsible for the fear and insecurity that families are feeling. Then we show how these threats, and our responses to them, steer our interactions with students—from our motivations and decisions to our actions and behaviors. We'll demonstrate how these well-intentioned responses hurt our students' performance and mental health.

Threat #1: Surviving in the "Real" World

Increased income inequality. The gig economy. Automation and globalization. Rising cost of living and stagnant wages. Social injustices. All of these factors make it seem harder than ever for someone to survive, let alone thrive, in today's economy. One of our biggest fears is that our students might not make it in the world—especially if they aren't elite performers (or extremely lucky). They'll struggle just to support themselves, much less find dignified, meaningful work. We worry that they'll spend years financially dependent, paying off loans, living in our basements. They might even end up on the streets. These are real fears, and can be felt by any parent, even the most economically advantaged. And as "Covid Hoarding" taught us, when we feel unsafe, we value material resources all the more. In a parallel way, many seek solace and salvation in another scarce commodity—higher education.

College has long been hailed as a great investment. With the exceptions of billionaires like Steve Jobs, Elon Musk, Bill Gates, and Mark Zuckerberg, the simple adage remains true: the more education you get, the more money you make.[5] College graduates enjoy more job security.[6] The great recession of 2008 erased more than 7.2 million American jobs.[7] When the economy bounced back, 95 percent of jobs created went to people with at least some college education.[8] And which college one attends is linked to salaries. Graduates of "elite" colleges can expect to earn more than graduates of other schools.[9]

These statistics suggest that in order to make it in today's economy, students need a college degree. And advantages seem stacked for those who go to elite colleges. Problem is, the high-stakes game of college feels like anything but a sure bet. Admission to top universities is like finding a golden ticket to Willy Wonka's Chocolate Factory. And as the numbers of applicants at the top colleges and universities have continued to rise, acceptance rates have dropped to near-record lows.[10]

Even for those accepted, the game isn't won: paying for college is punishing. Attending public college costs $21,950 a year (up 60 percent from 2000). Attending private college costs $49,870 a year (up 45 percent from 2000). Depending on how long it takes to earn a degree (less than half of college-goers finish in four years),[11] students can expect to pay anywhere from $85,000 to $300,00 for a diploma.

There's more bad news: the returns on this investment are diminishing; college prices have grown eight times faster than wages in the United States.[12] In response, students are taking on buckets of debt. As of 2021, Americans had racked up an astounding $1.75 trillion in loans.[13] The 43.4 million students who took out student loans graduated with an average debt of $37,113. And graduates feel the impact: 52 percent of those who took on student loan debt didn't feel it was worth it; 53 percent of millennials haven't bought a home because their student loan debt made it impossible to get a mortgage.[14]

This high-risk, high-reward scenario has turned higher education into a double-edged sword. If you want a good career that affords you financial security, you need to go to college. But doing so entails an enormous financial risk, with no guarantee that it will pay off. College has become the ultimate catch-22; you need it to make money, but it might bankrupt you. And so students are caught in a vicious feedback loop: the need for economic security drives college aspirations, but the rising costs of college and increased competition for quality jobs make people feel *more* insecure. College attendance used to ensure security, but now it drives our insecurity, which makes us want it more, which makes it all the more scarce.

The bottom line is that there are real threats to students' economic security. College has become an arms race. There are precious few seats at the so-called top schools. The greater problem than this reality, though, is our perception of it. Since economic success is correlated with attending these schools, we can adopt a certain self-destructive perception. We can view life as a zero-sum competition. We start to see success in college as a battle between winners and losers. People are either ahead or behind, and we better make sure it's not our student on the short end of the stick. There's a reality to the threats we worry over. Our students' real-world survival and success are on shaky ground, especially if we define success in terms of wealth, power, and prestige. In response to this threat, we view life as a vicious, dog-eat-dog game of survival. We call this life view the *performance mindset*.

Performance Mindset: Life Is a Zero-Sum Game

People with a performance mindset view life as a fierce, cutthroat competition. The goal is to *win*. The game is winner-take-all, and to the champion go the spoils. When we adopt this performance mindset, we pour our all into helping our kids *be successful*. And we will take down any obstacle in their paths to make it happen. This is the mindset that enabled Belle's parents to get to the United States, and because of all they risked, she felt the need to make good on their bet. *Winning* at school felt like the way to make her parents' sacrifice worth it.

This mindset is ubiquitous. Today's parents are also referred to as *snowplow parents*—a term that, while pejorative, captures our determination and skill at leveling any and all obstacles that stand between our kid and success. We make helicopter parents look like amateurs. As heroic, impressive, and well-intentioned as we are, the snowplow approach can do students harm. The college admissions scandal showed what happens when snowplow parents take it too far. People who bribe SAT proctors and pay off college coaches aren't the only ones guilty of snowplowing because of performance mindsets. Many of us would do anything short of breaking the law to ensure our kids' "success." In his book *Dream Hoarders,* Richard V. Reeves describes this as "opportunity hoarding," and it includes leveraging "legacy admissions," personal networks to land prestigious internships, and any means of helping your students become successful.[15]

So it's a bit like the pot calling the kettle black when we blame parents for losing their way as they try to ensure their kids' success. While most of us don't take it to the criminal extreme, we're on the continuum. We desire the same outcome of success, albeit via more acceptable means. The most common strategy is to identify what our students excel at and "help" them be the best at that thing. Be it math or writing, soccer or piano, we push them to seek achievement that will be recognized and rewarded. Performance mindset parents are eager to provide all sorts of opportunities for their kids to explore various sports, musical instruments, and other extracurricular activities in hopes of unearthing hidden talent. Better still if it's one that will make them appear "well rounded" and get them ahead in the college game. And once we detect these little sparks of special talent, we make it our mission to fan those flames—to coach, cajole, cheerlead our kids on to becoming the very best versions of themselves. We sign them up for travel soccer leagues, accelerated math courses, tutoring, private lessons.

We become all about "helping" our students reach their potential by pursuing whatever they're best at doing. We focus our energies on making sure they pursue exactly the right opportunities and paths that will lead to success. We goad them into using their special gifts. Never mind whether *they* view these little gems as representing their best selves. That would be an added bonus, but otherwise it's beside the point. The point is that they need to beat out the competition. Who can blame us? We are loving parents, desperate to help our students *make it in the world.*

Consider the following scenario. Six-year-old Talia joined a club soccer team. Her father wanted her to have fun, make some friends, and get some exercise and fresh air. However, he quickly realized that his motivations were very different from those of the parents around him. They had grander ambitions than playing for fun. They were vying for the competitive travel team, attainable for the sum of several thousand dollars. A small price to pay if the travel team (or robotics team, math or debate club, dance showcase, etc.) puts our students on a trajectory toward a competitive college. This example is just the tip of the iceberg.

At least two companies claimed they had DNA tests that could help match youngsters with the sports they are genetically hardwired to play best. For $160, parents bought up these DNA kits, swabbed their youngsters' cheeks, and sent saliva off to a lab to detect its levels of ACTN3—a protein supposedly associated with fast-twitch explosive muscles. Excitedly they awaited the results that would help them steer their children toward games they were most likely to win—and get scholarships to play. Kids overloaded with ACTN3 were blessed with strength and power and could go out for football, wrestling, boxing, and the like. Kids with an absence of ACTN3 were blessed with the endurance needed for long-distance running, cycling, and swimming. Kids with a little bit of ACTN3 were mixed-pattern athletes with strength *and* endurance— meaning they could take their pick of a sport. People clamored to get their hands on this test, believing that steering their students into the sport they were *made for* would increase their chances of success.

From a financial perspective, the plan makes sense. Athletics can help you get in and pay for college. Being an elite athlete dramatically increases your likelihood of being accepted into Harvard.[16] Derek Thompson reported that "nearly 90 percent of recruited athletes gain admission to Harvard versus about 6 percent of applicants overall. These athletes make up less than 1 percent of Harvard's applicant pool but more than 10 percent of its admitted class."[17] Savvy parents of child athletes are vying to tap into the $3 billion in athletic scholarships Division I and II colleges give out every year.[18]

In this era of performance mindset, where good snowplow parents must exploit every competitive edge for their children, is it any wonder that soccer for eight-year-olds can be not only fun and games, but an *investment* in future success?

End Destination vs. Stepping-Stone Goals

Performance mindset parents, coaches, educators, and mentors are strategic. We are practical people. We see short-term successes as *stepping-stones* to our *end destination goal.* This ultimate goal is to ensure the safety and security of our students. Achievement in school, on the soccer field, in the engineering club—these are all stepping-stone goals. Yes, they may feel good in the moment, but their real value is that they help us reach our bigger, more critical long-term goals. Today's success will ensure tomorrow's financial security. We convince ourselves that if our students succeed at these stepping-stone goals today, they're on the right path to safety, security, and belonging tomorrow. We hyper-focus on short-term success, but always keep in mind the long-term perspective and promise of economic security. We push our students hard, because the ends justify the means.

Seems sensible, but there's a catch. Focusing too closely on achieving these stepping-stone goals doesn't necessarily lead to our desired end destination. Our research reveals that the performance mindset does not actually guarantee success. It does the opposite; it *undercuts* students' performance and damages their psychological health. When we adopt a performance mindset to ensure the safety and well-being of young people, it actually does the opposite.

Why the Performance Mindset Backfires

There are three reasons the performance mindset does not help students in the long run. First, it insidiously ingrains in them a toxic message about the world they live in, one that is inaccurate and dangerous. Second, it doesn't actually lead to long-term success. Third, it's bad for their mental and physical health.

The performance mindset is a strategy for survival. It's also a set of beliefs about what's most important and of value in the world. Our subsequent actions are motivated by the worthiest of intentions: we just want what's best for our people. However, these intentions are different from the *message* we're sending them.

When we buy into the performance myth, we socialize students to embrace the side of human nature that is fundamentally competitive and self-interested. This perpetuates a vision of the world as hopeless and dangerous. Peter Railton, a University of Michigan philosopher, describes this worldview as "your great-grandfather's Social Darwinism," in which "all creatures great and small [are] pitted against one another in a life-or-death struggle to survive and reproduce."[19]

Not only do we raise young people to be anxious and afraid for their lives with this fear-based narrative, it's not entirely accurate. This hostile "survival of the fittest" view of life doesn't take into account the fuller understanding of evolution that's developed in the last several decades. Scientific evidence since the 1960s has converged with theological and spiritual beliefs that humans are created for so much more than the battlefield. Biologists have made major advances in discovering that we and the world we live in have been beautifully designed for altruistic cooperation—not just ruthless competition.[20] Humans are part of a larger context in which effective cooperation within and among different species enables us to survive and thrive. For example, the forest is a community in which trees of different species share nutrients (nitrogen, carbon, and phosphorous) by associating with each other. Older trees give beneficial nutrients to the younger trees around them. The laws of the jungle have proved that self-interest is often less beneficial than mutual cooperation in promoting growth and gains.

We can see the same principles played out in human communities. Just as ecosystems with rampant predation dissolve into chaotic states of starvation and violence, human societies fall apart when competition is too fierce. It's easier to survive and thrive when people come together, pool labor, share risk, and seek alliances. Rebecca Solnit, in *A Paradise Built in Hell: The Extraordinary Communities That Arise in Disaster,* documents the many examples of newfound purpose and communities that arise after disasters.[21] Hurricane Katrina, like many disasters, was marked by altruism—young people who decided to take on the responsibility of supplying material goods and protection to strangers stranded with them. In the same way, we see examples of people who have chosen to behave in ways that protect others in the face of COVID-19 and racial injustices. These altruistic, cooperative behaviors have led to the greater good of communities. In March 2020, as the severity of the pandemic was becoming clear, #Caremongering was born across Canada. #Caremongering was a community-led social movement that organically emerged as a way for Canadians to offer and seek out help, support, and information during lockdown. In just the first few days, hundreds of thousands of Canadians joined the movement, eager to offer their support.

Yet everywhere we look, the themes of predation continue to saturate popular culture. From superhero franchises, to professional sports, to zombie apocalypse dramas, we're immersed in and entertained by watching people fight to the death. In each of these situations, it's "everybody for themselves." Kindness equals weakness and is often fatal. A cutthroat competition dictates who will survive, who will prosper, and who will be no more. As scary as this worldview is, it's also highly seductive. We love seeing the underdog conquer obstacles, annihilate opponents, and claw to the top, victorious. While the stories we tell through arts, media, and sports perpetuate this vision of the world, reality is different, and thankfully so.

In 1967, biologist Lynn Margulis published a seminal article on the origin of Earth that had been rejected by fifteen journals.[22] She posited that hungry one-celled organisms nearly annihilated the planet in a fierce competition for food resources, before disaster was averted by different cells that entered communal arrangements. These mitochondria and chloroplasts exchanged nutrients that became the building blocks of all higher life forms. People thought Margulis's theories were absurd and largely ignored them until they were powerfully substantiated by genetic evidence. Similar to her generation, which placed a premium on competition, the performance mindset prevails today, such that students are terrified of skipping a beat for fear of losing their competitive edge. We've been conditioned to raise versions of one-celled organisms who will take over the world.

The performance mindset is built for this type of world. It's a strategy to help students "win" in this hyper-competitive zero-sum world of school, college, and career. The performance mindset says you win by beating others. It's a dangerous myth that leads to fear, futile striving, and collapse. Even if they don't agree with the mindset, many well-intentioned families feel they need it to survive. We don't want our students to be left behind. We don't want them to lose. And so we start with what's in front of us: helping them win *right now*.

Stepping-Stones Become End Destinations

The sad irony is that this mindset may win short-term gains, but cost dearly in the long run. This is due in part to adolescent brain development. Neuroscience findings show that *kids are short-term decision-makers*. Their prefrontal cortexes, the brain region that allows for self-regulation, envisioning the future, and making long-term decisions, don't fully develop until well into their twenties. Early adolescents aren't yet equipped to think through the long-term consequences of today's actions and decisions. Instead, they focus on what's right in front of them; research has shown that kids thirteen and younger are more likely to accept less money immediately than to wait for a delayed larger payoff, in contrast to those sixteen and older.[23]

A second key insight from neuroscience research is that adolescents are extremely sensitive to rewards and willing to take risks even for relatively small, short-term rewards (a great reason not to take them to casinos). In one study, young people took part in a driving simulation where they were tasked with getting to the finish line as fast as possible.[24] They had to decide whether to stop at yellow traffic lights. The downside of stopping was a slower time; the downside of not stopping was risking a car accident. Compared to people of any other age, teenagers were much more likely to run yellow lights. The short-term reward (i.e., a fast time) outweighed the risk of crashing. These and other studies show how strongly youth are attracted to rewards, regardless of risks.

We saw this when COVID-19 hit the United States. By mid-March 2020, the entire country was gripped in fear and panic about contracting the virus. Well, not everyone, actually. Quite a few young people were more concerned with celebrating spring break. And so, going against the CDC and common sense, these young people took YOLO to a whole other level by congregating, contracting the virus, and putting scores of other people at risk. How could they be so shortsighted? Neuroscience would explain their thinking—a good time now trumps long-term investment any day.

This is why the performance mindset fails. For adults, it's a long-term risk-minimization strategy. But young people are short-term reward-seekers. Their brains aren't yet wired to value the long-term economic security of the performance mindset that adults' brains are wired to value. For parents, students' short-term achievement is assurance of success in their future. This long-term reward is more important to us than to our students. Instead, they're tuned in to the short-term rewards for their hard work: recognition and approval.

Recognition rewards come in various shapes and sizes. Class grades. Grade point averages. Class rankings. Earning a starting position on the hockey team. An award in photography. Winning a robotics competition. A thousand likes on an Instagram post. One hundred new followers on TikTok. Youth with a performance mindset who succeed are rewarded with *social status* and *prestige*—which are *extrinsic motivations*.

Extrinsic motivation comes from *outside ourselves*. We're compelled to do something mainly because there is a reward associated with it, and we lose our intrinsic, or natural, interest in doing it.

For example, researcher Mark Lepper and his colleagues asked kids to play with Magic Markers.[25] Lepper knew that the kids in his study all were interested in Magic Markers because he picked the ones who had enjoyed them in a previous activity. Once in the experimental situation, the kids were exposed to one of three reward conditions. Group 1 was told there would be a reward for kids who colored with the Magic Markers. Group 2 was told nothing, but these kids were given the reward unexpectedly at the end of the session. Group 3 was simply asked to use the Magic Markers without any reward, expected or unexpected. Later, all three groups were given another chance to play with the Magic Markers, but this time they weren't urged to do so. Guess which kids were the most interested in using the Magic Markers again? The kids who had *not* been extrinsically rewarded.

Extrinsic motivations can also come in the form of punishments. If you threaten to take a cell phone away if a teenager breaks curfew, that is extrinsic motivation. This can work in the short term, especially when the adult is right there to enforce the sanctions. But experimental evidence has shown that extrinsic motivation in the form of punishments and coercion does *not* lead to long-lasting, dependable formation of habits or beliefs. Punishments simply are not effective when adults are absent (and thus can't dole out the punishment!). The more severe the threat of punishment, the *worse* the child's bad behavior becomes.[26]

Research on older adolescents and adults also showed that high extrinsic motivation was harmful for their mental and physical health. A meta-analysis on extrinsic motivation looked to see what happens when people aspire to make a lot of money. The findings were clear: the more people had an extrinsic drive for material goods, the worse off they were psychologically.[27]

College students who were extrinsically driven to do well (i.e., they were motivated to make money) faced similar challenges. They had lower rates of well-being than their less money-focused peers.[28] A separate study showed that materialistic college students also had greater levels of narcissism and physical symptoms.[29] Clearly, even if extrinsically motivated goals lead to money, they didn't lead to healthy and fulfilling lives.

There is a price to privilege. Students from wealthy, high-achieving backgrounds suffer from higher rates of depression, anxiety, and alcohol and drug abuse than do those from other socioeconomic backgrounds.[30] Paradoxically, many of these problems may be caused by struggles with self-esteem, despite the fact that privileged students tend to outperform students from lower income backgrounds in academics and extracurricular activities. Greater opportunity doesn't automatically lead to happiness and health.

In a study examining what it is about achievement pressure that causes distress, *social comparison* rose to the top as most responsible for anxious-depressed and withdrawn-depressed symptoms.[31] Our findings suggested that students from high-achieving schools and communities felt pressure to be extremely ambitious, smart, caring, fit, and more accomplished than their peers.[32] They strived to be essentially superhuman.

Young people are hearing it from all sides—home, school, the media— that success means all-around outstanding performance in order to get into prestigious colleges, which then leads to prestige and wealth—the ultimate measures of success. Students in our studies were stressed, depressed, full of fear that they might lose the rat race—even as they strove day and night for straight As, played musical instruments, engaged in sports, and performed "community service" (which probably should be called "self" service, given its role as a résumé padder). And here's the clincher: they said they were expected to do it with a smile. To come across as nice, cheerful, and enthusiastic. They felt pressured to "be all things to all people" for the sake of extrinsic success. All this effort led to little happiness. They reported overwhelming achievement pressures, perfectionistic strivings, and fears of failure. The performance mindset damages students' psyches and health.

The other big finding was that extrinsic motivation doesn't make students perform any better. It actually gets in the way of long-term performance. Extrinsically motivated youth are more likely to drink alcohol and smoke tobacco and pot.[33] And highly materialistic students had lower levels of academic engagement and achievement.[34] Typically, partaking in substances and disengaging from school aren't good strategies for success.

The bottom line is: the performance mindset backfires. Students *underperform* rather than succeed. One reason is that a performance mindset causes people to care too much about how others view them. It gives other people the power to decide how successful we are, how meaningful our contributions are, and what our place in the world is. The performance mindset says that what other people think of us should determine how we feel about ourselves.

In fact, it leaves us out of the equation altogether.

What if we want to pursue a vocation that is personally meaningful and fulfilling, but doesn't square with society's definition of success? By the rules of the performance mindset, it doesn't matter how meaningful an aspiration may be; if it doesn't lead to external achievement, improve our social status, or serve as a gateway to prestige, *it is not worth pursuing.* Ultimately, the performance mindset affords us little choice in what we do; we must follow the path that is most socially acceptable and leads to the greatest recognition and approval from others. The performance mindset fails to fulfill our psychological or spiritual needs and callings. Not attending to these essential needs decreases our quality of life, hurts our performance, and undermines our ability to achieve what caused us to adopt a performance mindset in the first place.

- - - - - - - - - - - - - - - - -

Passion Mindset: Don't Worry, Be Happy

Fortunately, not everyone succumbs to a performance mindset. You might be one of the few who sees through it. Perhaps being safe and secure is important to you, but you realize that money isn't everything.

You've come to the conclusion that money can't buy happiness. You know that if you support your students to pursue their passions in the world, you might not know where they will go, but chances are, they'll end up okay. Maybe you've experienced the hollowness that comes with a myopic focus on accumulating wealth. You realize that there's more to life than wealth, status, prestige, and power. This was Tim's mindset as a young adult. He cared much more about having fun and doing what made him happy than pursuing achievement or recognition. If you are like Tim, perhaps you'd much rather your students find their passion and do what they love. Where the performance mindset seeks economic and physical security, you prioritize *emotional security*. You much prefer the mantra: the goal of life isn't to win, but to be *happy*. We call this the *passion mindset*.

Whereas the performance mindset is a response to the fear and uncertainty we feel about our economic future and desire to find our place in the world, the passion mindset is also born of fear. It comes from the fear of not being happy and not being able to handle negative emotions. One of the biggest current threats to students is an internal struggle, the battle for mental health.

The mental health crisis is well documented and all signs point to it only getting worse. Following the suicide of a girl in the public high school of Belle's high-achieving community in the Boston suburbs, a *New York Times* article by Kyle Spencer described how painted rocks had been placed throughout the school's large campus by its students.[35] The rocks were inscribed with encouraging sayings such as "Mistakes are O.K." and "Don't worry, it will be over soon." These rocks speak volumes about the toxic messages they're pushing back against—"mistakes are *not* O.K., you must be perfect" and "there is a lot to worry about, the stress is overwhelming." These little rocks give us a tiny glimpse into our students' desperate attempts to fight against the dangerous currents they are swept up in. The waters they swim in every day perpetuate performance anxiety, even suicides. Sadly, this is just one small anecdote that illustrates a much larger crisis.

Dr. Marc Brackett, the director of social emotional intelligence at Yale

University, sums up the accumulating statistics on the mental health crisis this way:

> From 2016–2017, more than one in three students across 196 U.S. college campuses reported diagnosed mental health conditions. Some campuses have reported a 30 percent increase in mental health problems per year.
>
> According to the 2019 World Happiness Report, negative feelings, including worry, sadness, and anger, have been on the rise across the globe—up by 27 percent from 2010 to 2018.
>
> Anxiety disorders are the most common mental illness in the U.S., affecting 25 percent of adolescents between thirteen and eighteen years of age.[36]

It's no wonder we worry about our students. We are hearing about, and witnessing firsthand, mental health struggles associated with social media, screen time, bullying, social isolation, peer pressure, and academic and social stress. Sadly, the list goes on. Many of us know that irresistible urge to withhold nothing, to give our children the moon and the stars, and to protect them from pain, struggle, and heartache. Some fascinating research indicates how mothers are hardwired to respond to their babies' cries. Mothers from eleven countries consistently rushed to comfort (pick up, hold, talk to) their infants within *five* seconds of hearing them cry.[37] *Five* seconds. Why are we so desperate to jump to the rescue when our kids are struggling, even in the slightest way? The MRI scans of healthy mothers showed that hearing their babies' cries activated regions in the brain tied to caregiving, movement, and speech. These are considered "readiness" or "planning" areas of the brain. So, when these moms heard their babies' distress cries, they knew exactly what to do to remove the source of struggle. And many of us never stop doing this. We want our kids to be happy, and not suffer even five seconds of unhappiness. We're conditioned from our babies' first cries to remove all their obstacles, earning our titles as snowplow parents. Later, if they are uncomfortable in a class, if they are disengaged on a club team, if they are *unhappy,* we must do everything we can to remedy this: we call their teachers, we run interference for them, we fix their problems.

A second study suggested an additional physiological reason for our anxious response to our kids' distress. Oxytocin, a hormone tied to mother-infant bonding, seems to cause mothers to react to their babies' cries with a sense of urgency.[38] This urgency to comfort and rescue our children at all costs continues into their adolescence. In our desperation to protect them from any hint of distress or unhappiness, we may encourage them to find their happy place—a passion that makes their hearts sing. Just like parents with a performance mindset, these snowplow parents have the best of intentions. They can often be extremely empathetic and attuned to their child—hallmarks of great parenting. Unfortunately, their good intentions can send an unhelpful message:

If you feel bad, something is wrong.

The Dark Side of the Passion Mindset

The problem with this mindset is that we can mistake *mental health* for the *absence of negative emotions*. We think that if we can eliminate any sadness, anger, uncertainty, or uneasiness, and replace these with happiness, excitement, and pleasure, then: bingo! We've succeeded in keeping our students mentally healthy. The truth is we cannot keep them in a bubble. Ups and downs, highs and lows, joy, sadness, and, yes, suffering are inevitable parts of life. Our role is not to remove all suffering (because that's impossible) but to teach them how to bear it. We don't want to send the message to students that negative emotions are to be feared and avoided at all costs. When we attempt to avoid all negative emotions, and we put positive emotions on a pedestal and worship them above all else, it backfires. The more we value happiness, the more unhappy we become. The more we try to avoid negative emotions, the more they dominate our lives.

A Beautiful Day in the Neighborhood is a movie based on the real-life friendship between a journalist and children's TV icon Fred Rogers. The journalist is a tortured soul with angst over a broken relationship with his father. He fears sadness, and acts out in anger when sadness inevitably comes. Fred tells him, "There is no normal life that is free of pain. It's the very wrestling with our problems that can be the impetus for our growth." And even as the journalist's father is dying and the family is sitting around him anxiously and awkwardly, Fred pays them all a visit. He normalizes their pain and makes it possible for them to embrace their time together in this poignant period of suffering, saying, "To die is to be human, and anything human is mentionable. Anything mentionable is manageable."

Rogers taught people how to confront difficult feelings rather than run from them. He once said off camera:

> Confronting our feelings and giving them appropriate expression always takes strength, not weakness. It takes strength to acknowledge our anger, and sometimes more strength yet to curb the aggressive urges anger may bring and channel them into nonviolent outlets. It takes strength to face our sadness and to grieve and to let our grief and our anger flow in tears when they need to. It takes strength to talk about our feelings and to reach out for help and comfort when we need it.[39]

Research has revealed that the more we value happiness, the harder it is to attain.[40] This might be because the more important happiness becomes to us, the higher our expectations for happiness become. These expectations are harder to reach; and when we don't reach those expectations, that makes us even unhappier. Weddings are expected to be one of the pinnacles of life. As a result, people invest enormous time, energy, and resources to make sure that they don't have just a great wedding, *but a perfect one*. They want it to be a mind-blowing, awesome occasion. This need for the *ideal* wedding is what drives the $72 billion wedding industry and causes couples to spend an average of $32,000 on their wedding (not to mention the honeymoon!).[41] This puts a lot of pressure on the couple to make sure their investment pays off. The emotional expectations and the financial stakes could not be higher.

These expectations unfortunately work against the "happy" couple to be: they value happiness in the form of their dream wedding. But as we can imagine, the perfect wedding is hard to pull off. An unforeseen thunderstorm, a guest who drinks too much, a great-uncle vocalizing questionable political views are just a few of the looming threats to a perfect day. When something goes wrong, as it usually does, it can feel devastating. This was supposed to be the perfect day, and it isn't. We feel *worse*. A happiness focus creates a vicious feedback loop; the more we want to be happy, the sadder we feel when we aren't, and the more important being happy becomes, the harder it is to come by. This is the paradox of the passion mindset.

The passion mindset backfires most when people have the highest expectations for happiness, like vacations, birthdays, and going off to college. These situations put pressure on people to be happy, which unfortunately makes them less likely to attain said happiness. So, if you've been on a vacation that felt more stressful than relaxing, or you've seen kids cry at their own birthday parties or want to transfer colleges because they thought they'd be having the time of their lives, you've experienced the paradox of the passion mindset.

When we have *low expectations* for happiness, say while waiting in line at the DMV, doing our taxes, or going to a family reunion where conflict is expected, being unhappy doesn't impact us as much. When we enter situations not expecting to have the time of our lives, we aren't as disappointed. These reduced expectations allow us to navigate the inevitable ups and downs of everyday life with more grit and resolve. You aren't expecting today to be perfect, so when things go awry you think, "that's how the ball rolls," and you're not thrown for a loop. Because you have modest expectations, it's easier to be pleasantly surprised . . . and happy.

It's this dynamic that sets students up for disillusionment in the digital age. Social media is a huge driver of the expectation that life should be constantly happy and passionate; the picture-perfect digital identities presented online are scrubbed free of the blemishes, hassles, and mundane experiences of everyday life. If you've ever felt instantly worse about your own life after seeing a picture of the perfect vacation/dinner/life on Instagram, you know the feeling. Even when students know intellectually that social media is not an accurate reflection of real life, they're hugely affected by seeing their peers on social media consistently having the *time of their lives*. This raises our students' expectations for what they *should* be feeling, driving the passion mindset.

There is a large body of research that confirms this. Among adults, valuing happiness was associated with lower psychological well-being, higher levels of depression symptoms, greater loneliness, and even poorer college grades.[42] Similarly, kids who valued happiness too much were more depressed.[43] Just like the performance mindset increases the likelihood of abusing substances and spending more time staring at screens, the passion mindset can also promote unhealthy behavior. The tendency to engage in rash action in response to extreme positive affect (i.e., impulsive behavior when passionate) is associated with risky behaviors, such as alcohol consumption, binge eating, and drug use.[44] The passion mindset also makes it harder for young people to connect with their peers. An article in *Emotion* put it succinctly: the more people value happiness, the lonelier they feel on a daily basis.[45] The outcomes of the passion mindset are similar to those of the performance mindset. Both lead to what we most fear—poor performance and poor mental health.

The Antidote: The Purpose Mindset

We've discussed how and why the performance and passion mindsets are so deeply embedded in the ways we think and make life decisions and why decisions that evolve from these mindsets are tied to so much struggle and adversity. In this book, we present a very different lens for decision-making that is tied to radically different outcomes for students and society. Research from our lab informs this framework we call the *purpose mindset*. Students with this mindset thrive despite the inevitable stresses of navigating school and early careers. Findings from our research and other studies showed that compared with their peers, students with a purpose mindset were more engaged in school, got better grades, and had higher test scores.[46] They not only perform better, but also have increased subjective well-being.[47] They built stronger and longer-lasting relationships with their peers and teachers.[48] The benefits of the purpose mindset stretch beyond school. After graduating from college, people who find purpose in their careers are much more likely to be thriving in their lives. They report greater well-being, and are even living longer lives.[49] People with a purpose mindset are physically, emotionally, and financially thriving in a way their peers are not.

So, what is the purpose mindset? How is it different from the other two mindsets?

Picture a balance scale. On one end is performance mindset; outward success is king. On the other is passion mindset; inward well-being is king. The purpose mindset is the perfect balance between them. It's about pursuing goals that are of consequence in the world (satisfying the need for outward success) *and* personally meaningful (satisfying inward well-being). It's a mindset that's good for the world and for the soul. Here's how it reaps the external *and* internal rewards expected of (but not delivered by) the performance and passion mindsets.

First, the purpose mindset is about playing the *long game*. It's not immediately attainable. It's not a fleeting desire, a quick fix, or an impulsive purchase. Trying to finish your homework by nine o'clock isn't a purpose. Making honor roll or landing the lead in the school play isn't a purpose. But wanting to become a nurse or doctor to alleviate suffering, or wanting to get a degree in social work to advocate on behalf of child trauma survivors, or wanting to raise children in a healthy environment are long-term purposes. They persist. They can take a while. They require commitment.

Second, the purpose mindset is about pursuing something that's *personally meaningful*. No one can give you a purpose, or persuade you to pursue one. A parent can tell a student to work hard to get straight As in high school, or to submit internship applications, or to be a person of integrity. But if those things don't feel personally meaningful, and if a student is only doing something because a parent wants them to—that's not their purpose. If they're chasing after a dream that's fueled by society's values and not their own—that's not their purpose either. It's someone else's expectations, but not purpose. Purpose has to be owned, it has to be something you buy into and really want to do.

The third essential aspect is: purpose is not all about you.

That is, it's not *just* for your personal happiness, security, and advancement. It's pursuing a goal that *also* contributes to people and places beyond the self. A purposeful goal is one that, if accomplished, will contribute to the world. Research doesn't say what the contribution should be, whether large or small, and who gets to judge whether you're successful in accomplishing it, and whether it makes the world better or not. Purpose simply includes an intention to make a contribution to someone else besides yourself.

When these things (long game, personally meaningful, and contribution) are present and working in tandem, you will see all the benefits of the purpose mindset in action.

The purpose mindset can serve as a powerful motivator behind the immediate goals and motives that drive daily behavior. Kyle, a first-generation immigrant student, wanted to go to college. Many of his peers saw college as just an expected stop along their journey to success. But it meant much more to Kyle. He struggled academically and worked harder than any of his peers. He would stop at nothing to make his family's sacrifices as unskilled laborers worth it by achieving economic mobility. So, going to college in and of itself wasn't his purpose. It was a milestone on a longer journey. A stepping-stone goal toward his greater purpose of raising his family's economic and emotional security.

Adults hyper-focus on short-term goals students should pursue, while overlooking the deeper reasons and purposes behind these goals. We role-model and cajole and pressure young people so that they learn to live busy and chaotic lives chasing short-term goals. Getting straight As, getting into college, or landing a particular job. The problems arise when we don't support students to explore *why* these goals matter.

Purpose provides perspective and direction if we can see our long-term goals in the distance. When astronauts have seen Earth from afar for the first time, they've described the profoundness of this perspective shift. Astronaut Edgar Mitchell, who saw Earth from the moon in 1971, explained, "You develop an instant global consciousness, a people orientation, an intense dissatisfaction with the state of the world, and a compulsion to do something about it."[50] You suddenly understand the "big picture" and feel connected to your daily life and yet bigger than the daily minutiae.

In the same way, seeing our purpose clearly is like seeing Earth in the distance. We realize that *this* is where we're headed. That we have a role to play on the planet. This is our mission and calling, and it's beautiful. We develop a sense of compassion for a need beyond our own. And the will to be of service.

With a purposeful goal in mind, we connect our short-term goals to something greater. Purpose provides the long-view hope that gives our everyday tasks and responsibilities meaning.

So many students, from the poorest to the richest schools, are disengaged. Tell them to study for their algebra final and you will get no pulse. But Kyle had a different view. He wasn't just taking a test, he was taking a step toward liberating his family from poverty. Students who haven't seen the Earth from space lack direction and are easily influenced by others. Young people like Kyle have a better sense of their own identity, take more initiative, and are more self-directive. Purpose is the navigation tool that guides our actions, behaviors, and decisions. In an ever-changing and uncertain world, it's our North Star, guiding us in a meaningful direction, even if we don't know exactly where we will end up.

Yet, as any parent or mentor can attest, clarifying one's purpose takes time, and the process is different for every person. Discovering purpose can feel frustratingly random or serendipitous. Where some people seem to be born with a sense of purpose, others struggle to develop it despite immense effort and support. Students in our research and other studies fell into four groups:

- "The Adrift" (low search, low commitment): students who show little interest in exploring avenues for living purposefully;

- "The Too Soon Decided" (low search, high commitment): students who have latched on to causes or aspirations that may have more to do with someone else's expectations for them than a sense of personal meaning tied to who they are and what contribution they want to make in the world;

- "The Searchers + Samplers" (high search, low commitment): students who've participated in all sorts of meaningful activities but lack real commitment to any long-term aspiration;

- "The Purpose-Driven" (high search, high commitment): students who have engaged in a period of exploration and have identified something that matters to them, understand why it matters to them, and are currently engaged in activities related to their long-game goal.[51]

The purpose mindset is extremely beneficial, but getting there isn't second nature. It involves struggle. It requires guidance to expand our perspective and draw our attention to the aspects of life we don't typically notice. Writing about the Hubble Space Telescope in the *Atlantic Monthly*, Marina Koren explains the benefits of glimpsing places that exist beyond ourselves, especially during a global pandemic that has made so many people's lives smaller: "Imagine yourself at a scenic vista somewhere on Earth, such as the rim of the Grand Canyon or the shore of an ocean stretching out past the horizon line. As your brain processes the view and its sheer vastness, feelings of awe kick in."[52] With this awe can come feelings of smallness and insignificance in the face of something larger than ourselves. And yet research has shown that this can be a good thing. Awe can make us feel more connected with others. David Yaden, who has studied self-transcendence, including in astronauts, explained the paradox of seeing space images or Earth from afar. And it's true of seeing purpose: "[seeing this long view] can draw our attention to the preciousness of local meaning—our loved ones, people close to us, this Earth."[53] When we step back from our daily activities and people, and look at them from the perspective of our long-term purpose, we gain a greater appreciation of our lives. Kahlil Gibran wrote a poem that describes the clarity and appreciation that comes with stepping back from life:

> When you part from your friend, you grieve not;
> For that which you love most in him may be clearer in his absence,
> as the mountain to the climber is clearer from the plain.[54]

Our research and work are designed to help you see the bigger picture, and how your current life moves in a direction that is not so random after all. Drawing upon a combined fifty years of work in the field and findings from Belle's lab, we've written this book to help people in all stages and from all walks of life cultivate a purpose mindset, and use it to navigate life decisions.

We will dispel commonly held views about what purpose is and isn't. Often purpose is viewed as a singular entity that people need to "find" rather than something to be cultivated throughout life. And it is erroneously seen as a luxury for privileged people. In actuality, marginalized and underserved young people often develop more purpose than their privileged peers. Purpose is also misunderstood as an endeavor for touchy-feely, idealistic, self-sacrificing, silly people who don't want or need to "make a good living." But the reality is that purpose can be found within any job or career, and those who have it are *ten times* as likely to be happy and healthy.[55] They also don't have to sacrifice a paycheck for it.

Purpose is often conflated with passion, when actually passion is only half of the equation. Passion is defined by self-interest; purpose is defined by an interest in both self and others. Purposeful students are passionate about doing something with their lives that benefits more than just themselves. Purpose is even confused with happiness; happiness is a temporary emotional state determined by "positive" circumstances, whereas purpose is a higher aspiration that carries one through the most difficult of circumstances. All of this misinformation converges on a false message: that purpose is a luxury and a burden that's out of reach except for the privileged few.

Purpose is for everyone. It's the lifeblood that leads to success inside and out. Therefore, our first rule of navigation is to resist the passion and performance mindsets and commit to adopting a purpose mindset. In the next four chapters, using the five purpose principles, we will show you how to do just that.

2

Games

Play growth games even when competing in fixed games.

Life is a game. We must keep playing the game. The more
we play, the more we will understand the game of life.

—LAILAH GIFTY AKITA

Doers, Not Deciders

The course began predictably, with students introducing themselves by their names and majors. As students took their turns, an interesting pattern emerged: most had not one but two majors. Many listed two majors *plus* a minor. Then came a tidy articulation of their career aspirations: organizational psychologist, entrepreneur, human resources professional, high school principal, human rights attorney, to name a few. They were so impressive, so motivated. As they rattled off surefire plans for success, we side-eyed each other, thinking:

"This class is over, we've got nothing for them."

Such was the inauspicious start to our True North college program.

We had designed this empirically based curriculum to help students find their purpose. We had just delivered it to underserved high school students in Boston with great success. In a randomized control trial, program participants who applied our five purpose principles were significantly more motivated in school, got better grades, and were more likely to go to college than control group students. These results were cause for celebration, because most students of low socioeconomic backgrounds struggle to get into college—only 14 percent graduate from a four-year college within eight years of graduating from high school.[1] We adapted it for college students, because we felt sure that students from other backgrounds would benefit, too. Now, just fifteen minutes into the first class, they burst our bubble. These superstars were saying they already knew what they wanted in life. They seemed well on their way to executing their career plans.

Or so we thought.

Problems in Paradise

On the surface, they had it all together. They had the plan down. Enter a top university. Check. Excel in academics. Check. Take advantage of opportunities. Check. Jump through more hoops. Check. Pump up résumé. Check.

But as the semester progressed, their confidence began to crack. Despite having their pick of academic and professional opportunities, a cheering squad of parents and teachers, and a stellar record, they were terrified of the future. Why?

They had no clue how to *decide* what to do. They were struggling to find direction. They felt pressure to pursue goals that fit with their parents', peers', and society's definitions of success. They were busy applying to the crème de la crème of programs, internships, and jobs. But doing a lot didn't mean they felt solid about their choices. They agonized constantly. "Did *I* choose this or was the choice made for me?" "Am I doing the *right* thing?" "What even is the right thing?" "Is the right thing the right thing for *me*?"

When asked, "What're you up to after graduation?" it felt better to fake an answer than admit to not having one. But in truth they felt lost and uncertain. If these super-successful students were struggling, what about their less-privileged peers across the country?

Students everywhere feel overwhelming pressure to make the "right" decision—to make good with their educational investment. But they have no idea how. They don't know what to value. They aren't sure what's most important to them. As a result, they can't make big decisions. Should I follow the money or follow my heart? Should I be practical or passionate? Do I do what my parents want or what I want? They aren't taught how to grapple with these questions as they wander down the unmarked road into young adulthood.

Our students represent a generation that knows how to DO, DO, DO. Put a task in front of them, and consider it done. They're busy bumblebees. The problem isn't *doing,* it's *deciding.* Young people know what they *should* do, but how do they decide what *they* want to do?

- - - - - - - - - - - - - - - -

Playing the Long Game

When it comes to life advice, young people hear the same thing over and over again: "Figure out what you're *good* at, and do it." This platitude offers little practical value and is woefully misleading. Because what does it mean to be "good at" something? Today, our kids are objectively "good" at a whole range of things, making this question even more unanswerable and unhelpful. Despite this, people tend to consider themselves good at the things they've been successful doing. So our definition of strengths is determined by success. But that opens up a whole different can of worms: How do we define success?

We'll demonstrate how two opposing definitions of success (one that fuels the performance mindset, and the other a purpose mindset) make all the difference in how we view our strengths. We'll also dispel the myth that "it's your job to identify your students' strengths for them."

Instead, we'll show you how to help them identify their own strengths—the ones they most delight in. The ones they'll be self-motivated to grow and use their whole lives.

In the Eye of the Beholder

Tim Klein was a dominant tennis player in high school. Over his four-year career he amassed a record of 52–4. You read that right—he only lost four times total in his entire high school career. During his freshman year, his high school won the state championship, where Tim also placed second in the state doubles championship. During his senior year, he went undefeated and was a top-ten ranked player. Tim continued playing tennis in college. As a freshman, he went 7–4, helping his college win a conference championship while also setting a school record for the most team wins in a season.

By all metrics, Tim was incredibly "good at" tennis. And successful, to boot. However, we will admit that we omitted some vital details:

Tim is from Vermont.

While Vermont is a beautiful state and an amazing place to grow up, athletics, especially tennis, is not one of its strong suits. In fact, Vermont has one of the least-competitive high school tennis systems in the country. Tim began playing as a ten-year-old, which by national tennis standards is a *late* start. In Vermont, however, this gave Tim years of advantage over many of his competitors. Many Vermonters *start* playing in middle school or high school. It wasn't uncommon for Tim's high school to compete against students who had *never played a match before*. In addition to a lack of competition, Tim also benefited from the demographics of Vermont—it's a small state with under a million people in it. When his high school won the state championship, there were only eight other schools competing in the entire division. Tim was a big fish in a small pond, and his "success" in tennis reflected that.

Tim enjoyed more of the "big fish in a small pond" benefits when he played college tennis. We forgot to mention *where* Tim played college tennis—on a small Division III team. His teammates and opponents were not scholarship athletes who had devoted their lives to the sport—he was playing people with similar skill sets and commitment to the game that he had. So, when Tim boasts about breaking records, and winning titles and conference championships, perhaps he should include an asterisk providing context to his achievements.

Given this new information about Tim's tennis career, are we still feeling like Tim was incredibly "good at" tennis? He admits that the majority of his "success" came from the luck of being born in a small state where most people didn't care about tennis. If he'd been born a few hundred miles south, in New York or New Jersey, he would have been considered an average to below-average player with few accolades to boast about. If he'd gone forty-five miles north to a Division I team, there's a good chance he wouldn't have made the tennis team. Not to sleep on Tim's fantastic tennis career, but being "good at" something or "successful" is relative.

What's it even mean to be successful? Who gets to say? Definitions of "success" and being "good at" something are actually very arbitrary. Success (and strengths) are in the eye of the beholder.

Life Is a Game

Games are a powerful metaphor for life—they reflect principles for how the world works. "It's not how you win, it's how you play the game." "Winning isn't everything, it's the only thing." Games explain how business is done: that idea is a "slam dunk," we "dropped the ball" last quarter. Games describe what's going down politically: the election is a "toss-up," the candidate is a "wild card." Games even offer pro-tips for your love life: "Don't play mind games," "Don't hate the player, hate the game," and "Don't get played."

Games existed before written language. Games pass on the ideas of their cultures from generation to generation. Pieces that are still essential in most board games today were the basis of the oldest game . . . dice! They first appeared as small carved painted stones found at a burial mound in southeast Turkey—five thousand years ago.

Fast-forward to today, when games still form the foundation of our collective conscience. The global market value of board games was estimated at over $7 billion in 2017 and is expected to exceed $12 billion by 2023. And video games? Estimates are that by 2023, the game market will surpass $200 billion.[2] The streaming video game platform Twitch has on average 15 million people *watching other people play* video games each day.[3]

Games do more than entertain us, they reveal truths about how we pursue life goals. The game maker for the *New York Times* (yes, there is such a job) describes a game as a structure that you navigate by making a series of interesting choices. Each choice you make determines the course of play, exposing who you are and how you think. Similarly, pursuing your life goals involves making a series of interesting life choices. The choices you make determine the course of your life, and expose who you are and how you think.

Growth Games vs. Fixed Games

There are fundamentally two types of games—*fixed games* and *growth games*.[4]

Let's play a round of Hand Cricket, right now, so you can see what we're talking about. It's like Rock, Paper, Scissors. Shake your fist, "1, 2, 3, shoot!" and throw out any number of fingers. (We'll put our choice at the end of the chapter.) If our combined fingers total an even number, you win. Odd number, we win. This is a "fixed game"; there are limited and specific options to choose from (up to five fingers), and a limited, specific end goal—to defeat your opponent by selecting a number that, when added to their number, is even.

Now let's play Fortunately, Unfortunately. This is a storytelling game that gets you thinking about how much better (and worse) things can get. As the first team, we'll make up a premise: "Once there were two best friends who could hear each other's thoughts."

As the second team, you now add a turn-for-the-worse plot twist, like "Unfortunately, one of them got 'Leaving on a Jet Plane' stuck in her head."

Now, it's our turn again to add a turn-for-the-better plot twist, like "Fortunately, this gave the other a cool idea—to take a trip together to Timbuktu."

Then it's your turn again. And so on. We can play this story out as long as we want it to go, embellishing it into a masterful, unending adventure. This involves open-ended play. It's what we call a *growth* game; we can create anything we can imagine. In a growth game, there are fewer rules or restrictions. There's no end goal or outcome we're striving after. As long as we're playing and having fun, we're doing it right.

Open vs. Closed Play

LEGO has existed for eighty-plus years and is still widely considered the most popular building toy on the planet. But a lot has changed since the glory days when playing LEGOs meant creating something *you* conjured up from a box of assorted pieces of all shapes and sizes. There was nothing in particular you were tasked with making; you had the freedom to create whatever your heart desired. You could build cars, houses, cities, or stylish abstract sculptures—it was entirely up to you. Sky's the limit! Your only objective was to keep playing, to keep building, to keep having fun. A *growth game*.

LEGOs is a different game today. The LEGO website reassures you that "you can't go wrong, just follow the easy building instructions." These instructions dictate *exactly* what to build—a *Star Wars* Death Star, a *Pirates of the Caribbean* ghost ship, or the Indominus Rex from *Jurassic World*.

Cool creations, for sure—someone else had a great idea, and if you just follow their instructions to a T . . . Voilà! You've re-created their idea! The website leaves out: "you can go very wrong if you don't follow the instructions." And if you lose a piece, God be with you. And when that kit is built, game over—this $100 kit that got you pumped up last week is on a shelf collecting dust. A *fixed game*.

People play fixed games for the outcome, which is to win. And fixed games are defined by limitations. The rules tell you *what* you can and cannot do and *who* can or cannot play.

In contrast, people play growth games for the process; the goal is to enjoy playing and to keep on playing for as long as possible. Growth games are defined by possibility. There are no restrictions on what can be done and who can participate.

More than a Mindset

The terms "growth" and "fixed" are often associated with Carol Dweck's growth and fixed mindset theory. People with a growth mindset believe you can grow your abilities (through good strategies, hard work, and mentoring). Fixed-mindset people believe you're born with all the talents you will ever have and there's not much you can do to change them. Growth-mindset people do better in school, are more adventurous, and bounce back better from failures.[5] They achieve more overall because they're less worried about looking competent and more interested in actually learning.

Unfortunately, a growth mindset doesn't guarantee that good things will happen. We can have a growth mindset all we want, but if our settings (our school, workplace, career field) play the talent game (a fixed game), we'll be hard-pressed to practice growth-mindset behaviors, such as collaborating and sharing information, taking risks and innovating, and seeking feedback and admitting errors. In other words, the games we play influence the mindsets we adopt. We shouldn't expect a young person to have a growth mindset when they're only ever competing in fixed games.

In Suzanne Collins's dystopian series *The Hunger Games* there's a deadly tournament that pits children from thirteen districts in varying states of poverty against each other. There can be only one victor. Everyone else loses. You can imagine the mindset of the contestants. You better believe that they're doing all they can to survive by using whatever strengths help them to beat their opponents. No time to mess around with growing the strengths they most enjoy using. That's a luxury that can't be afforded here. School has become like *The Hunger Games*—a fixed game with limited winners leaving everyone else feeling like a loser. School promotes a fixed mindset (doing what you're naturally good at) and a performance mindset (where success is measured by how we compare with others). The subconscious strategy becomes: *figure out what you can do better than others* if you want to come out ahead. And you'll know you're better at doing the thing than other people by applying quantifiable metrics—acceptance into competitive colleges, number of trophies, number of followers, income, five-star reviews. The numbers and awards tell us who's good—and who isn't. Who's successful—and who isn't. Growth games are different. They aren't about competing with other people, but pushing to become the best version of ourselves. Where fixed games focus on what we want to *get*, growth games are more concerned with what we want to *do*.

What Game Are You Playing?

So the type of game you're playing makes all the difference. Context matters and shapes mindset. That said, it can be hard to know which games we're playing. Below we differentiate fixed and growth games based on three aspects of a game—its goals (outcomes that players are working toward), rules (specific ways players can/can't achieve the goal), and feedback (signs of players' progress).[6] Your responses to three questions (reflecting the three aspects of a game) can reveal which game you're playing:

- What's your endgame? (Goal)

- What rules do you play by? (Rules)

- What's your measure of success? (Feedback)

Fixed Games

What's Your Endgame?
In a fixed game, the goal is simply to win. And everyone's a loser except the winner. In a study conducted by Belle's lab,[7] data revealed four over-

arching sources of stress among high school students: (1) pressures to win, (2) narrow constructions of success, (3) peer competition, and (4) parents' expectations. These pressures to win the fixed game of school ramped up from one year to the next, like a freight train building momentum until it reached breakneck speed by junior year. Sixth- and seventh-graders complained about some stress from the desire to meet teachers' expectations, but described such stressors as still manageable, all in all. These kids didn't focus solely on "winning," because time was on their side. They felt a freedom to try new things and interests because performance "still didn't count." Many were playing a growth game, but this didn't last long. They anticipated the rising tide of performance expectations to come. One student put it this way:

> When I get a bad grade, I'm like, "Oh. Is this going to affect my future? I really hope it doesn't." But I sort of push it off. I'm like, "I'm not in high school yet. It's not going to affect college."

Eighth- and ninth-graders transitioning to high school began to feel pressured to meet academic and extracurricular demands and balance all these "responsibilities." They said things like: "It's just really stressful trying to get it all done." They were rapidly losing sight of the "want-tos" of their growth game. And any previous sense of joy and freedom in their activities gave way to the "have-tos" of their fixed game. By eleventh grade, students' stress levels were through the roof. Every little failure seemed increasingly high stakes—a threat to winning the fixed game. An eleventh-grader captured the stress and stakes this way:

> I think 10th grade stress is "in the moment" stress . . . If I fail this test, then I might fail this class. But then, junior year it's like if I fail this test, I won't get into college . . . I won't have a good job.

These are the signs of being *all in* to win a fixed game. Unfortunately, being *all in* for a fixed game means that *if you're not winning, you're losing*. If you don't have the best grades and test scores, and the leadership positions in clubs and teams, then you're losing. Prominent in the students' narratives was a fixation on getting "good grades" to get into a "good college" to secure a "good career." "Good grades" meant straight As, "good colleges" meant the most elite universities, and "good careers" meant those that were the highest paid and highest status. And while they believed that happiness would come through achieving this end-game, this zero-sum game was costing them their self-esteem and mental health.

What Rules Are You Playing By?

In fixed games, the rules are rigid—they place structural limits on what you can and can't do. We want to believe that rules are in place to make sure no one has an unfair advantage. We want to believe in the American dream, where everyone who works hard can get ahead. Unfortunately, this vision of meritocracy is a myth. There is *no* level playing field. Rules will always advantage some people and disadvantage others. For example, we'd like to think that the NBA is a perfect meritocracy—the very *best* players have earned the right to play. Yet the rules of basketball advantage some people and disadvantage others. An NBA basketball hoop must be exactly ten feet tall—an obvious plus for tall people. A player who's seven feet tall is twenty times more likely to play in the NBA than someone who is six foot six.[8] Even if rules in basketball exist for the sake of fairness, the reality is they aren't always fair.

Similarly, the rules of the college admission process are supposed to ensure that any student who works hard and deserves to be admitted can get in fair and square. But the Varsity Blues scandal proved this isn't the case when wealthy, white families exploited the rules. The National Bureau of Economics reported that students from the top 1 percent income bracket are 77 percent more likely to attend an Ivy League university than are those from the bottom income quintile. At five of the eight Ivy League schools, there are more "1 percenters" than low-income and middle-income students *combined*. High-income students of color are less likely to attend prestigious institutions than middle-income white students.[9]

These rigged rules ripple into the workforce. White men and women "earn" 22 percent more than Black men and 34 percent more than Black women with the *same* work experience. Up to 80 percent of the wage gaps are due to inequalities in access to and completion of higher education. Students from the top quartile of family income and parental education who have low test scores still have a 71 percent chance of graduating from college and getting a good job by their mid-twenties. But students from low-income backgrounds with top test scores have only a 31 percent chance of doing so.[10]

Structural inequities on the basis of skin color, gender, or other demographic characteristics are the results of *unfair rules of a fixed game.* Isabel Wilkerson defines *caste* as "the granting or withholding of respect, status, honor, attention, privileges, resources, benefit of the doubt, and human kindness to someone on the basis of their perceived rank or standing in the hierarchy." She explains how *caste is the rule system of most fixed games:* "we are all born into a silent war-game, centuries old, enlisted in teams not of our own choosing. The side to which we are assigned in the American system of categorizing people is proclaimed by the team uniform that each caste wears, signaling our presumed worth and potential."[11]

Our kids get it. Studies show that they (more than any other generation, even baby boomers) are sensitive to social injustices. Rules that are rigged. For example, they strongly believe that women are discriminated against in getting a college education and in jobs.[12]

What's Your Measure of Success?

In fixed games, feedback on how you're doing in the game comes in the form of external rewards. Grades. Class ranks. Trophies. Raises. Approval from others. Apart from these incentives, what's the point in playing? We play fixed games mainly for the win, and less for the joy of playing.

And even when we do win, it can be anticlimactic. Because playing solely for external rewards leaves us feeling empty. Research suggests that grades don't actually inspire students to learn more or work harder.[13] They actually detract from academic motivation and inhibit learning.[14] Extrinsically motivated students are more likely to use "shallow-learning" strategies, and they struggle to push through adversities or challenges.[15] Gunning for external rewards is also tied to poorer mental health. Extrinsically motivated business students had "lower psychological well-being, showed more signs of internal distress, and engaged in more substance use than those who cared less about extrinsic goals."[16] And these findings hold true in the world of work. A study of 2000 U.S. lawyers found that those working in high-powered, high-paying private firms were far *less* happy than those serving in public service roles, even though the latter were paid far less.[17] The "high-powered" attorneys had attained the American dream and achieved our shared cultural definition of success. They were winners. Why were they so unhappy?

It's not the money itself that causes poor outcomes. People who pursued money for intrinsic reasons—personal growth, community service, and leisure—had improved well-being and happiness.[18] But not so for people who were after money for extrinsic reasons—prestige, status, and power. Their well-being suffered even if they accomplished their goals. People who pursue money in the service of fixed games don't benefit.

Growth Games

What's Your Endgame?

Growth games are a different story. When playing growth games, your goal is to play for as long as you can. To keep learning, growing, and enjoying the game.

What Rules Are You Playing By?

In contrast to fixed games, where you're forced to play by the rules, in growth games there are rules of thumb that are informative, not restrictive. They take the form of wisdom passed down from other players who have accumulated experience and knowledge from their own successes in growth games. We know we're playing a growth game when we *seek out rules* to learn from. The "rules" are resources that help all players get better at their growth game.

What's Your Measure of Success?

In growth games, you know you're doing well when the game is fun. Not necessarily all the time, but you want to keep playing and getting better at it. Growth games are inherently rewarding because you get to use the strengths you delight in (as opposed to only those necessary for the win). Growth games aren't about winning by beating others; they are about a sense of mastery, competence, fulfilling one's purpose, and most importantly, contributing to needs in the world, rather than just serving oneself. And so success in growth games is measured by *personal progress* and *positive impact beyond yourself.* Is your hard work paying off? Are you learning from your mistakes? Can you feel yourself improving? And can you feel the world around you improving? These questions are important because we want to keep improving—not to beat others, but to keep playing.

Notice what happens when students *choose* their own activities or their own goals, rather than being made to do something. They're more self-directed, engaged, and resilient. This is the same motivation that drives growth games. Intrinsically motivated students do better—they work harder, learn more, and thrive in school. They're also more positive and self-regulated, better problem solvers, and more likely to use deep-learning skills. When people *want* to play, they bring their A game. Intrinsic motivation improves performance.

Growth games also spark self-perpetuating feedback loops. Because we enjoy growth-oriented games, we're more likely to play hard, to excel, and to go after the next goal we set. What does this super-satisfying feedback loop do for strengths? The act of using the strengths we most delight in is good for the mind, body, and performance. People who use their strengths at school do better academically, and feel better.[19] People who use their strengths at work are more engaged, perform better, and are more likely to stay.[20]

Refer to this summary table whenever you need a heart check about whether you're playing a fixed game or growth game.

	Fixed Games	**Growth Games**
Goal	To win (outcome-oriented)	To keep playing (process-oriented)
Rules	Rigid	Flexible
Feedback	Extrinsic rewards	Intrinsic rewards

Are you playing *to win* or *to keep playing*? Are the rules *rigid* or *flexible*? Are your rewards mostly *extrinsic* or *intrinsic*?

It's Not All or Nothing: Choose Growth Games First

Your first thought might be: "Give me some growth games! Doing what I love, playing by my own rules, nothing to lose or prove . . . It's a no-brainer!"

Until a little voice reminds you, "I have bills to pay, kids to feed, responsibilities . . . And my kids have responsibilities—they've got to do well in school to land a decent job so they can pay their bills, feed their kids, etc."

And suddenly our practical minds land right back where we started: "I have to play fixed games—whether I like it or not." I must do so for survival's sake and for success's sake. Growth games might even seem like a distraction from the full commitment needed to succeed in fixed games—getting into college, internships, graduate school, and careers that pay.

The truth is, it's not all or nothing. *You can compete in a fixed game while playing a growth game.* In fact, you'll be better at your fixed game if you first figure out what your growth game is and prioritize it. For example, if you are interested in going to medical school, mainly because it is a prestigious goal and you think you can be good at it, you will be entering a grueling, fixed game. But if your motivation is your love for learning about the subject matter, your desire to meet certain needs in the world through the practice of medicine, you'll be in a growth game. Identifying your growth game first will help you succeed in the fixed game.

At the height of his career, John Wooden coached the UCLA men's basketball team to win a record-breaking ten NCAA championships in a twelve-year span, including seven titles in a row. The secret to his success was how he defined his team's growth game: "Success is peace of mind, which is a direct result of self-satisfaction in knowing you made the effort to do your best to become the best that you are capable of becoming."[21]

Notice how his definition of success says nothing of outcomes, other competitors, or wins and losses. Instead, it's about being the best versions of themselves. A goal that won't grow old. This coach got upset when his team wasn't playing up to their potential, even if they won the game. Other times he beamed with pride when they had played their hearts out, even if they lost the game! This is prioritizing your growth game, not living to win the fixed game. It's the full use of the strengths you most delight in. The freedom and joy of working toward your best self.

Finding Strength: How to Play the Game

Research from Belle's lab suggests that purpose is a long-term aspiration that gets you using the strengths you love using. These are the strengths you *want* to keep using in your long game. These findings held true with both affluent and impoverished students. In an impoverished community that works and lives in a Guatemala City garbage dump, students who graduated from high school against all odds had an aspiration that involved using strengths they delighted in. They noticed ways to use their strengths even in the most mundane jobs and tasks. So while it's easy to assume that purpose is a luxury, and only the privileged get to use the strengths they delight in, the data tell a different story.[22] Even those who needed to work for survival's sake (and had limited work options) were more likely to overcome obstacles and achieve goals when playing their growth game. You know you're playing a growth game when you're using strengths you delight in.

That said, two out of three people are not aware of their strengths, let alone the strengths they most delight in.[23] To help you identify your strengths, check out the VIA Institute's Character Strength Survey—a validated tool, easily accessible at www.viacharacter.org. In just a few minutes, this diagnostic test can provide you with a comprehensive profile of your strengths. It will give you a sense of your character strengths, and then it's up to you to discern *why* these are your character strengths.

In purpose work, understanding *why* we value certain strengths is just as important as knowing what they are. Engage in a dialogue with students after they take the VIA survey. Ask if they agree with the results or if they would change any of the strengths attributed to them. Then, explore how they apply these strengths:

- Where in your life have you found success using these strengths?

- Why are these strengths important to you?

- Do you feel you've always had these strengths, or that you developed them over time?

- Where/how can you continue developing these strengths you value?

High school students we will call Aran and Corinne were vying to get into the same selective university. Both had stellar academic records—many AP classes, strong GPAs and standardized test scores, and high class rankings. Both had résumés loaded with extracurricular activities signaling their "well-roundedness." On paper, they were indistinguishable. But something did distinguish them: one was playing a growth game, and one was not.

Aran's motivation to enter this university was to prove himself. He had two older brothers who had both gone to Ivies. Seeing his parents' glowing with pride sent a clear message about the value of this accomplishment. Now it was his turn to prove himself by achieving the same. Aran was playing a fixed game; his goal was to win, and winning was having an acceptance letter in hand.

Corinne's obsession since childhood was Egypt. All things Egypt. The bottomless reservoir of discoveries about this fascinating land. She pored over the architecture of the pyramids. Examined the ornate jewelry of the pharaohs. Soaked up the historical drama of Cleopatra and other historical figures. And other subjects were passions, too, because they served to unlock more of the mysteries of Egypt. Math helped her understand the ancient Egyptian sciences of astronomy and astrology. History provided tools for accessing resources for researching the past. These endeavors never grew old. Each discovery was the key to opening yet another door, building upon a deep and significant area of expertise. Studying ancient Egypt was her growth game; she played for its own sake and found it inherently pleasurable. During her college search, she discovered a way to keep playing this game—by applying for a little-known program at the university of her top choice called the Department of Egyptology and Assyriology. Finding this program inspired Corinne to double down on her already stellar grades; her primary motivation for attending this university was to continue pursuing her passion.

Both students were in the race for entry into one of the most competitive universities in the country. On the surface, they were both competing for the same prize. But below the surface, only one of these students was playing a growth game. Corinne was shooting for a chance to build on her Egyptian scholarship. Aran was competing to measure up to his brothers and every other applicant to this university. Same goal (get admitted to university); different game.

You can bring your growth game to a fixed game. You may be playing someone else's fixed game, but a growth game is yours alone. Some of the most influential people are thriving in a fixed game because of their growth game:

- Oprah Winfrey's fixed game is to increase her TV ratings. Her growth game is to inspire people to be more than they think they can be.

- Martin Luther King Jr.'s fixed game was to leverage political power. His growth game was to promote racial equity.

- Elon Musk's fixed game is to sell electric cars. His growth game is to get people to Mars.

- Ruth Bader Ginsberg's fixed game was to practice American law. Her growth game was to advance gender equity.

- MacArthur "Genius" award winner Tressie McMillan Cottom's fixed game is to write sociology books. Her growth game is to reimagine societies to better serve marginalized populations.

Get in the Game

What's your endgame? What rules do you play by? What's your measure of success? If answering these questions helped you realize you've been missing out on growth games, tomorrow is a new day. Research points to how to get in the game. In one study, a class of psychology students was explicitly told at the start of the semester that the goal of the class was to improve their learning by building skills for understanding and synthesizing the class content.[24] One group of students was given learning goals every class that built on the last class while also giving them specific things to learn during the next class. Another group was given a test before class to see which student performed the best. This subtle change in language shifted students' emphasis from a fixed game (getting a good grade/being the best) to a growth game (learning the content to the best of their ability). The impact of this intervention was dramatic: those playing the growth game closed the achievement gap between low- and high-income students. Helping students shift to a mastery orientation was profound. Low-income students' grades improved enough to go from failing to passing.

Students can go from fixed to growth games with even small shifts in language. They *want* to play growth games. Even in early adolescence, many of the video games they're most drawn to, such as Minecraft, Roblox, or Animal Crossing, are appealing because of their constant opportunities for advancement and growth.

Below find more pro-tips and activities for helping your people find and grow the strengths *they* want to use, and the games *they* want to play. Here are a few initial ideas. First, encourage them to try different activities and interact with people outside of their typical social circles to expand their thinking about who they are in the world. This is different from figuring it all out for them—telling them that they should pursue x, y, and z because it's what they're good at. What *you* think is not nearly as important as what *they* think. Instead, a powerful role you can play in your students' lives is to *affirm strengths that you see them delight in*. Your people already have an inkling about their gifts. They might just lack the confidence in their strengths or the language to articulate them. Your validation can provide the encouragement they need to integrate these strengths into their identity. Self-determination theory refers to this as "autonomy-supportive" parenting/guidance—actively taking students' perspectives, as well as providing support for self-expression, initiation, and self-endorsed activities.

Autonomy-supportive parenting can encourage students to play growth games. When they do, they thrive.[25] A meta-analysis of thirty-six parenting studies showed that autonomy-supportive parenting led to growth games, which in turn led to other positive outcomes—increased psychological health and school engagement.[26]

Bringing It All Together

Playing growth games = success and well-being. We want to play growth games. Playing them is good for us . . . and for the world around us.

The opposite is true for fixed games. We feel forced to play them. And then we're disillusioned even if we win them.

Corinne wanted to go to a university to study Egyptology. She enjoyed the process of studying it and delighted in being able to exercise these muscles, these strengths. Aran, on the other hand, felt forced to apply to this university to prove his worth. He didn't get the gratification of using his unique strengths to pursue this goal. Instead, he did whatever it took to increase his chances of admission. During application season, he was a stressed-out mess.

Aran was admitted to his dream university . . . and his elation lasted about six weeks. Once the initial excitement wore off, he was back to stressing over the next fixed game—how to succeed at an Ivy League university. Being accepted here didn't liberate him from his demons. Threats to his self-worth continued to plague him in the next fixed game with higher stakes.

Corinne was not admitted to her dream university. Perhaps the rules were rigged against her; she wasn't a legacy candidate like Aran was. She was understandably disappointed, but not for long. She was playing a growth game, so this outcome wasn't a dead end, just a bump in the road. After receiving her rejection letter, she began researching graduate programs that focused on Egypt. Her eyes never wavered from her true purpose. Her purpose lasted beyond admission into a particular university. Corinne entered another university as a history major. There she enthusiastically continued her growth game, honing her strengths, learning new skills, while enjoying the ride immensely.

It's never too late to help our students find their growth game. We can start by helping them see their strengths, and then fanning those flames. We must resist comparing them to other people. Their development isn't a race, it's a journey. One to be eased into, not forced or feared. Playing is winning enough. As long as they commit to growth, they're headed in the right direction. Success is not defined by anyone but themselves. These countercultural truths are key to winning whichever games they're playing.

- - - - - - - - - - - - - - -

Conclusion: True North

Now, back to the story about our students who seemed confident, but actually felt lost over their future directions. Uncovering their growth games clarified what they wanted in their lives. It gave them resolve to take some risks. Their self-exploration inspired their desire to contribute in the world—as principals, counselors, HR professionals, lawyers, corporate leaders. They recognized that their peers—some with plans to go into similar jobs—had different motivations. Some were on the fast track to fame and fortune via fixed games. They needed to ask themselves, were they committing to a life of poverty by not aiming for fame and fortune? Were they making a mistake?

Growth games helped them see what was truly important to them. Affirming their strengths gave them the resolve to make hard decisions that were right for them. Seeing their true strengths helped some change direction. For others, it strengthened their resolve about choices they were making. For all, recognizing their authentic strengths and their growth games provided an intentionality behind their decisions. They recognized that it was okay for them not to fall for the siren call of status, prestige, and power. That their trajectory wasn't right for everyone, but it was right for them. They had a sense of what they wanted to do. Now they could explain why.

That's the power of playing growth games.

(By the way, if you're here for Hand Cricket, we pick two. Did you win?)

3

Skill Sets

Future-proof your skills as a creator, facilitator, or driver.

Before I can tell *my life* what I want to do with it,
I must listen to *my life* telling me who I am.

—PARKER PALMER

Mastering Your Superpowers

The wonder of parenting is witnessing your child's disposition unfold over time like the petals of a blooming flower. The universal aspects. And the unique aspects. The parts you know and the parts you don't know. Of course, humans come into the world with slight variations, but the similarities are mind-boggling. The Dalai Lama went so far as to say: "Basically we are the same human being—different faith, different race, different language, even different cultures. These are secondary. When we come from [the] womb—no difference of religion, no difference of nationality, no difference of culture . . . We are the same human being—mentally, emotionally, physically the same . . . everybody has a sense of self and experience of pleasure, pain, suffering, happiness." This is the *Dalai Lama* speaking—recipient of the Nobel Peace Prize for uniting diverse groups of people. And yet he points out that when it comes down to it, we—the 7.8 billion people in the world—are not that different.

This universality means we can draw on a wealth of research (and wisdom of generations) to do right by our students. Sure, there are dicey moments when we don't know what to do. But thanks to the countless parenting books and websites hawking advice on major milestones and experiences from birth through young adulthood, we have good intel at our fingertips. How to help them sleep through the night. Recover from tantrums. Eat their veggies. Mind their manners. Ride a bike. Be a good friend. Get off their phone. Read for pleasure. Not blame us for everything in therapy. And have good taste in music.

But there's a mysterious part of parenting that doesn't come with a manual. Genetic predictability has its limits. No matter how similarly we parent our children, the siblings each have a unique essence. It's this elusive, unique core of an individual that's hard to put a finger on. Students often lack this deep self-awareness. We must observe them closely to catch glimpses of this essence—their unique predispositions. Their way of being in the world. Parker Palmer likened one's true self or soul to a wild animal: "tough, resilient, savvy, self-sufficient, and yet exceedingly shy. If we want to see a wild animal, the last thing we should do is to go crashing through the woods, shouting for the creature to come out. But if we are willing to walk quietly into the woods and sit silently for an hour or two at the base of a tree, the creature we are waiting for may well emerge, and out of the corner of an eye we will catch a glimpse of the precious wildness we seek."[1]

It's this true essence of our students (what truly matters to them, and what makes them tick) that we have to tune in to as good mentors. And we should bring these parts of ourselves into the relationship, too. When we know our own true strengths and motivations, we can support our students to know theirs.

A student's activity in the physical world is a window into their hidden world—their unique persona. And this hidden world (of their strengths and motivations) is what fuels them in the physical world. So there's a reality beyond what we see. A reality that we have to wait for patiently . . . like watching for that wild creature in the woods. We can also call it forth.

It's this mysterious aspect of parenting/mentoring—how to welcome and water these predispositions—that we discuss in this chapter. So far we've introduced how to navigate life when you *commit to one mindset* and *play two games*. Now, we introduce a third navigation principle: *future-proof three skill sets*.

We'll show you how to build skills that have lasting relevance. Strengths and skills are two types of competency. By strengths we mean the abilities, curiosities, and character qualities you most delight in. When you're using these strengths in growth and fixed games, you feel like your best self. By skills we mean the expertise you need to do a job or perform a role. You master these competencies through zeroing in on activities and settings where you can practice them.

Mastering and future-proofing skills boost purpose in two related ways. The first is pragmatic. Building relevant skills enables you to become gainfully employed in a rapidly changing economy. The second is psychological. Building skills fulfills our innate psychological need for mastery. Skills help us navigate toward the activities, careers, and other pursuits aligned with our purpose.

Respect the Tech(nology)

Four of the world's largest companies—Apple, Amazon, Google, and Facebook—are worth a combined $4 trillion. Together, the wealth of these four companies makes them richer than Germany, the fourth-wealthiest country in the world. Apple was the first-ever multi-trillion-dollar company. More than four of five US households have an Amazon Prime membership.[2] Eighty-eight percent of all internet searches,[3] over 8.5 billion a day,[4] use Google. More than one in three people *on the entire planet* are active Facebook users.[5]

How did these companies become so dominant? What's behind their mind-blowing influence and growth? It's simple—they've leveraged emerging technology. Whether we like it or not, technology rules over the economy, as well as our lives. So what can we do to prepare our students to survive in "the real world"? To start, we need to get a better grasp of how technology is impacting the world they're stepping into.

Times They Are A-Changin'

Technology is responsible for the dramatic upgrade in quality of life we take for granted. Life expectancy has doubled in the last hundred years.[6] The infant mortality rate has dropped over 20 percent since 1960.[7] Thanks to the phone in your pocket, which has more power than the computers that first put humans on the moon,[8] you can access almost any article, book, or piece of music at the tap and swipe of your finger. A lion's share of societal progress directly results from technology.

Perhaps technology's most visceral impact is how it *replaces* the old with the new. We used to *call* a cab for a ride to the airport; now we push a button on our phone. We used to *push a button* to turn on the radio; now we *ask* the radio to turn itself on. We *dialed up* friends and family on rotary phones; now we *text* them. We *drove* to in-person doctors' visits; now we can *Zoom* in. Technology's long reach replacing old for new is felt in every nook and cranny of life.

A foundational theory in labor economics is *creative destruction*.[9] Its premise is that any economic innovation will destroy old ways of working and introduce new, more efficient ones. The theory first referenced industrial and manufacturing innovations, but it holds true today. What's changed is that digital technology—as opposed to the steam engine or the assembly line—is now the harbinger of employment destruction and growth. Automation, machine learning, and artificial learning are replacing human jobs by the day.

Over 36 million US jobs are at "high risk" of being automated.[10] Nearly 10 percent of all global manufacturing jobs, over 20 million in total, may be done by robots by 2030.[11] About one of three jobs in the world (1 billion in total) will be transformed by technology.[12]

Routine Is the Enemy

Technology replaces jobs, but not *all* jobs. Tech is on the prowl for routine tasks, especially the ones requiring minimal skill. This is called *routine-biased technological change* (RBTC).[13] If you've withdrawn cash from an ATM, used the self-checkout line at the supermarket, or been greeted by a machine when calling customer service about your phone bill—you've rumbled with tech that's replaced human jobs. A young fan of the Netflix series *Stranger Things* posted a question to fellow aficionados about the purpose of the "red room" on the show—"we frequently see Jonathan go inside this to 'refine' his photos or something. I don't quite understand what happens here. He puts the photo in water, and somehow this makes it more clear?"[14] He'd never heard of a darkroom! Tech has so rapidly automated photography that kids don't know that an entire industry was once devoted to developing photos. This is the power of *creative destruction*. Creative destruction first came for manual labor and blue-collar jobs. In the 1850s, over half of all American jobs were agrarian; it took half of the country's entire workforce to produce enough food for people. They worked hard at routine tasks like digging holes, harvesting crops, and tilling land. Machines have now upended manual labor. Less than 1.5 percent of US workers remain in agriculture.[15]

And that's not all. Bots are scanning for ways to transform our digital lives. They're watching our every move and capturing previously invisible human patterns—tracking mouse patterns, clicks, and communication. They do our chores, pay our bills on time, and get our appliances to obey our every thought. Anything we do on a computer repetitively or routinely, machines can do more efficiently. Routines consist of patterns; and if there's a pattern, a system can be designed. And if a system can be designed, an algorithm can be built. And if an algorithm can be built, a machine can automate our work. With each day, tech gets smarter at picking out patterns. Where machine tech automated the farming industry, automation is now coming for high-skilled, white-collar work.

College-educated workers are four times more likely to be negatively impacted by automation than those with just a high school degree.[16] Over 100,000 legal jobs, such as junior lawyers and paralegals, will be replaced by automation by 2036.[17] Artificial intelligence (AI) experts predict that there's a 50 percent chance that AI will automate 90 percent of human tasks in the next fifteen years.[18]

Like a plant, automation needs the right conditions to grow. It needs rigid settings and work characterized by rules, concrete thinking, and routine skills. Rules and skills, like compliance, memorization, and un-questioned rule following, are fertile ground for creative destruction.

If we're serious about preparing students for their future careers, we have to ask: Are schools prioritizing skills that will be evergreen, or the ones that will soon be automated? If aliens from outer space spent a day in an average US high school, what would they make of grade point averages, standardized test scores, and AP exams? All reward routinized behavior. How many of the tasks that are rewarded in school rely on compliance, rote memorization, and recall—routine skills that can be performed by the devices in students' pockets? Would an alien think we were designing robots, or preparing students for the future?

Worse yet, would it seem that our current education systems penalize students for being creative and original—two skills that are impossible to automate? Adam Grant, author of *Originals,* noted:

> . . . the most creative children . . . are the least likely to become the teacher's pet. In one study, elementary school teachers listed their favorite and least favorite students, and then rated both groups on a list of characteristics. The least favorite students were the non-conformists who made up their own rules. Teachers tend to discriminate against highly creative students, labeling them as troublemakers. In response, many children quickly learn to get with the program, keeping their original ideas to themselves.[19]

When students rebel against the rote, routine, and repetitive, they're met with resistance. It's easier to teach a classroom of conforming, unoriginal students than to teach the type who change the world. We prefer well-behaved students to the ones who question everything. Education systems are not well designed to cultivate the very skill sets and roles essential in the race against technology.

Tech Is the Terminator (of Tech!)

Schools are really into preparing students for this tech-centered future by doubling down on STEM (science, technology, engineering, and math). A persistent narrative in the education world is that technical/STEM skills reign supreme over other skills. Here's why. First, people associate "skill-building" with *technical* skills. Second, RBTC suggests that automation is replacing more middle- and low-skill jobs than high-skill jobs, especially those that require technical/STEM skills.[20] Third, we assume STEM careers are more lucrative.

New graduates experience what economists call "rapid earnings growth."[21] Overnight, broke college students subsisting on ramen noodles and thrift store purchases make the leap to salaried positions with benefits. This jump, called the "college wage premium," represents on average an 85 percent increase in wages over those with a high school diploma.[22] The highest-paid entry-level workers of them all are those entering STEM fields.[23] They succeed on the job market because they're up against limited applicants for high-paying jobs. And employers value their skill set because it's tangible and coveted outside of STEM fields, including in finance, business administration, and law.

What Got You Here Will Not Get You There

Little wonder everyone's so pumped about getting students into STEM fields. And students are heeding this advice. Since the great recession, while the number of humanities majors have been tumbling, the fields that have risen are almost entirely STEM majors.[24] Sixty-eight percent of students are mainly motivated to pursue STEM to follow the money.[25] They're thinking: technical skills = well-paying, stable jobs.

But here's the twist. STEM majors make more money at the *beginning* of their careers, but not necessarily *throughout* their careers. The wage premium STEM majors enjoy over liberal arts majors doesn't last. Harvard University economists David Deming and Kadeem Noray found that "the relative earnings advantage for graduates majoring in applied subjects like STEM is highest at labor market entry and declines rapidly over time."[26] The Academy of Arts and Sciences explained that "vocational training focused on narrow job-related skills helps students find jobs when they are young . . . but they are often not prepared to adapt to changes over time and thus are more likely to be unemployed or have lower salaries when older compared to those who received a more academic general education."[27] STEM majors are the hares of the career race, but liberal arts majors are the tortoises—starting off slow and building momentum over time. This is because STEM occupations have a steep learning curve and a declining value curve. Specific technical skills *depreciate* over time. Highly skilled workers who know how to use technology are needed. But if these professionals are not diligent in constantly upgrading their skills to keep pace with the times, their skills are quickly left behind as innovation marches forward.

Take, for example, learning to drive a car. You're on a steep curve while you're learning to parallel park, separate the gas and brake pedals, keep to the speed limit, avoid hitting pedestrians, and obey traffic laws. Over time, your skills become second nature. The initial learning curve pays off because it means you'll be set with skills that last a lifetime.

Or will it?

Driving is going out of fashion. Learning to drive among teens is down 50 percent since 1983.[28] Why learn to drive when Uber and Lyft can do it for you? With autonomous vehicles coming soon, driving skills will be obsolete before we know it.

Tech-centric professionals face the same conundrum—the skills they're investing in are always on their way out. The speed at which a skill gets outdated is called "the rate of skill change." Occupations with the highest rate are in STEM fields.[29] STEM professionals are beholden to a vicious cycle: learn skill, tech makes it obsolete, learn new skill. Repeat.

This *learn-rinse-repeat cycle* is a reason that people leave STEM: "STEM Majors with higher academic aptitude scores leave STEM careers more often and at younger ages."[30] It's a disincentive to invest so much in skills that are gone by tomorrow.

We certainly are *not* trying to dissuade students from STEM pursuits if it's their growth game. But if money and a cushy life are why you're going into STEM? Buyer beware. Investing years in learning skills that'll be replaced in less time than it took to learn them isn't a wealth-building strategy! The steep learning curve of STEM occupations comes with commensurate potential sunk costs. Learning a specific job or skill set makes it easier to get a good-paying job when you start your career in STEM, but is much harder to keep up as you advance.

At the Speed of Light

Just when we think that the creative destruction rate is at its peak, it accelerates exponentially. For example, computers become twice as fast and half as expensive as their predecessors every eighteen to twenty-four months.[31]

To illustrate the power of exponential growth, suppose we make you a deal. We give you $1,000 every day for 30 days and you give us a penny on day one and double the amount every day for 30 days (2 cents on the second day, 4 cents on the third day, etc.). Any takers?

On the thirtieth day you would have $30,000. Not too shabby. But we would be getting $5,368,709.12!

Now apply this exponential function to technological progress. When households first had dial-up internet, we connected at 28.8 kilobytes per second, then 56k, 128k, and so on. Today, average Wi-Fi speeds are over *2000 percent* faster than dial-up speeds of the past. Soon, 5G will increase internet speeds to a nearly 40,000 percent increase over today's speed. A

1,115,970 percent increase from dial-up. The PlayStation 5 is over twice as powerful as the PlayStation 4, but it is over *850 times faster* than the original PlayStation that came out twenty-five years ago.[32] Author Tim Urban drives home the rate of progress this way:

> *If you divide the 100,000 years of human history to a 500-page book (with each page being 200 years), on the first 499 pages we had 1 billion people or fewer. Then, on the 500th page, we've crossed the 1, 2, 3, 4, 5, 6, and 7 billion person threshold. For the first 499 pages of the book, we barely used any energy at all—we got around with sailboats and walking and running and horses; we developed submarines and cars and planes and space travel all on page 500 alone. Communication was just talking—and maybe letter writing— for the first 499 pages; on page 500, we have FaceTime and the internet.*[33]

Who knows what'll be on page 501! We might not be vacationing on Mars or flying to work via jet pack, but the next chapter will surely bring advances beyond imagination. Exponential change mapped on a graph looks like a hockey stick; the curve is steadily flat until it dramatically rises, almost vertically. The bigger surprise is that tech innovation accelerates during economic downturns.[34] Why? The opportunity cost to invest in new technology is reduced during a recession or bear market. When things are good, people are buying things and business is growing. Business leaders don't want to fix what isn't broken. They hate to take a foot off the gas to make an investment in tech that won't pay off for a while. When the economy is bad, the decision is easier and essential. It's a cold reality that firms trade off humans for new tech. Organizations shift their strategy from growth to efficiency—this makes tech very appealing.

In 2020, we saw a historic disruption that has thrown our economy into a tailspin that will take years to stabilize. In just weeks, it's estimated that COVID-19 destroyed 22 million jobs. More than triple *all* jobs lost during the great recession of 2008. Labor economists predict that 42 percent of these jobs are permanently eliminated. In addition, McKinsey estimates that 45 million Americans could lose their jobs to automation by 2030.[35] COVID-19 ushered in the perfect storm for creative destruction and permanently altered the labor market our young people are entering. So, are students doomed to be swallowed whole by this tech revolution?

No.

We can prepare them to thrive in the face of it.

Future-Proof and Future-Ready

There's another highly valued set of skills in the workplace. We call them *universal human skills*. These skills, also commonly known as "soft skills," "twenty-first-century skills," or "power skills," differ from tech skills in some critical ways. First, where tech skills are narrow and specific to one domain, universal human skills are broad. Second, where tech skills depreciate over time, universal human skills appreciate. Third, universal human skills are future-proof. Never to be replaced by automation, machine learning, or artificial intelligence. In fact, the more technology dominates the world of work, the *more* valuable universal human skills become.

Technical Skills	Universal Human Skills
Narrow	Broad
Depreciates over time	Appreciates over time
Dependent on technology	Leverages technology

Universal Human Skills

Three essential ingredients make any skill human. First, they're *universally applicable*. Unlike tech skills, which are domain specific, these skills can be applied anywhere, anytime. In an analysis of 150 million online job postings, universal skills, such as problem-solving, critical thinking, collaboration, communication, and ethical reasoning, were the most in-demand skills across *all* labor markets.[36] A majority of *all* job openings required at least one of these skills. "Demand for [these] skills outpaces all other skills and spans a diverse range of careers and industries."[37]

Second, these skills are *universally valued,* especially by employers. In a series of large sample surveys, CEOs and other employers across the globe overwhelmingly endorsed universal human skills over all others. *Creativity* and *management of complexity.*[38] *Problem solving* and *teamwork.*[39] *Written communication.*[40] Employers get that these skills *predict* success in careers.[41] These skills *cause* success to happen.[42] Students with universal human skills were more successful at landing jobs and had higher salaries than their peers.[43] When Google analyzed their most productive workers, they found that it wasn't technical skills, but universal human skills, including being "a good team player," "communication," "possessing insights into others," "empathy toward colleagues," "critical thinking," and "ingenuity" that best predicted success.[44]

The final ingredient of universal human skills is that they can be learned, developed, and mastered anywhere, anytime, by anyone. The designer Peter Skillman created a challenge to see which groups of people could make the tallest tower that could hold a marshmallow using only spaghetti and tape. Guess which of the teams were the best at tower building. College students? Lawyers? High-powered CEOs?

Nope. Kindergartners.

What did five-year-olds have over adults that made them the winners? Universal human skills—like collaboration and problem-solving. Skills that are maybe lost on adults after years of playing fixed games.

To sum it up, the best skills to develop are: Applicable. Transferable. Widely valued. In-demand. We invite you to look at our list of universal human skills and put a check next to those you're most motivated to master. Now, circle the ones you think you or your students are most interested in.

Universal Human Skills

☐ **Critical Thinking**
Identify problems and access available information to come up with a novel solution.

☐ **Collaboration**
Help other people and work with them in effective ways, using

communication, coordination, empathy/perspective taking, trust, service orientation, conflict resolution, and negotiation.

☐ **Accountability**
Consistently follow through on one's responsibilities and be seen as reliable.

☐ **Ingenuity**
Create novel ideas by cleverly combining existing constructs.

☐ **Cross-Cultural Skills**
Meaningfully connect with a diverse population of individuals and groups in a variety of different settings.

☐ **Technology Skills**
Identify different types of media, understand the messages they're sending, and use them agilely.

☐ **Initiative and Self-Direction**
Independently create and follow through on a goal one is motivated to achieve.

☐ **Social Skills**
Meaningfully engage with people in one-on-one and group situations.

☐ **Productivity**
Create systems to complete tasks as efficiently and quickly as possible.

☐ **Media/Communication Literacy**
Seamlessly adapt to and communicate through emerging digital environments.

☐ **Flexibility and Adaptability**
Effectively and appropriately respond to any changes that may occur.

☐ **Responsibility**
Act independently and make the correct decision without needing authorization.

What's Your Role?

We present three universal roles that represent three skill clusters drawn from a competency framework developed by the National Research Council.[45] Each skill set and role will be essential in the future of work. They are needed in all workplaces, and they complement each other. We call these professional roles the Creator, the Facilitator, and the Driver.

Creator Competencies	Facilitator Competencies	Driver Competencies
Critical Thinking The ability to identify and question problems and access available information to come up with a novel solution.	**Collaboration** The ability to help other people and work with them in effective ways, using communication, coordination, empathy/perspective taking, trust, service orientation, conflict resolution, and negotiation.	**Accountability** The ability to consistently follow through on one's responsibilities and to be seen as reliable.
Ingenuity The ability to create novel ideas by cleverly combining existing constructs.	**Cross-Cultural Skills** The ability to meaningfully connect with a diverse population of individuals and groups in a variety of different settings.	**Technology Skills** The ability to identify different types of media, understand the messages they're sending, and use them agilely.
Initiative and Self-Direction The ability to independently create and follow through on a goal one is motivated to achieve.	**Social Skills** The ability to meaningfully engage with people in one-on-one and group situations.	**Productivity** The ability to create systems to complete tasks as efficiently and quickly as possible.
Media/Communication Literacy The ability to seamlessly adapt to and communicate through emerging digital environments.	**Flexibility and Adaptability** The ability to effectively and appropriately respond to any changes that may occur.	**Responsibility** The ability to act independently and make the correct decision without needing authorization.

The Creator

Creators are visionaries who see beyond what is to what could be. They are all about bringing into existence new things, or bringing together old things in new ways. They are critical thinkers who question the status quo. What emerges from the rich soil of their imagination, creativity, and ingenuity are ideas, solutions, media, art. The skills they draw from include *ingenuity, critical thinking, problem-solving,* and *self-direction.* Research on the characteristics of top businesses and business leaders reveal the top skills that high-profile creators, like Indra Nooyi, Jeff Bezos, Mark Zuckerberg, and Tim Cook, have in common.[46] Forward thinking. Creative problem-solving. Persuasion. A study of two hundred founders and CEOs of game-changing organizations identified five similar "discovery skills":[47]

- Questioning: posing queries that challenge common wisdom

- Observing: scrutinizing the behavior of customers, suppliers, and competitors to identify new ways of doing things

- Experimenting: constructing interactive experiences and provoking unorthodox responses to see what insights emerge

- Associating: making connections between questions, problems, or ideas from unrelated fields

- Networking: meeting people with different ideas and perspectives

The ability to innovate depends not just on our minds, but on our behaviors. Blending Creator skills into our daily lives can boost our innovation aptitude.

Rising Passion + The No Code Revolution

Workers have been negotiating wages and benefits for decades. Automation and the decline of unions have dealt a serious blow to the middle class. Workers of the industrial economy in the twentieth century needed to conform (they needed reliable and routinized skills).

Are You a Creator?

- Are you a question asker? Are you inherently curious and eager to challenge the status quo? If so, you have *critical thinking skills*.

- Are you a problem solver? Are you inherently drawn to try to fix things? Do you love coming up with novel solutions, often to problems other people aren't aware of? If so, you have *ingenuity skills*.

- Are you a self-starter? Do you expect to win? Are you more likely to ask for forgiveness than permission? If so, you have *initiative skills*.

- Are you a bit of a rebel? Are you excited about making life changes? Does your style seem a bit "out there" to others? Do you question everything? If so, you have *self-direction skills*.

- Are you a trendsetter? Are you an early adopter of new technology, fashion, or slang? Are you a hypebeast? If so, you have *media literacy skills*.

We need a different skill set today—one more original and creative, in keeping with today's "passion economy." Any Creators out there? This is your moment to shine. People who excel at creating content. Solving problems. Inventing solutions for specific communities. If you have these skills, you're golden. Content creators on the membership platform site Patreon make an estimated $1 billion annually.[48]

Tech has supercharged the Creator's skill set. Through the no code revolution, creatives can leverage sophisticated tech without hiring a programmer to help them. With little to no training, Creators can now whip up their own beautiful websites, shoot and edit high-definition videos on their phones, or create professional-sounding podcasts. The no code revolution has shifted the value from tech skills to creative skills.

Young people with their tech agility are leading the charge. See platforms like TikTok, Medium, Instagram, and Twitter. Among three thousand youths, the most common response to the survey question "What do you want to be when you grow up?" was *a YouTuber*. More kids reported YouTuber than pro athlete.[49]

We're *not* suggesting students drop out of school to make it as YouTubers. Just saying that *creating, problem-solving,* and *critical thinking* are skill sets that'll pay off in the long run.

Pro-Tip for Creators: Join with Facilitators and Drivers who share your vision, and leverage their skill sets to help turn your ideas into fruition.

The Facilitator

Facilitators are the glue that holds people together. They are community builders and team players who unify people behind a shared vision. Teams work better together when they are around. They're emotionally intelligent, adaptable, and relationally savvy. Communication skills, including writing, speaking, and cross-cultural adaptability, are their toolkit staples. Facilitators are awesome at collaboration and getting their points across. They can even get obstinate people on board with a plan or a change. They help people to feel heard, brave, and open in all kinds of situations.

The Rise of Sharing + Amplifying Collaboration

The Facilitator's skill set is of particular value in today's *collaborative or "sharing"* economy. This economy joins people holding particular assets with those who want to use these assets. For example, Airbnb joins homeowners with travelers. Uber joins car owners with passengers. Kickstarter joins creators with their fans. And this is just a sampling of sharing economy businesses.

Tech amplifies Facilitator skills through collaborative technology. Broadband internet tech and remote work further elevate the value of communication skills. Where work once happened in boardrooms, now it's on Zoom, email, and various communication and project manage-

Are You a Facilitator?

- Are you a team player? Do you play nice with others and promote harmony within groups? If so, you have *collaboration skills*.

- Are you a code switcher? Are you good at adapting to the situation? In other words, do you feel comfortable in a variety of situations and with different people? If so, you have *cross-cultural skills*.

- Are you a spokesperson? Do you love communicating ideas and making connections with people through shared experiences? If so, you have good *social skills*.

- Are you an improviser? Are you good at thinking on your feet and changing on the fly as needed? If so, you have *flexibility* and *adaptability skills*.

ment platforms like Discord, Slack, and Salesforce. Businesses have moved marketing and sales online. More than four out of five businesses post video content on Facebook as a way to engage customers.[50] These conditions make communication and collaboration invaluable to employers. They want employees who communicate well inside the organization and outside with clients.

It's interesting that these skills can be gained through activities that students enjoy and parents worry about—posting life stories as captions on their Instagram selfies, texting, and tweeting. No matter how these skills are gained, communicating effectively, whether in written or visual form, is the digital equivalent of gold.

Pro-Tip for Facilitators: Notice whether there are assumptions, rules, or red tape that prevent people from diverse backgrounds from working well together. Figure out how to work around these barriers to allow for more progressive strategies that think outside the box.

The Driver

Drivers have a bias toward action. They are movers and shakers. While others may do a fine job thinking and talking about the job, Drivers get it done. Whether through self-discipline, reliability, or obsession with progress, they meet deadlines and expectations. Their skills include flexibility, productivity, responsibility, and accountability. Drivers are really good at creating and managing systems to stay organized and get things done. If you know someone who's into making to-do lists, never has to be reminded to clean their room, and loves managing projects, you may have a Driver in your midst.

Rise of the Gig Economy + Project Management Technology

The Driver's skill set is a boon in the gig economy, which emerged from the shift from full-time employment to shorter-term (even one-off) contracts with workers. As a result, workers who can *execute* specific tasks are in hot demand. It's estimated that by 2027, close to six out of ten

---

Are You a Driver?

- Have you been the "grown-up" among your friends? Do you like to be in charge of important tasks? If so, you have *responsibility skills.*

- Are you reliable? Do you consistently follow through on what you say you will do? If so, you have *accountability skills.*

- Are you an organizer? Do you love to build and maintain systems? Do you maintain your own checklist and get immense joy from crossing items off the list? If so, you have *productivity skills.*

- Are you a techie? Do you love staying up-to-date on (and are you an early adopter of) the latest technology? If so, you have *technology skills.*

Americans will be or will have been gig workers.[51] This economy signals a shifting trend toward unbundling tasks from workers. Organizations used to hire full-time workers responsible for a mix of tasks. But today, similar to how the Industrial Revolution caused workers to mono-task, technology makes it possible for companies to find workers who specialize in specific tasks.

Content Is Not King

Give a five-year-old a brick and a two-by-four and they'll come up with endless, imaginative ways to entertain themselves. This is the beauty of being a human. Observe your students and notice how they are constantly developing their universal human skills while engaged in the activities they most enjoy. Minecraft fosters innovation and collaboration. Fortnite is built on effective communication skills. Knowing when to pass out of a double-team takes critical thinking skills. The editing suites of TikTok and Instagram cultivate creativity.

When it comes to universal human skills, *what* students are learning to do is much more important than *where* they're learning it. You don't need to take up an international relations class or violin lessons to learn these skills. They can be developed in vast ways beyond academic or extracurricular content, as long as you become attuned to these skills and roles.

Not Just Facts

So, should students drop out of school? No. There are no shortcuts to developing the skills and mindsets that enable people to learn how to learn, embrace responsibilities and challenges, collaborate with diverse people, and think outside the box. Albert Einstein noted, "Education is not learning of facts, but training of the mind to think." Students who attend college, compared with those who don't, are much more likely to have opportunities to gain these skills in various ways. Especially in high-impact practices like writing-intensive classes, mentored research experiences, and community service and internships.

And then there's the power of a liberal arts education. Philosophy teaches students to think critically, to challenge assumptions, and to use reasoning to solve complex problems. An English degree teaches people how to make coherent arguments, organize information, and persuasively communicate across mediums. A history degree teaches people to curate and contextualize information from disparate sources. Because of their emphasis on universal human skills, liberal arts programs teach people *how to learn*. In the future of work, a professional's value will rest not on a specific skill, but on the ability to *acquire any skill*.

A common narrative of policy-makers is that a liberal arts education doesn't prepare workers for the twenty-first-century workplace. They think short-term certificate programs are the solution for teaching workers "real" and "tangible" skills needed *now*. While short-term, vocational programs are a good fit for many students, evidence doesn't support the claim that they best prepare workers for the twenty-first-century workplace.

Cutting back educational and personal development in the interest of immediate economic productivity is shortsighted. The students in short-term training programs are disproportionately from historically under-privileged backgrounds. They make up the majority of students who were misled by various for-profit institutions promising to deliver a good return on investment. Those who complete four-year college degrees tend to come from more privileged backgrounds; they remain more privileged because of their exposure to universal human skills—the ones needed in the future of work.

From Makeup to Grown-Up

A high school senior we will call Mya declared the day she started post-secondary planning with Tim that she "despised school." School triggered feelings of shame and failure for her. Until Mya discovered makeup artistry. Through this medium, she expanded her sense of self beyond the narrow identity imposed by her previous school experiences. She pored over YouTube videos, volunteered at a salon in exchange for free samples, and did makeup for friends, family, and strangers, pro bono. This investment began to pay off. Mya started her own YouTube makeup channel, which grew to five thousand subscribers. Her cadre of paying customers grew.

She was very disappointed to find out that cosmetology school could cost as much as college tuition and that many graduates have trouble making a living in makeup artistry. Mya and Tim identified three skills that drew her to makeup artistry:

- Constant learning of current trends in a fast-moving industry.

- Novelty in approaching every face as a fresh canvas.

- Collaboration with clients.

Mya's interest in makeup was tied to her interest in being a Creator and Facilitator. She enjoyed critical thinking and problem-solving; creativity and innovation; communication and collaboration. When Tim asked whether she could be happy using these skills in another career, Mya's interest was sparked. As they brainstormed, they landed on web design. She believed designing websites would be a creative outlet for solving challenging problems while providing the economic mobility important to her.

Mya went to college and majored in graphic design. She still loves makeup artistry, but currently uses and grows similar skills as a designer.

Hardwired for Mastery

Most students have a fire in their bellies. They won't be content lying on their parents' couches with a bag of chips and playing Xbox every day for years and years.

If you question your students' work ethic and ambition, be encouraged—humans are born *wanting* to learn skills. We've never come across a young person who didn't want to work hard, to get better, to make something of themselves. Finding aims worth getting up for in the morning gives them a direction for that energy. We have an innate desire to learn and grow new skills. "How do I teach my students these skills?" is the wrong question. Instead ask yourself: "What skills are they already pursuing?" Angela Duckworth (MacArthur "Genius" award recipient) and colleagues have identified "mastery behaviors" associated with "grit."[52] People with these behaviors have better learning and emotion-management strategies. They have more positive attitudes and stick-with-it-ness in the face of difficult tasks. When we have mastery behaviors, universal human skills follow. So, to understand which skills your young person gravitates toward, look for these four mastery behaviors.

Mastery Behavior #1: Lean In

Mastery starts with throwing your weight into meaningful activities. Exerting some serious energy in the direction of the skills you want to learn. It's not sitting back passively and waiting for money to grow on trees. Where do you proactively invest time and energy? Where do you focus your efforts? What are the things you get lost in? Video designers differentiate between *lean-in* and *lean-back* activities or moments in a game. You know you're having a lean-in experience when you're on the edge of your seat, fully engaged in a task. Maybe even forgetting to eat, drink, sleep, or go to the bathroom. Lean-back energy is laid-back energy. You're relaxed and more passive. Think lying on the couch Netflix bingeing or Pinterest scrolling. Where we invest our time and energy is where we lean in.

Where do you and your people lean in, rather than lean back?

Mastery Behavior #2: Do Hard Things

Now that you're leaning in, consider what *direction* you're leaning in. Mastery comes with leaning into *challenges*. You push yourself and want to be pushed by others. You stop taking safe shortcuts. Instead of the Magic Kingdom ferryboat, you line up for Splash Mountain. It's choosing "hard" over "easy." Yes, it sounds crazy. But when you're hot on the trail pursuing mastery, you have a whole new take on challenges. No longer a threat to your success, challenges are now fuel for learning, growing, upping your game. Instead of dodging a good challenge, you seek them out and master them! Now we're having fun.

Where do you and your people choose hard instead of easy?

Mastery Behavior #3: Stay the Course

Challenges are *hard*. You will hit some bumps in the road. You may get tired or stuck. But when it's an activity or role you're determined to master, you *push through the challenges*. You stay the course even when the going gets tough. Mastery isn't just about tackling challenges but *persisting through them*. In fact, mastery comes when the challenge makes you even *more* focused. It's as if that challenge triggers your engagement and other superpowers. Staying the course means persisting through challenges, especially where other people quit. While others get distracted or defeated by adversity, you come to life.

Where do you (and your people) stay the course no matter how difficult?
When does the onset of challenges get you pumped?

Mastery Behavior #4: Flop Forward

Leaning in, doing hard things, and *sticking with it* inevitably exposes you to "failure." When you go "all in" with challenges, life isn't as uneventful as it is for people who choose the easy road. By having the audacity to lean in, you've increased your opportunities for failure. You've joined the ranks of the most accomplished leaders who failed frequently (and sometimes epically):

- In the 1970s, Oprah Winfrey worked as a news anchor at Baltimore's WJZ station and was told by supervisors that she was "the wrong color, the wrong size, and showed too much emotion." She was unceremoniously "demoted" to co-host of *People Are Talking* with Richard Sher, and it was through this "failure" that she realized that her true passion was human interest stories rather than hard news. The rest is history.

- A desegregation campaign in 1961, called the Albany Movement, ended in the jailing of hundreds of Black protesters, including Martin Luther King Jr. While it was considered a failure by many of its leaders and the media, King used the lessons learned to help build a movement even more powerful and beautiful.

- Elon Musk got ousted as CEO of his own company, Zip2, fired from PayPal during his honeymoon, and watched his company's rockets explode multiple times. He told himself, "No worries, these are experimental landings." They taught him just what he needed to know for subsequent successful landings.

- Ruth Bader Ginsberg once wrote to a five-year-old who asked if she had ever made a mistake: "I have made many mistakes, but I try to learn from them so that I will not make the same mistake twice."

When you're dedicated to mastering something, you have ways of handling the inevitable failures. Many people who've been told repeatedly that they're awesome are afraid to not be awesome. They're fearful of underperforming, so they are reluctant to try new things. This perfectionism and image-consciousness makes them afraid to show up as their full selves. They quit prematurely because they somehow think that if it was meant to be, it would've gone their way without a hitch.

But when you're determined to master something, a switch turns on, and instead of evaluating yourself by your failures, you're dialed into your response to them. You tell yourself, "Of course I'm going to fail at times, because mastery is a process of constantly learning things that are new to me."

Let's be real; failure doesn't feel as good as success. But it's an opportunity to use the lessons learned to get better and smarter. It's also a heck of a better story to tell yourself. Doing something successfully the first time is a fact, but saying, "I couldn't XY and got knocked on my butt, then figured out that if I did AB, it might work. And after three tries, I XY'd!" is a good story. *Flopping forward,* even for colossal failures, always looks ahead. Instead of "I failed at this relationship," you say, "I struggled with communicating in this relationship. I'm learning to communicate better now." You use failures to learn what works and what doesn't so that you can keep honing your skills and craft. Failures are your training ground, and your mantra is "Learn to fail or fail to learn."

What would you (and your people) do even if you knew you're going to fail? Where and when have you bounced back from failure?

Finding Mastery

Mastery behaviors provide clues to which skills students are motivated to master. What are the things they're already investing in? Think about how they spend their time—are they most often creating, facilitating, or driving? The language of universal human skills can help young people understand how the skills they're into now can be the ones they'll still find purposeful in their future work.

Feel free to think of ways to cultivate students' universal skills inside and outside traditional education. We don't have to stress over academics as the end-all and be-all. We can meet our students where they are. How can they get the most out of things they already enjoy doing? As long as they're developing universal human skills, it doesn't matter where they learn them.

This opens up a whole new landscape for cultivating skills. No need to fixate on content-knowledge; students can make skill-building their learning goal wherever they are. They can pick the content they're interested in and build universal skills within that content. This means that the activities we thought were wasting their time—video games, social media, socializing—are actually ripe with opportunity. As long as students are leaning in and learning new skills, the time will be well spent.

Below we've made these lessons actionable for your own self-care and for your role working with students.

Self-Care

Knowing where and when you use mastery superpowers will show you which activities or roles reflect your purpose and which specific skills you're motivated to master.

1. **THINK.** What's an activity or role that you're really into (even obsessed with)—one that inspires you to lean in and challenge yourself? One that you find yourself pushing through even when there are rough patches?

2. **WRITE.** Voilà—these activities or roles are ones you're motivated to master! Write them down! (For example: "authoring a book" or "training for *American Ninja Warrior*.")

3. **THINK.** Now break it down further. Which specific skills (on pages 75–76) do you use when engaged in these activities/tasks/roles (e.g., *ingenuity* and *cross-cultural skills*)?

4. **WRITE.** Record these as the skills you're motivated to master while doing the activities that matter!

5. **PLAN & ACT.** How can you lean in and challenge yourself even more in these activities? Come up with one or two actionable plans. (For example: "say yes to public-speaking gigs despite my stage fright" or "run two extra miles this week").

Case Example:

Belle's son (a high school student) is constantly devouring documentaries to collect facts and information about spectacularly far-flung topics, including the ability of ants to navigate by sensing the Earth's magnetic field, the controversy over whether Goofy is a dog or a Scottish cow, and the plight of child soldiers in Myanmar. His particular expertise is in history, ranging from an encyclopedic knowledge of the Greek city-states to contemporary global politics. He's always asked "why" questions and isn't satisfied with surface-level answers (sometimes to the chagrin of his exhausted parents and teachers). This love of learning extends to a love of sharing knowledge through teaching, mentoring, and leading others. These choices of activities and patterns of thinking are evidence of the skills he's motivated to master, including synthesizing information quickly and drawing connections between disparate ideas and concepts. To build these skills, parents and educators give him ample learning opportunities on various topics, investing in piles of books and multimedia resources. He eats it all up. His parents have also engaged him in debates and taught him to build solid arguments and rebuttals using CER (claim-evidence-reasoning). And they sometimes regret it.

What You Can Do for Your Student

Role-modeling mastery behaviors—leaning in, doing hard things, staying the course, and flopping forward—is the best thing you can do to support your student to do the same. Once you've practiced self-care in the above section, reflect on the times you've seen your students exhibit these behaviors.

1. **THINK.** Where do they spend their time and energy? Where are they leaning in? Is it in academics? Video games? Other hobbies? Are they making YouTube videos? Are they playing sports, painting, editing photos on their computer? Wherever they are actively engaged is where you will find mastery happening.

2. **WRITE.** Write down the one or two activities where they are exercising mastery superpowers!

3. **THINK.** Where we find a mastery orientation, universal human skills will follow. As you reflect on those activities your student is mastering, what specific skills are they practicing there (see skill list, pages 75–76)?

4. **PLAN & ACT.** Talk with your student about their skills. Students often struggle to identify where and when they practice mastery behaviors and specific skills.

   a. *Share examples of your own mastery behaviors and skills, as well as what you've observed about theirs.*

   b. *Ask if they agree with your assessment.* Affirming and validating the mastery behaviors you see in your student can be an uplifting "aha" experience!

   c. *Help them find activities or hobbies they enjoy.* If you can't identify an area where your student is applying mastery behaviors, that's a warning sign. Give them opportunities to explore different activities where they can practice mastery. Mastery behaviors are like muscles; use them or lose them.

4

Value Archetypes

Add your value as a Trailblazer, Builder, Champion, or Guardian.

Love recognizes no barriers. It jumps hurdles, leaps fences,
penetrates walls to arrive at its destination full of hope.

—MAYA ANGELOU

The Value of Values

Strengths are what make us our best selves. *Skills* are what make us able to do the job. *Core values* are what *move* us—they are another huge directional force that orients you toward purposeful decisions. What *motivates* you and your people? What drives you? One parent quipped, "I don't see any motivation in my fifteen-year-old, except for being a couch potato. Every free moment he plays this multiplayer video game. So, is his core value *gaming*?" No, but his core values pull him to gaming. Gaming aligns with his desire for *mastery, self-direction,* and *community.* Core values are the motives that underlie our behavior. They represent our aspirational best selves. They are like the air we breathe—essential yet invisible. But if we don't get what our core values are, we will struggle to live and relate to people authentically.

Core values help us connect with people in ways that are the most meaningful to us. And we especially long for meaningful connection with our students. Using a shared language of core values enables us to understand and communicate more clearly. This is easier said than done. A Harvard University study showed that parents and teachers tend to send mixed messages. Most parents and teachers say they want their students to be caring above all else, but roughly 80 percent of students say that these adults value achievement and happiness over caring.[1]

Why the huge gap between what we claim to value and what we actually communicate?

What's missing is a language and framework for having conversations about values. It's easier to explain *what* we want our students to do than *why* we want them to do it. Finish your homework. Clean your room. Do the extra-credit assignment. We can rattle off these directives in our sleep—they come so naturally to us. But how do we explain the importance of helping a struggling classmate? How do we get our students to understand *why* it's important to do the *right* thing rather than whatever is easy or convenient? How do we get our students to make decisions that align with what's truly important in life? Too often our explanations feel abstract, arbitrary, inauthentic.

Core values provide a powerful language to drive these conversations. In this chapter, we'll show you how core values can help you understand what motivates your young people. We'll show you how to identify specific core values, and how these core values are applicable in the world of work. Specifically we will take you through a process where you will:

- See core values for what they are—perceive how they divide and connect us.

- Find inflection points—identify the formative experiences that shape values.

- Zero in on your value archetype—pick the one that explains your motivations.

- Add value with your archetype—identify the settings you'll thrive in.

- Communicate with core values—acquire language for deep connection.

See Core Values for What They Are

Before we go any further, let's share what core values actually are. Below is a list of them. Try to pick the three core values that represent your best, most authentic self.

☐ **Compassion**
Genuine concern for the needs and suffering of others.

☐ **Equality**
Treating everyone with fairness and respect to ensure a level playing field.

☐ **Wisdom**
Constantly striving to learn more about yourself and the world around you.

☐ **Freedom**
Having the ability to act, think, and speak the way you want without fear of mistreatment.

☐ **Adventure**
The world is a big place, and you want to experience all that it has to offer.

☐ **Service**
Putting in work to benefit others.

☐ **Justice**
Ensuring that everyone is treated impartially.

☐ **Mastery**
Having the desire to learn and accomplish the things you commit to.

☐ **Knowledge**
Striving to increase intelligence by learning, either in school or in the world.

☐ **Fun**
Seeking sensory stimulation and a wide variety of experiences.

☐ **Community**
Includes the people and places that align with your attitudes, interests, and beliefs.

☐ **Friendship**
Having the ability to make and keep old friendships.

☐ **Humor**
Having appreciation for seeing the humor in things.

☐ **Respect**
Desiring the admiration of others because of the way you act and because of the qualities you possess.

☐ **Authenticity**
You keep it real and remain true to yourself no matter where you are or who you are with.

☐ **Tradition**
Protecting the beliefs and customs that are passed from one generation to the next.

☐ **Integrity**
Always following through on what you say you are going to do.

☐ **Fairness**
Making sure that everyone has an opportunity to do their best.

☐ **Achievement**
Having the ability to accomplish things, typically by effort, courage, and skill.

☐ **Independence**
You go your own way, pursue your own goals, and are not easily influenced.

☐ **Family**
Blood-related or otherwise, these are the people closest to you.

☐ **Loyalty**
You stand up for and stick by those who are closest to you, no matter what.

☐ **Security**
Keeping those closest to you both financially secure and physically safe.

☐ **Recognition**
People see you, and they see your talents and impact on the world.

☐ **Power**
Having influence over other people and situations.

Core Values Connect

If you struggled to choose just three, you're not alone. They are called "values" for a reason: they *all* feel important. This is because humans across time and place share a universal set of values. More than two hundred studies involving tens of thousands of people in seventy-plus countries have shown that every culture has core values.[2] And even across the most diverse cultures, core values are amazingly similar. Pioneering research by Shalom Schwartz found that no matter where you go in the world, people consider the same twenty or so core values important.[3] Just think of it! We are *connected* with the rest of humanity through valuing the *same set of values.*

Of course, we don't all *prioritize* the same core values. We feel more connected to people who share the *same specific* core values. This is what we mean when we say "we found our people." When freshmen start college with a sea of strangers and struggle to find "their people," these aren't just people to party with, but kindred spirits who "get them" because they share core values.

Find Inflection Points

How do we figure out our *core* values—the ones we prioritize above all others? Teasing them out from a list can feel like looking for needles in a haystack. Here, the old adage holds a universal truth: actions speak louder than words. We can locate our core values by reflecting on big decisions we have made in our lives. There are three key actions that serve to illuminate our core values. In the name of our core values, we will:

- Embrace risks worth taking.

- Lean in to noble sacrifices.

- Fight the good fight.

Embracing Risks Worth Taking

LeBron James is a four-time NBA MVP with two Olympic gold medals. Beyond his superior strength and court vision, one asset has made James truly special: his durability. For eighteen years, he has dominated his sport, ranking in the top ten in all-time minutes played. Yet he never seems to tire. Where does his consistent motivation to play at the highest levels come from? It may seem that he's driven solely by person-focused values of achievement, recognition, and desire to make his mark in the world. Less known are his deeply held collective values. Especially *family*.

James reported to *Sports Illustrated* that by age seventeen, "I saw drugs, guns, killings; it was crazy . . . But my mom kept food in my mouth and clothes on my back." When his basketball skills gave him the opportunity to escape his chaotic neighborhood in Akron, Ohio, for the NBA, he insisted on having one of his longtime friends, Maverick Carter, serve as his agent, rather than more experienced agents. Barely an adult, James entrusted his fortunes to a friend with little experience. This choice was widely criticized in the world of professional basketball, and perhaps with fair reason, given how risky it was. But James saw this as a *risk worth taking* because it aligned with his core values. When he made the decision to return to his hometown Cleveland Cavaliers after leaving them for the Miami Heat in 2014, he wrote this letter:

> *Before anyone ever cared where I would play basketball, I was a kid from Northeast Ohio. It's where I walked. It's where I ran. It's where I cried. It's where I bled. It holds a special place in my heart. People there have seen me grow up. I sometimes feel like I'm their son.*

He explained how these deep roots shaped his values and behavior:

> *Their passion can be overwhelming. But it drives me. I want to give them hope when I can. I want to inspire them when I can. My relationship with Northeast Ohio is bigger than basketball. I didn't realize that four years ago. I do now.*

James was taking another major risk. He was leaving one of the most successful franchises in NBA history to return to one of the most dysfunctional. But his values made it clear—he had to do what was best for his extended family, the people of Cleveland and Akron.

James's values have shaped decisions beyond the court. When you walk into the school he opened for low-income youth in Akron, the "I Promise School," his motto appears: "We Are Family." And he referred to this school and his family as more important than being at the top of his game: "Besides having three kids and marrying my wife, putting my mom in a position where she never has to worry about anything ever again for the rest of her life, this is right up there. Championships, MVPs, I mean, points, rebounds and assists, that stuff is, whatever." What makes family more than an important commitment, but a core value, is the way it serves as a filter for the decisions he makes in life.

As you can see, there's a story behind LeBron's core values. They didn't just come out of thin air because he's a caring person. His particular kind of caring evolved from some very specific early experiences. And his story grounds his values in experience rather than abstraction, preserving their true meaning and conveying not only what they are, but also where they came from.

Leaning In to Noble Sacrifices

Patagonia is a 200 million–dollar company that creates high-quality clothing for outdoor enthusiasts. They're known for their emphasis on sustainability and stability. But ask anyone who works for Patagonia and they'll tell you Patagonia is more than a clothing company. Since their founding fifty-plus years ago, Patagonia has striven to make choices that prioritize the environment. They are all about making high-quality outdoor gear (core value: build the best product) that will limit the ecological imprint (core value: use business to protect nature). Standing by these values has pushed the envelope, and has been costly. For example, Patagonia implements a self-imposed "Earth Tax," donating 1 percent of all revenue—not just profits—to environmental nonprofits.[5] They've also sued the federal government for eliminating three million acres of public land. And if that weren't enough, they donated the entirety of their 2018 tax break (over $10 million) to environmental nonprofits.

Filing amicus briefs. Funding activist groups. Suing the federal government. Giving away tax breaks. These are not the actions of a business that prioritizes short-term stability, safety, and traditional strategies for generating revenue. On paper, Patagonia has sacrificed millions of dollars in revenue for court fees alone. Yet Patagonia doesn't see this as a sacrifice at all; rather, it's a noble investment in their core values that prioritize the long-term preservation of the environment. Patagonia CEO Rose Marcario explained in an interview: "These decisions were in our

DNA . . . Our company was founded on the love of the outdoors. If you love something you want to preserve it and protect it . . . It was an easy decision."[6]

A powerful statement by the CEO, but the greater proof is in the pudding. Patagonia's core values ("build the best product" and "use business to protect nature") are proved by the company's actions. We can often gauge how important a core value is to us by the degree to which we have sacrificed for it. Parents sacrifice their sleep to comfort their crying infants in the middle of the night. These same parents later sacrifice financially to support their students' college education. We make both small and large sacrifices every day on behalf of what's most important to us.

Fighting the Good Fight

In 2016, a generation-defining gesture happened in the middle of a meaningless exhibition. It was the fourth and final preseason game for the San Francisco 49ers, and the stakes couldn't have been lower; the team's main objective was to get through the game without any injuries. This was a dress rehearsal, a chance to go through the motions as a prelude to what really mattered: the start of the regular season. But before the game even started, the 49ers quarterback made a gesture that proved bigger than any play of the season.

Colin Kaepernick took a knee during the National Anthem to raise awareness of police brutality toward Black Americans: "To me, this is bigger than football, and it would be selfish on my part to look the other way. There are bodies in the street and people . . . getting away with murder."

Although Kaepernick knew that acting on his collective justice and equity core values might cost him his career, he acted anyway, explaining: "I have to stand up for people that are oppressed . . . If they take football away, my endorsements from me, I know that I stood up for what is right."[7] In January 2016, Kaepernick played his final NFL game. He joins a long line of civil rights activists who fought to uphold their core values.

Rosa Parks was arrested for violating Montgomery city code. John Lewis referred to fighting for equality as "good trouble." Muhammad Ali gave up his freedom and heavyweight world titles to fight against the United States' involvement in the Vietnam War.

Zero in on Your Value Archetype

We don't have to be famous athletes, legacy clothing brands, or civil rights leaders to tap into our core values. We've all got them, whether we know it or not. Think about your life experiences:

What risks have you taken? Think about turning-point moments in your life. What are some big risks that you took? Was it moving to a new city? Quitting a stable job? Traveling the world? Or was there a risk you *wish* you had taken, but didn't? *What made these decisions worth the risk?*

What noble sacrifices have you made? Have there been times in your life when you were willing to make a big sacrifice for what you believed in? Has there been a time when you made a decision *that made your life harder,* but was worth it? This could be a personal sacrifice or a professional one. *What made these sacrifices worthwhile?*

What's worth fighting for? Have there been times when you welcomed conflict to stand up for what you believe in? When have you ruffled feathers or made waves? What fights have you been willing to have throughout your life? *What made these fights worth having?*

Taking risks, sacrificing, and fighting are all formative moments that reflect our core values. Go back and take another look at the core values at the beginning of the chapter. Consider: What core values was I prioritizing when I was taking risks, sacrificing, or fighting? Are the same core values connected to my risks, sacrifices, and fights? Only our true values are worth risking, sacrificing, and fighting for. You can consider the same for your students: What risks are they willing to take? What sacrifices will they make? What do they fight for? Ask yourself: *Why?* The answers to these questions will lead to our core values.

Core Values Conflict and Complement

Since we risk, sacrifice, and fight for our core values, we know that they don't all live in perfect harmony. It's important to understand how core values relate to one another because some values complement one another, while others conflict.[8] When aunts and uncles at the holiday dinner are talking past each other about politics while the food gets cold, a conflict in core values is often at the root of the argument. Whether core values complement or conflict can be the difference between a harmonious and a contentious relationship with a loved one. This is why it's important not only to understand our own core values, but also to work to understand those of our people.

Understanding and communicating well with others has a lot to do with becoming aware of differences in values. The source of most arguments or disagreements (big or small) often comes down to a conflict in core values. Research suggests that in most families, conflicts tend not to result from serious matters such as drug use and addiction, or disagreements about religion and other core values, but more often are about differences in superficial preferences and styles, in such areas as clothing, music, and leisure time. Often a struggle for increasing autonomy among adolescents underlies conflicts with parents.

Sometimes it can be easier to identify what our core values are by considering them in relation to each other. We can only realize how important a core value is to us by comparing it with others. For example, we can more readily recognize independence as a core value if we're asked to prioritize it relative to tradition or conformity. Core values don't exist in a vacuum; we subconsciously rank and organize them.

There are two major continua of core values: (1) individual- versus collective-focused core values and (2) growth- versus stability-oriented values.

Individual vs. Collective Values

People with collective values, such as compassion, community, and equality, prioritize the concerns of their community or group over individualistic concerns. They're more likely to adapt themselves to fit their environment and privilege the needs and preferences of others. They value connecting with others and responding to their needs and interests. They think of "*we* before *me*." At the opposite end of this spectrum are people who prioritize individually focused values, such as achievement, recognition, and authenticity. These people are driven to make their mark in the world—to distinguish themselves from others and to act freely based on their motivations, goals, and preferences. They want to influence the environments they find themselves in, as opposed to being influenced by them. They think of "*me* before *we*."

Individual- and collective-oriented goals conflict with each other. Ask yourself: Do you prioritize self- or other-focused goals? Do you prefer cooperating or competing? Do you like going your own way, or traveling with the pack? You can't have it both ways: the more you prefer individual goals, the less you prefer collective ones, and vice versa. It's hard to prioritize both simultaneously.

Growth vs. Stability Values

Growth and stability values are also diametrically opposed on a second continuum. People who prioritize growth values embrace change, adventure, and freedom. They seek out new experiences and are eager to grow as people. They envision how things could be and see change as an opportunity. People with stability-oriented values care about preserving and conserving the status quo and prioritize values of safety such as tradition, loyalty, and security. They seek out ritual and tradition. They tend to like the way things are and to see change as a threat.

Ask yourself: Do you prefer growth or stability? How about adventure or tradition? Is change good or bad? What about your students' or other family members' values? Do their values complement or conflict with yours?

The Four Value Archetypes

Each of us has a combination of values that orients us toward either individualistic or collectivistic values and growth or stability values. There are four archetypes that represent the intersections of these two continua of value sets. We call them the Trailblazer, the Builder, the Champion, and the Guardian. Each of these captures a motivation style of approaching work and life. They are a "filter" for what we tune in to and how we handle responsibilities and relationships.

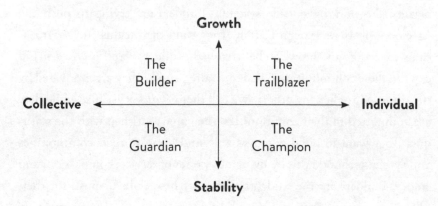

You can read the brief descriptions below to see which one (or two) seem to fit you the best. Of course, these descriptions are not comprehensive but include highlights of each type.

Type One: The Trailblazer
Trailblazers gravitate toward individual- and growth-oriented values. These include independence, mastery, wisdom, and adventure. Trailblazers are motivated by autonomy. They love breaking down walls and pushing the envelope way beyond what more risk-averse peers are comfortable with. They go their own way and pride themselves on being different and doing things differently. Because they are independent and individualistic, they tend not to worry about other people's opinions. They love their own ideas and always see change as an opportunity. They do not cling to safety and security. This combination of values can cause Trailblazers to gravitate to innovating *outside* of traditional systems, rather than within them. They resist following rules dictated by other people or systems. Trailblazers have little interest in playing by

the traditional rules of school or workplace; they can often be viewed as rebels or even outcasts.

Type Two: The Builder

Builders most value collective- and growth-oriented values. Like Trailblazers, Builders are also all about growth and change. But where Trailblazers like working outside systems, Builders are trying to push the envelope within their organization. They want their teams and organizations to change and grow. To be stretched. Builders want to *broaden* and expand these communities to include more people. They are motivated by the simple joy of helping others. We call them *Builders* because while they are committed to their communities, they aren't satisfied with the status quo. They want to build onto, expand, and improve their communities and systems. They do this by living out values of service, compassion, and equity. Builders are the students who start new clubs or push for their schools to change their policies to be more inclusive. They often care more about changing the culture and climate of a school than their own personal success.

Type Three: The Champion

Champions are the polar opposites of Builders. They prioritize individual-focused and stability-oriented values, such as achievement, recognition, and power. Where Builders focus on broadening their community, Champions strive for *individual* success within existing systems, such as school, business, or sports teams. They always strive to be the best version of themselves. They love clear rules and expectations and excel at following directions. Champions value stability because it allows them to *optimize* their performance. They view change as a threat because it may undermine their own success. They work hard to understand how things work and are very self-disciplined in following through on strategies that will help them win. Champions love to compete; specific metrics of success motivate them to try their hardest. Champions excel in traditional academic settings; they are the students who strive for the best grades and to be at the very top of their class.

Type Four: The Guardian

In many ways, Guardians are the polar opposite of Trailblazers, and that's why they can sometimes clash. Where Trailblazers prioritize individual- and growth-oriented values, Guardians are motivated by collective- and stability-oriented values, such as community, tradition, and loyalty. Guardians are motivated to *protect and preserve* what's tried and true. They love feeling connected to something larger than themselves. Guardians have a great appreciation for their history and culture. Where Builders work to change systems, Guardians serve to *sustain* their communities—their families, neighborhoods, schools, and so on. Guardians are often the glue of a group; they focus on creating and upholding rituals that bind a community together. Guardians are the students who love being part of a team and upholding the traditions of the school culture. They live for spirit week and any other activity that promotes the rituals of the community.

If you're still having difficulty choosing your archetype, take our quick and easy quiz.

Value Archetype Quick Quiz

Instructions:

- In questions 1 and 2, select the statement, A or B, which best reflects your *current* values or general approach to work.

- You don't have to agree with the statement 100 percent of the time. You should just agree with the general philosophy of the statement you choose.

- Don't overthink your choices. Just go with your initial "gut reaction" as to which statement reflects your motivations best.

Question 1:

A. Change is an opportunity.

B. Change is a threat.

Question 2:

A. When I win, we win.

B. When we win, I win.

We approach work in a way that reflects the combination of these values or motivations. The two letters you picked form a two-letter code. To find out your value archetype based on our quiz, see the codes below.

Q. 1	Q. 2	Value Types
A	A	**Type 1: The Trailblazer**—thrives in settings that encourage self-direction and innovation and seeks opportunities to choose their own projects and goals; challenged in settings that micromanage and limit personal growth.
A	B	**Type 2: The Builder**—thrives in settings that value commitment to the community, pushing it to be better (sometimes out of its comfort zone); challenged in systems that are resistant to change, or that stifle dissent.
B	A	**Type 3: The Champion**—thrives in settings where personal achievement and consistent progress on projects is celebrated; challenged in settings that relegate success to group efforts and create hurdles that thwart progress.
B	B	**Type 4: The Guardian**—thrives in settings that value loyalty, community, tradition, structure, and organizational clarity; challenged when forced to break with customs and disrupt what is tried and true.

You don't need to agree with every word of these archetype descriptions. There are, of course, variations across people within categories. While everyone is a particular mix of these archetypes, one of these motivational types is our home base, and we keep returning to it.

None of them is inherently better or worse than any other. We are not better or worse people if we prioritize individual over collective values, or stability over growth values. Each type has its unique assets. However, some types can be more valued in certain settings or organizations. Champions clearly thrive in traditional academic settings, where Trailblazers do not. If you're wondering right now whether you can convert your Trailblazer into a Champion, we advise against this. In the larger world outside of school, each archetype plays important and valued roles. Instead of changing their values, consider the settings that will most appreciate your young people and the values they hold.

Add Value with Your Archetype

To be sure, value types and skill sets can't tell us everything about ourselves (for example, our history, integrity, character strengths). But they do tell us about how we view the world, the values we prioritize, what motivates us, the kinds of choices we make, and even how we might respond to stress. Knowing our type is not the final destination, but it gives us a jumping-off point for a much greater journey.

One of the benefits of value archetypes is that they remind us of our fundamental unity as human beings. When we search below the differences of gender, race, socioeconomic status, and so on, we discover a deeper layer of commonality. Trailblazers are like other Trailblazers, and they share the same value sets as others of their type. Instead of emphasizing "culture fit," which is often a way of weeding out people who don't look and act like us due to cultural differences, organizations can tune in to "value add." When we think in terms of "value add" versus "culture fit," what we're doing is recognizing that people with very different motivational types can share the same purpose. They can contribute to organizations and beyond in their unique ways. They can complement the values that others bring into the place.

Organization Archetypes

Just as individuals have sets of core values, so too do schools, businesses, and other organizations. We're not talking about the core values organizations might *say* they value on their websites or have painted on their walls, we are referring to what they *actually* value through their actions, decisions, and behaviors. The same four archetypes apply to organizations and departments within organizations. Organizations take on different value sets depending on their unique organizational life cycle. Understanding the values of organizations can help us understand where our young people will thrive.

Trailblazing Organizations

Start-ups or brand-new companies will naturally adopt Trailblazer values because they will need to *innovate* to survive. A tech start-up racing to develop a flying car is likely to emphasize innovating and "failing fast." They would not be about conforming to existing standards or following the leads of others. Rather they would want to be pioneers, motivated by growth and disruption, instead of stability.

Building Organizations

Fairly new companies with some traction may fall in line with the Builder archetype as they have moved beyond innovation to *broadening and building* their business to scale and grow. A company that has found traction and is rapidly growing will need a Builder to come in and operationalize their processes and standardize their systems. Where Trailblazers create new ideas, Builders make them operational.

Champion Organizations

Fairly mature companies with an established market and solid track record will look for Champions who can optimize their existing strategies. These companies have figured out what works and will look for high performers who strive toward individual success. These companies need Champions who won't need to change or disrupt the status quo.

Guardian Organizations

When organizations become established institutions they may function as Guardians focused on *sustaining* their organization. A 150-year-old financial institution or a long-established automobile company that prides itself on its tradition of trustworthiness and reliability will seek out Guardians to protect their brand. These organizations value stability more than risky growth.

Life Cycle of a Company	Strategic Values
Start-up	Type 1: The Trailblazer (*Innovate*)
Grow up	Type 2: The Builder (*Broaden*)
Maturity	Type 3: The Champion (*Optimize*)
Maintain	Type 4: The Guardian (*Sustain*)

Recognizing the life cycle of a company can help us pinpoint its values. When we do that, we know what the company is looking for in its employees. Early-stage start-ups will look for people who are creative critical thinkers who can generate new ideas. Organizations that are growing up will look for people who can operationalize processes and scale existing systems. More mature organizations will look for people who can optimize their proven strategies to drive performance. Finally, established legacy institutions will look for workers who are committed to sustaining the legacy and tradition that's made them successful.

Where Will You Be Valued?

Identifying our value archetypes can be revolutionary, as it provides clarity for why we live and work the way we do. Our value types also help us understand why we feel frustrated or blocked in a particular club, school, or work setting.

So ask yourself: "In what type of environment would I thrive given my values?" Where are you a "value add"? In what setting or department would your values and approach be aligned with the approach and needs of the setting? *In other words, what organization would value your values? Where are your values needed most?*

Within organizations all four types are needed. Purposeful organizations are very intentional in making sure the values of an individual are aligned with and being honored in their department, and that the values of the department are in harmony with the larger organization's values.

- *Trailblazers* in the organization may do well in departments or on projects that involve innovation and start-up. They may be given opportunities and freedom to experiment, learn, and grow. This may include drumming up new customers and serving stakeholders in ways that think outside the box. Projects may have guardrails in place, but wide boundaries for open and free exploration.

- *Builders* may add value in roles that focus on growing and stretching the organization itself. They would thrive in roles that allow them to operationalize core processes and expand the scope of work. They may be invited to engage in initiatives tied to equity and opportunities for underrepresented members of the organization, like the diversity, equity, and inclusion department. Organization leaders would need to be open to Builders pushing the envelope in order to make the organization stronger and more inclusive.

- *Champions* who value their freedom to achieve independently may be given roles that come with clear instruction and structure, but not multiple layers of oversight. They may enjoy optimizing and expanding the reach of the organization by participating in development or sales and marketing.

- *Guardians* may be happy in roles focused on preserving the established institution and keeping the organization stable, such as general counsel of the legal department, accounting, or human resources. They may be invited to help uphold organizational traditions and rituals by planning important community events. And they may be recruited to help with initiatives that create connection and preserve the organization's culture.

Working where you are a value add does not necessarily mean you must stick with a department or organization that shares your same archetype. It's simply paying attention to where you will be needed or personally energized even if it means butting heads with people who think differently from the way you do. For example, you may be a CFO Guardian archetype who is fiscally very responsible, and you are needed and energized by working in Trailblazer organizations (e.g., start-ups).

Hiding in Plain Sight

A seventeen-year-old high school student we'll call Lydia was engaged in college and career counseling with Tim during her junior and senior years. She was a motivated young woman on track to be the first in her family to go to college. Not only was she an outstanding student, she was passionate about combating social injustices. For years, she focused on fighting for sustainable and humane food policies to be adopted in western Massachusetts. She regularly burst into Tim's office urging him to watch the latest Netflix documentary exposing troubling practices of America's corporate-controlled food industry. Early in her senior year, she organized a campaign to serve more locally grown and organic food in various high schools' cafeterias. It was clear that her vocational aspirations would involve social advocacy, which would draw on her fearlessness, independent spirit, and determination to take down oppressive authorities

and systems. Because Tim understood Lydia's core values, when she announced her plan to enlist in the army, he knew that expressing curiosity might be needed more than simply congratulations. Indeed, it didn't
take long before she came out with her fears about failing in the college
admissions process. As a first-generation prospective college student, she
was anxious and unsure about her abilities. Rather than pooh-pooh her
decision, Tim worked with Lydia to revisit her core values, and to consider whether the army was a good fit with them.

Lydia recalled that her core values were equality, individuality, creativity, and social justice. Together they googled the US Army's core values: loyalty, duty, respect, selfless service, honor, integrity, and personal
courage. Through an honest and open dialogue comparing these with her
own core values, Lydia recognized that the army wasn't a good fit for her.
She realized that joining the army might stifle her style of self-expression,
and she also worried about how her independent and defiant personality
would mesh with the army's culture of discipline.

When Tim asked what had instigated her interest in the army in
the first place, Lydia tearfully admitted that paying for college might
bankrupt her family. She saw the military as a "free pass" to college.
And so more core values surfaced: family, security, and independence.
For Lydia, going to college threatened these values. After viewing her
decision-making through the lens of these core values, she recognized
that her motives for joining the army were fear-based. Together, Tim
and Lydia worked to overcome her fears of failing in college and to explore financially viable college options given her family's needs. Lydia has
matriculated to a state college in Massachusetts and is majoring in political science. What's more, the college's in-state tuition made attending
eminently affordable, alleviating Lydia's financial fears.

The truth is, we all know what it's like to have a conversation with a student who is *clearly* making the wrong decision. They're hanging with the
wrong crowd, dating the wrong person, taking up the wrong major or a
career path that's unrealistic. Getting them to see the error of their ways

is usually not that easy. As they get older and become their own bosses, all the persuasion, manipulation, and guilt-tripping in the world can fail to do any good. The reality is, we can't make all their decisions for them. But we *can* teach them to make wise decisions for themselves.

Let's be honest, some of us wonder if we can trust our young people enough to relinquish our control. But what if we knew that there was a way to help students make truly wise and effective decisions for themselves—wouldn't it be such a relief to hand the rudder over to them? By the time our people are heading to college, our goal is to serve as crew members of their team, rather than as their skippers.

Let's revisit how Tim helped Lydia with decision-making. He helped her uncover her fears and aspirations in the college search process though the language and power of core values. Then, when Lydia was clear on her own core values, rather than making decisions for her, he asked a simple question: Which choices align with your values and which don't?

It's through the power of identifying core values that we can teach young people to make the right decision, instead of making it for them.

So What? (Core Values Aren't Just a Nice Thing)

Research shows that good things happen when we align our life choices with our core values. Core values put us in the zone: we perform better, we get unstuck, our mental health and quality of life improve.

They are also powerful mood boosters; aligning with our core values makes us feel better about ourselves. They boost our self-esteem, confidence, and self-worth.[9] They improve our relationships, too. They make us feel more loved and connected to others, which in turn makes our own lives richer.[10] Just reflecting on our core values makes us happier, less depressed, and less anxious.[11] And when students are living out core values, they bring their A game to school. Students who tap into their core values are more academically motivated, get better grades, and are less likely to drop out.[12]

How does living life aligned with core values do all this? By *connecting* us to others and by *motivating* us to become our best selves.

The Answer's in the Question

A remarkable set of interventions have proved that simply asking young people to talk, write, or think about their intrinsic core values can have outsized benefits. These values-affirmation exercises engage students in identifying their core values and then writing about why they're important and the roles they play.[13] In one study, students in the affirmation intervention were asked to indicate their most important values from a list of core values and then write a brief paragraph about why these values were important to them. Control students indicated their least-important values and why these might be important to someone else. The simple affirmation exercise had astounding results: in just one year, the intervention reduced the academic gap between Black and white students by 40 percent.[14] A follow-up study showed that affirmed Black and Latinx students continued to earn higher GPAs than their nonaffirmed peers even two years later![15]

Values affirmation also helped women perform better on their course exams and earn higher grades.[16] How could such a small intervention have such powerful effects? The combined findings of these experiments suggest that reminding yourself of your core values strengthens your self-worth and confidence and buffers the psychological threats to your academic potential. This gift keeps on giving, because affirmed students perform better on tests, and when they perform better, they feel more affirmed, and on and on it goes. A positive spiral up. Too often, underrepresented students' core values, such as community and family, are crowded out by achievement, power, and recognition. The affirmation exercise may allow students to recognize and become buoyed by strengths they would otherwise overlook. Other studies have shown that values affirmation not only increases self-worth and academic performance, but also reduces bad behavior, bullying, and aggression.[17]

Adults also benefit from these reflection exercises. When asked to identify their intrinsic core values and then consider how they would live differently if they lived by these values, they reported decreases in materialistic desires and dramatic increases in self-esteem three months later.[18]

Values Exercises

Below we have designed some exercises based on the research we shared in the previous section. Feel free to do these activities with your students.

Ranking of Personal Characteristics and Values
Here is a list of characteristics and values.[19] Some may be important to you, some may not. Please rank these values and qualities in order of their importance to you, from 1 to 10 (1 = most important, 10 = least important). Use each number only once.

Core Value	Ranking
Being good at art	
Creativity	
Relationships with family and friends	
Government or politics	
Independence	
Learning and gaining knowledge	
Athletic ability	
Belonging to a social group (e.g., a community, racial group, or school club)	
Music	
Career	
Spiritual or religious values	
Sense of humor	

Now choose one of your top three values and write about a personal experience that highlights why this value was important to you and made you feel good about yourself. A friendly reminder: your list should represent what *you* truly value and which values happily take up time in your brain or life. *Not* what you think you "should" care about.

Bringing It All Together

Better grades. Improved self-esteem. All from asking a simple question: What do you value? The power of this question has to do with how it shifts our attention. While we all have authentic core values, we can get distracted by our materialistic culture. When we're asked what we value, this question gives us permission to reconnect to what *we* truly care about. Instead of instinctively pining away for status and prestige, we can intentionally affirm our authentic core values. When we affirm the values that matter most to us, that endure, and that we're willing to sacrifice for, something important happens. We are reminded of *our* value and potential. We receive a fresh infusion of confidence in our ability to pursue important goals in life.

Our work with students largely involves *asking them questions* rather than providing answers. It doesn't help to just tell students who they are—what their core values are, what strengths make them their best selves, what skills they want to master, or what impact they want to make. Even if we are spot-on, it does no good if students don't arrive at these truths for themselves. They will do little to internalize our words and pursue their purpose if they haven't reflected on these critical questions for themselves. No other human, no matter how well-meaning, can give another the answers to their purpose questions.

Purpose comes from within us. That is the beauty of the purpose mindset; it takes shape in unique ways for each of us. It's our job as educators, parents, and mentors to scaffold students in discovering their purpose *for themselves*.

Asking the right question at a moment in time when a student is brave enough to ponder the answer is at the heart of impactful mentoring.

5

Needs in the World

Play your part by meeting the Big Five Needs.

Don't ask yourself what the world needs; ask yourself
what makes you come alive, and then go do that. Because
what the world needs are people who are alive.

—HOWARD THURMAN

Being of Service

Using our strengths and skills in a way that aligns with our values is *how* we do life. The fifth and final principle of purpose is *what* we do with life. Specifically, what will be our contribution? What positive impact will we make? What will we leave behind? What will be our legacy? In psychology, this intention goes by many names. It's an other-oriented, prosocial, or noble purpose. We refer to it as *being of service*. It's about honoring your interests, strengths, and skills by applying them toward a *need* in the world. It's what sets the purpose mindset apart from "just me" performance and passion mindsets. "Make *yourself* successful" (performance mindset). "Make *yourself* happy" (passion mindset). Exhausting and insatiable self-occupations.

The purpose mindset frees us from that rat race. The voice of purpose says, "No more scampering up the ladder toward these imaginary targets. No more feeding a bottomless pit."

You might be wondering whether "purposeful service" is just another burden to shoulder. *Off* comes the weight of making *yourself* successful and happy, and *on* comes the weight of *serving others*. How is *that* freedom?

We were made for this—that's how. When we're working toward goals that meet real needs in the world, our lives make sense. We have reasons to get up in the morning. The tools we've been given (i.e., strengths, skill sets, motivations/values) feel useful. When our work matters, we feel *we* matter. Whether we're contributing to a social cause, helping our families and communities to thrive, or making the world more livable and beautiful by protecting the environment or cultivating the arts.

Students in Belle's research studies have described this intention to make a personally meaningful contribution in a variety of ways. Tania described inspiring youths in her marginalized community as the reason behind her business aspirations: "I want children who come after me, from the youngest one, not to just look at me but to look at others as well so that we can be real models for them to press on." Antoine described his desire to leave a legacy as an engineer: "to build something that the world will remember. Something that will stick for a long time. Years. Decades, even . . . Because for a product to stick around that long, you have to have changed a lot in how we live our lives . . . which is, in the end, one of the main goals for almost any engineer."

A question that's often raised is whether purposeful service is a luxury for privileged people whose own needs have already been met. Are less-privileged people, with their limited opportunities and practical concerns like day-to-day survival, less purposeful? Are they less generous because they have less to give? No. Studies show that a commitment to contribute is highly prevalent among marginalized young people.[1] This may be because marginalized youth have done the work of self-reflection to make meaning of their marginalization or adversity. With reflection comes insights into the connections between themselves and other people and systems. And these insights lead to an awareness of their purpose. For example, students often take on civic purposes that redress the very social ills they've experienced.[2]

Young people are stereotyped as "vulnerable and flawed"—as problems to be fixed. But it's time to see them more accurately. Even the most disadvantaged young people can be supported to help themselves and others. They have the "capacity to change their own behavior, develop new cognitive and behavioral skills, cultivate different interests, and establish new social relationships." They have the power to "shape policies, cultural practices, and social norms" that affect them.[3]

Throughout the generations, purposeful students have driven major social transformations. Four college freshmen in the 1960s led the first civil rights sit-ins. Child coal miners in 1903 marched from Philadelphia to New York to protest child labor. Students in Tiananmen Square in 1989 fought for greater freedoms and democratic reforms. High schoolers in 2018 helped to reform gun laws. In the most critical crises of the day—including equity, democracy, diversity, and violence—youths are the sparks that keep society moving forward.

Living out purpose doesn't require doing great or extraordinary things in the eyes of others. Purpose comes alive in the small moments of everyday life. It's giving a heartfelt compliment, sending a thoughtful text to a childhood friend, or offering a well-timed hug in a moment of distress.

The secret of giving is that it's often the best way to help ourselves. Compared with their peers, students who are driven by the intention to contribute beyond themselves have a greater sense of self-efficacy and perform better.[4] Among urban, low-income youth, commitment to serve others is correlated with increased academic motivation and engagement in school. When adolescents and young adults have "self-transcending" purposes for learning in the classroom, they have higher levels of self-regulation and persistence, and get better grades. More self-oriented motives for learning, like wanting an enjoyable or interesting career, did not produce the same benefits.[5]

These benefits extend to the workplace as well. People who focus on helping other people in their jobs, like a mortgage broker who helps a family buy their first home, or a preschool teacher who helps kids learn to read, are happier, healthier, more likely to be employed with higher salaries, and more productive.[6] In one study, salespeople who were asked to reflect on how their job helped other people generated 50 percent more annual revenue than those who were not asked.[7] Similarly, people who volunteer are less depressed, more satisfied with their lives, and happier on a day-to-day basis. Research shows that volunteering is correlated with a 44 percent lower mortality rate.[8]

Organizations driven by such purpose also excel. Over a ten-year period, businesses whose primary motives were to make a social impact outperformed those on the S&P 500 by 400 percent.[9] In short, doing good for others improves *your* mental and physical health, *your* performance, and *your* relationships, as well.

Built for Good

Biology explains why giving is so beneficial. The ventral striatum (VS), reward center of the brain, gets increasingly engaged when people contribute to others. Activating the VS also reduces stress and ultimately improves psychological and physical health. Compared to a control group, adolescents randomly assigned to provide companionship and support to the elderly had lower circulating levels of inflammation, a marker of various chronic health problems.[10] Contributing to others on a daily basis also improves adolescents' moods, especially among those struggling with depression.[11]

Being of service impacts not just our bodies, but our brains as well. Striving to meet others' needs fulfills our own psychological needs for relatedness, competence, and autonomy. When we intentionally contribute to the lives of others, we're connecting with them. We're gaining a sense of efficacy that fuels competence. And we're acting out of agency and autonomy. We're also feeding our *need to belong* by playing our parts.

Contribution and giving have effects on adolescents that go way beyond traditional developmental tasks such as identity and intimacy. They promote a sense of purpose and generosity more than any other activity. "Making an impact in the world" or "leaving a legacy for future generations" are themes that adolescents consistently mention when reflecting on their hopes and aspirations. We often associate these themes with people entering middle age or beyond, but actually they start mattering during adolescence.

How Self-Reflection Makes Us Generous

Research shows that we are hardwired to do good in the world. The challenge is in discovering the *type* of service that best suits us. How do we decide what needs we want to commit to addressing in the world? Where does the desire to help others come from?

Two major sources of the drive to do good are *adversity* and *advantages*. These two sides of the coin—extreme negative and positive experiences—shape our identities. Both provide deep insight needed to serve others in a way that reflects our own lived experiences. The first has to do with personal hardships—our troubles, mistakes, wrong turns.

Why in the world would we want to spend even a second longer than we have to thinking about adversities? Because hidden in them are clues to our purpose—the change we want to effect in the world.

Adversity

Every generation has walked through pain and adversity. Every individual, family, culture, and society. We inhabit imperfect, mortal bodies and minds, on a vacillating planet with unchecked injustice. Sometimes we reap what we sow, and sometimes we reap what others sow. There are different reasons each person suffers, but we are united in suffering.

Suffering is not a good thing. As therapists, mentors, and parents, we try to help our students become aware of and avoid the unintentional things they do that add unnecessary suffering to their lives. We are very eager to help with that!

But not even the best therapy, mentoring, and parenting can create a suffering-free, perfected life. Try as we might, there isn't a way to help our people sidestep the painful stuff that is the price of admission to the human condition. The loss of loved ones. The breakdown of physical bodies. The inevitability of failures and frustrations. The injustices of people and systems that remain broken. The impossibility of constant bliss. We can try to avoid our painful feelings toward these unavoidable experiences, but they happen to us nonetheless.

Before we say another word, we must insert several crucial caveats. First, we strongly caution against minimizing or putting a Pollyanna spin on your (and your students') pain. Youth who've suffered environmental adversity—such as poverty, mistreatment, or a tragic loss—have an increased risk of mental and physical health problems, poor school performance, and relationship difficulties.[12] Chronic negative experiences and emotions can spiral into serious psychiatric problems, including post-traumatic stress disorder (PTSD). Eight to ten million people in the United States are diagnosed with PTSD, and many more go undiagnosed. So we are definitely *not* suggesting that adversity is good. Nor are we suggesting that we should be less sensitive to the effects of trauma and adversity on young people, believing that these are "the very experiences embedded in daily life that they need in order to become strong and healthy."[13]

Freud explained that the goal of analysis/therapy is to help people overcome "neurotic misery" so that they can face "normal human unhappiness."[14] Since some amount of suffering and adversity is built into life, the goal of therapy isn't to try to escape it, but to learn how to respond to it. To learn to bear it. Address it. Move through it. And often to even be a part of the solution on a larger scale.

Fortunately, 90 percent of people who experience trauma will not experience PTSD.[15] What's more, many people report experiencing post-traumatic growth (PTG) in the aftermath of adverse life events. PTG is a positive psychological change resulting from adversity that leads to a level of functioning higher than that pre-adversity. Out of stress exposure can emerge resilience,[16] and the motivation to make a meaningful contribution in the world. People with the greatest empathy and compassion for others in need are the ones who've experienced the most severe stress and adversity.[17] And it's this compassion that leads them to altruistic acts.[18] When people have survived acute stress or suffering, they're a lot more trusting, trustworthy, open to sharing, and altruistic.[19] "Survivor mission" is that phenomenon of helping others who've experienced something similar to our own adversity.[20] Every day, people are converting the pain and suffering they've experienced from their own adversity into a will to help others.

People who've experienced post-traumatic growth aren't *glad* about their losses or crises. But they do recognize that they've been changed in meaningful ways. These "changes" occur in five areas:

- **Possibilities:** A sense that new opportunities have emerged from the struggle.

- **Relationships:** Closer relationships with people, or a greater sense of connection with others who are suffering.

- **Strength:** A sense that they are stronger than they thought. "If I lived through that, I can face anything."

- **Gratitude:** A greater appreciation for life.

- **Spiritual growth:** A change in beliefs about life and purpose.

The Rose That Grows from Concrete

These personal changes grow into a desire to create change beyond oneself. When people reflect on their experiences of adversity, stressors, or problems, it can clarify how they want to serve.[21] This critical reflection is an opportunity to sharpen a sense of the purpose elements. Wanting to commit to a purpose mindset. Wanting to play growth games even when competing in fixed games. Leaning in to mastering skills and roles. Adding their value where it's needed most. And knowing where they will make their contribution.

That said, the journey from adversity to purposeful service is not a cakewalk. It must be fought for. It involves navigating the brambles of cynicism, fear, anger, and shame in the world. While there is no cookie-cutter road map, we provide a general guide informed by research in re-silience and post-traumatic growth.

Recovery and resiliency involve coming to terms with our adversities, including making meaning of our experiences, and bringing all of our personal experiences, including unresolved and challenging ones, to bear in helping and healing others. Cultivating a desire to contribute begins in our minds. Shapes our expectations. Crystalizes through our words. And eventually breaks through to our actions. You can tell when you come across someone who's gone through this process. You see emotional freedom and generosity. Elisabeth Kübler-Ross wrote: "The most beau-tiful people we have known are those who have known defeat, known suffering, known struggle, known loss, and have found their way out of the depths. These persons have an appreciation, a sensitivity, and an un-derstanding of life that fills them with compassion, gentleness, and a deep loving concern. Beautiful people do not just happen."[22]

All this points to a profound truth: adversities often activate personal growth and purpose. This certainly does not mean that a student who has sailed through life with a supportive home environment and little strug-gle is doomed to lack purpose. Tedeschi and Calhoun emphasize that personal growth after trauma should be viewed as originating not from the event, but from within individuals themselves through their process of grappling with the event and its meaning.[23] Those without trauma can grapple with suffering in the world as well if they have other motivations for doing so, such as an awareness of suffering and healthy empathy.

Students who feel disempowered or come from underprivileged back-grounds have some of the highest levels of empathy and compassionate behavior on a daily basis.[24] Marginalization is tied to increased stress and adversity and, in turn, reflection on these experiences. *Reflecting* on stress and adversity is tied to developing a sense of purpose.[25] People from impoverished and war-torn countries, as well as those who have survived traumatic events like natural disasters, are most likely to report a sense of purpose.[26] Within the United States, too, those who come from poverty, or have been affected by crimes or homelessness, are more likely to consider their life purpose.[27] In sum, experiencing adversity makes us think *about* life more. The more we think about our lives, the more likely we are to find purpose in them.

As we've written, people are *not* glad for their experiences of marginalization, trauma, or systemic racism. And we must fight for systemic changes, not just help people cope better. Still, we're left with the findings that adversity informs purpose, and can catalyze a desire to meet needs. Clearly, students are change agents. Not just problems to be fixed.

Our research and work with students documents their journeys as change agents who heal, fix, and crush the very adversities that have hurt them. They become experts in their own adversity. We see their wisdom, insight, and compassion as they tackle personal and systemic adversity. They listen. They express compassion. They advocate. They take action. They point out systemic injustices to be addressed by policy change. They understand they're not responsible for abolishing the social ills that have harmed them. But they seek to be part of the solution and call others to do the same.

The Examined Life

Adversity changes how we view ourselves, other people, and the world we live in. And this changed view has a special impact on our principles of purpose. Adversity can crystalize our authentic *core values,* uncover our unique *strengths* and *skills,* and compel us to go beyond ourselves and help others. Adversity doesn't just cause a psychological or spiritual response that cultivates purpose. It creates a biological response that readies us for purpose as well.

Our main biological response to adversity is stress. And we tend to view stress as a very "bad" thing. This culturally bound take on stress calls to mind the "fight-or-flight" response. We think of pounding hearts. Rapid breathing. Bodies trembling. Pupils dilating. All the signs that we're preparing to fight or run for our lives.

But there's more to "fight or flight." And it's important to understand the other parts of the picture.[28] Stress in and of itself is not a bad thing. It can help us rise to a challenge by amping up our physical and psychological capacities. It can spur us to strengthen our support networks. It can change the way we see ourselves, or our view of what's important in life.

In other words, stress can set off psychological and biological responses that mobilize each element of purpose. Here's how.

Adversity Reveals True Strengths

It's human nature to sell ourselves short. We *underestimate* our ability to endure pain and *overestimate* the negative impact adversity will have on us.[29] As mentioned in chapter 2, we're often not fully aware of our strengths—we're strengths-blind.

Adversity tests our strength and can reveal to us what we're made of. We react to these events in ways that are diagnostic of our strengths, and that provide life insights, including how to overcome challenges.[30] A common sentiment among trauma survivors is that they're much more vulnerable than they thought, but also much *stronger* than they ever could have imagined.[31]

The Challenge Response
Stress energizes the body to mobilize strength—our livers pump fat and sugar into our bloodstreams that our bodies convert to energy. We breathe deeper to provide more oxygen to our hearts. Our heart rates quicken to deliver a burst of energy to our brains and muscles. Adrenaline and cortisol kick in to help us use this energy efficiently. The combination of these biological reactions makes us able to run faster, lift more, and gain overall physical strength.

This "challenge response" also jacks up our intellectual strength and acuity. Pupils dilate to let in more light so that vision improves. Hearing sharpens and the brain processes information more efficiently. A cocktail of endorphins, testosterone, and dopamine rush in to create laser focus and motivation. So, if we feel we've discovered new strengths from adversity, it's true in more ways than we realize. This biological response to stress makes us physically and mentally stronger.

> *Try this: Ask yourself what personal strengths you discovered or grew as you navigated an individual and specific life challenge.*

Adversity Creates Opportunities for Skill-Building

Traumas are "seismic events" that shape our life narratives. For example, if your student's self-narrative includes being an excellent student, failing multiple exams during a difficult semester can challenge that narrative. If your narrative includes the belief that you live in a safe and secure neighborhood, getting mugged or having your car broken into might disrupt that story.

Recovery involves grappling with new, sometimes seismic events to make new meaning of your life and the world. This can be a painful process that involves coming to terms with losses, including what you formerly believed and felt capable of. At the same time, your eyes may be opened to new life paths and possibilities.[32] As you journey down unexpected paths, opportunities may arise for developing new life skills.

> *Try this: Consider how a challenge or adversity opened up new doors and opportunities for you. What skills were you motivated to learn as a result?*

Adversity Overhauls Values

When bad things happen to us, our knee-jerk response is to think about it over and over. We're highly motivated to make sense of traumatic events.[33] We will repeatedly ask ourselves: *Why did this happen? Why did it happen to me? What type of world do I live in, and what is my place in it? What does the future hold for me?* Sometimes, thinking over these questions can take the form of unhealthy perseveration, or what researchers call *intrusive rumination*. Intentional rumination, however, is making sense of the events and often just the thing we need to come to terms with adversity.

Still, grappling with these questions can be as painful as the adverse experience itself. But the silver lining is that the more we contemplate our lives, the more meaningful and purposeful they become. This is why adversity so commonly results in a greater appreciation of life—the mundane moments as well as the bigger picture. Adverse events can remind us that life is precious and that we have limited time to pursue what matters most. In other words, adversity can help us see what we truly value in life.[34]

The Learn and Grow Response

There are biological reactions to adversity that actually support these value shifts. One response to stress is for our brains to release the hormone DHEA. Known as the "learn and grow response," DHEA makes us receptive to new information so that we can make sense of adverse events. And so, as we replay a stressful event in our minds, the "learn and grow response" changes how we view it and what we value in life.

> **Try this:** *Reflect on a challenging event. Did it change what you valued or thought was important in life? Did it change what motivates you? If so, how?*

Adversity Inspires Us to Do Good

Experiencing loss or tragedy can connect us with others. Not only do we draw support from others, but we can relate to fellow travelers who have suffered as well. We're reminded of the profound importance of meaningful relationships.

Adversity improves our emotional intelligence; it increases our awareness of and compassion toward others' pain and struggles. We want to lessen the pain and suffering of others.

The Tend and Befriend Response

In response to stress, our bodies release high levels of oxytocin, known as the "snuggle hormone." This "tend and befriend response" causes us to crave social connection and motivates us to build and strengthen social bonds. Stress makes us want to talk to people, usually about our stressors. And this desire makes us feel more connected to others. Oxytocin also improves intuition, empathy, and willingness to trust others by enabling our brains to tune in to what others are thinking and feeling.

If you ever commiserate with another parent over a conflict with your adolescent, or vent with a colleague after a frustrating meeting with your boss, then you've activated the tend and befriend response. Your students, too, bond with peers over all sorts of stress. Heartbreaks. Harsh teachers. Too much work. And yes, even overbearing parents.

We've sealed the deal to many of our most significant relationships by bonding over stressful situations. A Harvard University survey found that 70 percent of fathers felt that the global pandemic caused them to spend more time with their kids, and they had stronger, more caring relationships with them as a result.[35]

Try this: Ask yourself: How has adversity impacted your relationships? Has it influenced how you see yourself contributing to the lives of others?

--- --- --- --- --- --- --- --

(Dis)Advantages

Not everyone faces the same amount of adversity in their lives. In fact, we often work hard to avoid adversity for ourselves and our people. Does the absence of adversity mean we lack empathy for others? Not at all. The other side of the adversity coin—advantages—can be just as powerful a motivator to do good in the world.

Each of us benefits from different privileges—some earned, some unearned. For example, we're born into certain identities in terms of race, gender, ability, class, citizenship, to name a few. For each category, society unconsciously arranges the corresponding identities on a continuum, from closest to farthest from the position of power. So, if our identities closely match the identities of decision-makers, we may enjoy unearned benefits. Marginalized identities are those that are farthest from those in power.

When we acknowledge where identities fall on this continuum, we're not making value judgments. Just acknowledging the objective data about the identities of people in our country who tend to occupy decision-making positions, like governmental policy-makers, CEOs, media moguls, and so on.

Just because we have privilege in areas of our lives doesn't necessarily mean we have "easy" lives. Privilege isn't a reason for guilt. It's an opportunity for meeting needs with the advantages we've been given.

The national conversation has put privilege front and center, and yet it can *still* be hard to grasp the impact of privilege. One way to understand it is to reflect on what an able-bodied student needs to think about to walk in the front door of school. Usually without a thought, they just walk through it. Compare this with a student in a wheelchair about to enter the school. They have a lot more to think about. Location of ramps. Curbs. Stairs. Obstacles. Obviously this doesn't mean the able-bodied student is a bad person or doesn't have other struggles and pain. It just means they have one less obstacle to getting to where they're going than the student in the wheelchair does.

So, too, do white Americans have well-documented unearned advantages compared with minorities. Better access to healthcare. Better-quality education. Greater lifetime earnings. Longer life expectancies. Yet policy-makers frequently debate whether racial privilege exists and whether to address inequities. Everyday citizens resist reflecting on and admitting to their privileges. If we're honest, this is because we don't like to admit to privileges we benefit from. Sometimes we feel guilty for having them. We also worry that acknowledging privilege minimizes our own role in success. If we've worked hard, we don't like the thought that our success came through unfair advantages. For example, five of the fastest men's marathon times in history have been set by runners in Nike Vaporfly shoes. A study showed that these shoes significantly boost running economy—wearers do less work to run at the same speed, thanks to a carbon fiber plate and rapid energy-returning foam core.[36] Just like a corked bat or pine tar on a baseball is performance-enhancing, these shoes are performance-enhancing and give runners an edge. Were these record-breaking marathoners really the fastest of all time, or did they overly benefit from the advantages the Vaporfly shoes provided?

We feel better thinking we earned our successes through hard work and talent, not via birthright or a fancy pair of shoes. So denying inherent benefits is a form of self-protection and self-aggrandizement. Privilege is easy for us to deny because it's often invisible—taking the form of an absence of economic insecurity, racial profiling, or stereotyping by others. Only honest reflection can reveal these often invisible truths.

> *Try this:* Ask yourself and your students: In what ways might one aspect of your social status give you an edge—even if you didn't ask for or earn this advantage? What about an aspect that puts you at a disadvantage? Are there certain groups who've been denied these privileges? What impact do you think the lack of privilege might have had on their lives?

Pay It Forward

Just as purpose can change our relationship with our adversity, purpose can also change our relationship with our advantages. Acknowledging our advantages means we can leverage them to help others who don't benefit from them. In turn, opening our eyes to inequalities and injustices can raise our awareness of our own advantages.

Using our social position this way changes our relationship with our privilege. Rather than something to hide, privilege becomes a meaningful resource we can use to give back. We can convert privilege into purpose. This doesn't mean we swoop in as saviors. Recognizing our privileges isn't

Practicing Gratitude

What's something that has made your life better . . .

- In the last year?

- In the last month?

- In the last twenty-four hours?

- In the last ten minutes?

the same as feeling entitled to them. It's being grateful for our advantages that is the engine for change.

Practicing gratitude for our privileges is a strong impetus for giving back. Gratitude transforms the way we see our responsibilities to others in multiple ways.[37] It helps us form and maintain strong and healthy relationships. We become motivated to help others, often in creative and thoughtful ways.[38] The more grateful we are, the more likely we are to help others.[39] Naming our good fortune inspires us to pay it forward. When we understand our advantages and our adversity, we better understand the needs we're driven to meet in the world.

Raising Critical Consciousness

Critical consciousness (CC) is the process of becoming aware of societal ills connected to our lived experiences and doing something about them. Its benefits for diverse youth and communities are well documented. CC involves perceiving a challenge in the world, understanding it, recognizing the possibility of a response, and then acting. Whether and how we take action depends on whether and how we understand the challenge first.

The three steps to this process are critical reflection, critical motivation, and critical action. Critical reflection is learning about social injustices and how they shape the world. Critical motivation is reflecting on how they shape our advantages and adversity. From this reflection, we gain the critical motivation to do something about these injustices. This motivation moves us from reflection to action. Let's use critical consciousness to understand how we can act to meet the big five needs in the world.

Universal Needs

The big five needs are things every human needs to thrive. Advantages *protect* and *promote* these needs. Adversities *threaten* these needs. Whether our needs are met versus unmet is typically the difference between an advantage and an adversity. Reflecting on how our own needs have been met can help to clarify the needs we are uniquely positioned to help meet in the world.

Consider how the big five have affected you. If a need has not been met, reflect on the adversity it may have caused in your life. If a need has been met, it's an advantage. Consider how your adversities and advantages might help you to address others' needs in a way that feels meaningful to you. Note that our descriptions aren't comprehensive, just starting points for considering how we might meet a need.

Physical Needs

At a minimum, everyone needs access to healthy food, clean water, basic healthcare, and safe, affordable housing. If these needs aren't satisfied, our bodies can't function.

Related Issues:

- More than 35 million people struggled with food insecurity in the United States in 2019.[40]

- Water scarcity impacts 40 percent of the entire global population.[41]

- Almost one in three American households don't have access to affordable housing.[42]

- One in four Americans skip medical care because they can't afford it.[43]

Critical reflection: Have my physical needs been met?

Critical motivation: What advantages or adversity have these needs created in my life?

Critical action: How could I use my advantages to help others whose basic needs are not met? How can my experiences of adversity be used to help others experiencing something similar?

Personal Needs

People need psychological, spiritual, and relational health, including a sense of security and safety, love and belonging, and self-esteem. These needs can be satisfied through resources and opportunities, such as mental health and medical care, schools, places of worship, spiritual and psychological supports, and other caring and contributing communities described in the next section.

Related Issues:

- Almost one in ten young people suffer from major depression.[44]

- Over 40 million American adults suffer from anxiety each year, and only one in three receive treatment.[45]

- One in three adults suffer from loneliness.[46]

- Only 14 percent of adults say they are happy, a historic low.[47]

Critical reflection: Have my personal needs been met?

Critical motivation: What advantages or adversity have these needs created in my life?

Critical action: How could I use my advantages to help others whose personal needs are not met? How can my experiences of adversity be used to help others experiencing something similar?

Community Needs

People need to belong in supportive communities. Not only do communities, such as schools, faith/affiliation communities, and work places, provide an opportunity to contribute as valued members, people also need access to quality education and dignified work that will provide economic security.

Related Issues:

- Fifty-three million American workers age eighteen to sixty-four make less than $18,000 a year.[48]

- Only 14 percent of low-income students will earn a college degree within eight years of graduating high school.[49]

- One in five young people around the world are not in education, training, or employment settings.[50]

Critical reflection: Have my economic needs been met?

Critical motivation: What advantages or adversity have these needs created in my life?

Critical action: How could I use my advantages to help others whose community needs are not met? How can my experiences of adversity be used to help others experiencing something similar?

Just Society Needs

Everyone deserves equal opportunities to participate in and benefit from a just, fair, and democratic society.

Related Issues:

- The richest 20 percent of American households own 77 percent of all wealth in the United States.[51]

- Black people in the United States are three times more likely to be killed by police than are white people.[52]

- Women make 81 cents for every dollar a man makes in the United States.[53]

- Only 40 percent of polling places fully accommodate people with disabilities, and one in three people with disabilities report difficulty voting.[54]

Critical reflection: Have my societal needs been met?

Critical motivation: What advantages or adversity have these needs created in my life?

Critical action: How could I use my advantages to help others whose just society needs are not met? How can my experiences of adversity be used to help others experiencing something similar?

Environmental Needs

Everyone has the right to environmental and/or planetary sustainability.

Related Issues:

- Average wildlife populations have reduced by 60 percent in the last forty years.[55]

- Carbon emission rates are rising at faster rates than ever reported in human history.[56]

- The World Economic Forum cites climate change as the biggest threat to earth.[57]

- The last five years have all been recorded as the hottest years on record.[58]

Critical reflection: Have my environmental needs been met?

Critical motivation: What advantages or adversity have these needs created in my life?

Critical action: How could I use my advantages to help others whose environmental needs are not met? How can my experiences of adversity be used to help others experiencing something similar?

Meeting Needs Both Big and Small

These lists demonstrate that there is much need in the world, and much work to be done. And there are infinite ways of being of service. Virtually any job or organization, whether for-profit or nonprofit, can address pressing needs. It can be argued that *every* effective business meets a need in the world. Jim Stengel, a former Proctor & Gamble executive and thought leader in helping companies find their purpose, has identified five needs that *any* company may meet:

- **Eliciting joy:** Activating experiences of happiness, wonder, and limitless possibility.

- **Enabling connection:** Enhancing the ability of people to connect with one another and the world in meaningful ways.

- **Inspiring exploration:** Helping people explore new horizons and new experiences.

- **Evoking pride:** Giving people increased confidence, strength, security, and vitality.

- **Impacting society:** Affecting society broadly, including by challenging the status quo and redefining categories.[59]

When your students consider what needs they intend to meet in the world, this doesn't necessarily mean they must choose to solve a pressing global problem. Meeting a need starts from contributing to the most basic of needs on a daily basis. Sometimes it means offering an encouraging word or holding open a door. Other times, it's picking up trash along the side of a road. Or it's voting or taking to the streets to protest racial injustice. Whether the context is personal or professional, meeting *a* need (big or small) requires our intentionality.

A critical piece of what's necessary to meet needs in the world is caring for our own essential needs. It's hard to meet others' needs when our own needs go unmet. When we're coping with adversity from an unmet need, we need to put on our own oxygen masks first. Over the long term, the most successful people balance the two: they find a way to meet their own needs *by* meeting the needs of others.

Next, we explore the science of how people turn their pain and privilege into purpose.

In Their Feelings

Psychology in the United States has come a long way in destigmatizing mental health issues. It's more acceptable now than it's ever been to acknowledge depression, anxiety, and mental health disorders. The rapper Drake's most popular song, "In My Feelings," explores difficult emotions he encountered in a significant relationship. His 2020 video for the song "Laugh Now, Cry Later" features a close-up of him with tears streaming down his face, asking a friend, "You got a tissue?" Drake's vulnerability is symbolic of the emotional rawness of young people today. It seems like they are always "in their feelings." It's never been more accepted to own up to the emotional roller coaster that's part of life. Psychologist Jean Twenge, in her book *iGen: Why Today's Super-Connected Kids Are Growing Up Less Rebellious, More Tolerant, Less Happy—and Completely Unprepared for Adulthood—and What That Means for the Rest of Us*, explains that with the increase in mental health problems among youth has come a shift in norms toward honest self-expression.[60] Social media has been their place to share feelings, for better and for worse.

Social and emotional learning (SEL) has become a huge area of focus in education. Schools are talking about teaching "the whole child" and changing their school schedules to include advisory periods for the sole purpose of helping teachers build meaningful relationships with students to help them navigate the vicissitudes of life. Now more than ever, young people are encouraged to "open up" about their feelings.

What's less understood is *why* talking through emotions is a key to thriving and *how* we can help our students do so. Opening up has real, tangible benefits that go well beyond "feeling better." It improves mental and physical health, and the ability to succeed in life. Opening up enables us to let go, think it through, and connect the dots.

Let Go

Research has revealed that we shouldn't be so quick to assume that "talking about a problem won't make it go away."[61] Opening up actually has a palpable effect on our brains and bodies.

Thought exercise: Imagine holding your breath while reading right now. In the first few moments, it may be light work. You can probably focus on reading these words with little effort. But as time goes on, your body will begin to crave oxygen, distracting you from the task at hand. You'll start to feel the physical strain of holding your breath in. Your stomach and chest will tighten; your lungs will feel pressed in on themselves. This physical exertion will coincide with a mental strain. The longer you go without breath, the harder it is to think about what you're reading. Go long enough and you won't be able to think about anything but *oxygen*. Your focus will move entirely inward.

Now, imagine taking a lovely deep breath after holding it all in. How does it feel to let go and let your breath return to you? What word would you use to describe it? For us, it's *relief*.

Holding in your emotions has the same impact. Both are physical acts of repression that take up energy. When you hold in your emotions, your heart races, you sweat, and you strain your cardiovascular system. You may not notice this exertion in the short term, but holding in your emotions long enough will lead to big problems, including physical and mental health ailments. Our bodies exert precious energy to hold in thoughts and emotions. It drains us over time.

The antidote to "holding in" is "letting go." Imagine again how it feels to take those first few breaths after holding your breath for too long. Huge relief. Your body and mind relax. The same is true when you release emotions you've been working hard to repress. Compared to their peers, college students who expressed painful experiences and feelings in writing were much less likely to visit the health center six months later.[62] Even taking a few minutes to write about deeply felt personal experiences or adversity can heal emotional wounds, decrease stress, increase your sense of well-being, and improve your relationships. It even boosts your immune system.[63] Similar results have been found in hospital patients: opening up has been shown to improve lung functions and joint health.[64]

There's great mental benefit to opening up as well. When students opened up about their worries before big tests, their scores improved dramatically.[65] When workers who were laid off or fired let go of feelings of guilt and shame, they were more likely to get hired in subsequent job interviews.[66]

Supporting your students to let go, and process their emotions in a healthy way, is the best way to overcome the negative effects of holding things in.

Think It Through

The next step to processing negative experiences is to think them through. When we experience a traumatic or stressful event, the typical response is to think about it over and over. This repeated thinking, called "rumination," includes reminiscing, problem-solving, and trying to make sense of what happened.[67] We replay upsetting key moments—a first heartbreak, a particularly cringey moment, various regrets. We obsess over where we went wrong and how we could've done things differently. Rumination is a natural coping mechanism. We ruminate to learn from difficult times.

But rumination can be a terribly painful process. We might realize that we'll never see a loved one again, or that after heart failure we'll never be as active as we once were. Rumination can plunge us to the depths of despair. We can be going about our day when out of the blue—bam!—a negative memory from our past takes over. This is the *intrusive rumination* we mentioned above. It affects waking thoughts, dreams, and every aspect of our internal worlds. These random thoughts trigger intense negative feelings, often at the worst times. No one wants to burst into tears during a job interview or in the checkout line at CVS. So, we try to beat back these intrusive thoughts. Force them out of our minds. Focus on the brighter side. Keep ourselves busy, surround ourselves with others, turn on the TV even when we aren't watching it, doom scroll through our digital feeds. Anything to *not* be left alone with our own thoughts.

But working hard to block intrusive thoughts is like holding our breaths; the longer we do it, the more it consumes us. Try as we might, adversity is not easily forgotten. Maybe that's for the best. Maybe we shouldn't be so hasty in deleting adverse events from our memories. Fortunately, automatic rumination isn't the only way to review our adverse experiences. *Deliberate rumination* is intentional and reflective thought. People who deliberately ruminate seek out space and support for reflection. These are common practices in AA, counseling, or other support groups. Automatic rumination makes us want to run from painful memories and emotions. Deliberate rumination involves *putting your arms around them*. It's meeting them head-on through active contemplation. It's a tool for *repairing, restructuring, or rebuilding* our understanding of how the world works.[68] The difference between continuing to suffer from adversity and growing from it is thinking through adversity very intentionally. We make sense of our lives. Strategize ways to manage adversity. Accept things outside our control.

Deliberate rumination takes a lot of different forms. Talking. Writing. Other forms of self-expression. Thinking through pain, problems in the world, and unearned privileges can come with negative emotions. Facing them, rather than fearing them, can help us to accept, move forward, and make meaning from them.

Three stages of deliberate rumination lead to post-traumatic growth.

- **Comprehensibility:** Accepting that the event happened, or that the feeling exists, rather than denying it. This stage is about *acceptance*.

- **Manageability:** Figuring out ways to cope with the consequences of the trauma. This stage is about *problem-solving* and *coping*.

- **Meaningfulness:** Finding meaning from the event, which can lead to post-traumatic growth. This stage is about *creating purpose*.

Adversity forces us to change the stories we tell about ourselves and the world. Intentional deliberation is choosing to tell a new story that makes sense to us, that aligns with our purpose, and allows us to move on in our lives. This is how many of the most influential and successful people in the world have turned their pain into their purpose.

Connecting the Dots

Opening up allows us to let go of our emotions. Thinking them through helps us make sense of and come to peace with life challenges. Connecting the dots leads to the purpose mindset. There is no easy recipe for arriving at your purpose. But this we know: the more we actively reflect on the connections between who we are, who we want to become, and the impact we want to have, the more purposeful our lives become. This is true for each principle of purpose. The more we think about our strengths, skills, values/motivations, and contributions, the more we can integrate them into daily life. This is why adversity can cultivate purpose—it causes us to *question* our lives. It's through this exploration and curiosity that we make meaning in life. When faced with a life-altering event, we tend to ask: "What's the point of my life? What's important to me? Who am I, and what am I capable of?"

Asking these questions clarifies the answers. Just asking people to reflect on the elements of purpose we've discussed can lead to other realizations. Students of color who journaled about their authentic core values did so much better in school that they closed the achievement gap.[69] Reflecting about their strengths made people better at, and more satisfied with their jobs.[70] Writing about who they wanted to become in the future, including the skills they wanted to develop, significantly and lastingly improved people's well-being.[71] When students were given an opportunity to write about their prosocial reasons for learning, they became more academically self-disciplined and learned more in school than when they focused only on self-oriented motives such as the desire to have an enjoyable career.[72] Reflecting on how their work would make a positive impact in the world made all the difference.

Connecting the dots, through talking or writing, reveals the thread joining the pieces that matter most to us. It's the process by which we make meaning of our lives, the good, bad, and ugly. It's how we connect our lived experiences to our sense of purpose. Our lives inform our purpose, and our purpose informs the needs we choose to meet in the world. This bond connects us to something bigger than ourselves. When we ask the questions: "Why me? Why did this happen to *me*?" this search for answers can reveal the connections between our life experiences and our purpose. Connecting the dots is how we construct a meaningful narrative.

Sink or Swim

The most decorated Olympian of all time, American swimmer Michael Phelps, competed in four Olympics (2004 to 2016) and earned an astonishing twenty-eight medals, including an Olympic record of twenty-three gold medals. Amid his triumphs, Phelps battled substance abuse, anxiety, and depression. He was arrested twice and served probation for drunk driving. At the top of his (fixed) game, after bringing home four gold medals and two silvers in the 2012 Olympics, he holed up for days in his hotel room not eating or sleeping, contemplating suicide.[73] An obsessive performance mindset had brought him to the brink of emotional ruin. Fortunately, he opened up to counselors and family members, and ultimately found healing and purpose. He channeled his energies into philanthropy, partnering with the Boys and Girls Club of America to promote healthy coping for youth—a focus inspired by his own challenges with mental health. During a live interview, he explained how his adversities had inspired him to be a part of saving lives. He claimed that this purpose was "way more powerful" and "light years better" than Olympic gold.

His story is a reminder to care for ourselves, and once our needs are met, adversity can give us insight and expertise to aid fellow travelers.

No "One Right Way" to Do Good

Phrases like "meeting a need in the world," "doing good," and "being of service" can stoke guilt, intimidation, and misinterpretation. Maybe we think it means living 100 percent selflessly, swearing off material possessions, and solving the biggest problems in the world all by ourselves. Refusing to fly on planes due to high carbon emissions, like environmental activist Greta Thunberg. Working to tackle misinformation on COVID-19, like Nelson Kwaje in South Sudan. Creating an anti-violence awareness campaign, like teenage Chicago activist RaSia Khepra. Inventing energy-efficient gadgets using scrap electronics for poor communities, like the teenage engineer Kelvin Doe in Sierra Leone. Using media to stand up for girls' access to free quality education and winning the Nobel Peace Prize, like Malala Yousafzai. Reciting the words of a poem to heal and unify a divided country at the 2021 presidential inauguration, like Amanda Gorman.

Without question, these are wonderful role models and exemplars of purpose. What a beautiful world it would be if there were more like them. But they also represent an image of purpose that is not for everyone. One that causes some people to question whether they should even bother to make service a part of their life equation. For some students, "meeting a need" sounds like *too great an ask*. They wonder, "How does my interest in making money or in full-time Netflix watching have anything to do with meeting needs in the world? What would I have to sacrifice to do good?"

For others, "meeting a need" sounds *too tiny an ask*. Overwhelmed by the thought of all the needs in the world, they wonder, "Where do I even start? What do I have to offer that would even scratch the surface of the vast needs in the world? How can befriending one lonely classmate, shoveling snow off my elderly neighbor's driveway, tutoring a second-grader, or donating my time and money to one charity, for example, make the slightest dent in meeting massive global needs?" For that one lonely classmate, elderly neighbor, or child, it's everything. And for your student, every act of empathy and generosity in daily life is a building block in the practice of purpose that meets needs in the world.

If the Shoe Fits

Psychologist Scott Kaufman explains how generous purpose has been misunderstood. In what Kaufman refers to as the *Surrender Yourself* model, Maslow's "hierarchy of needs" has been misinterpreted to suggest that meeting your own basic needs is a necessary evil and not as noble as sacrificing your needs to make the world better. [74]

The *Fully Human* model, in contrast, honors everyone's individual journey to purpose. Personal needs aren't less noble than the world's needs. We have to meet our needs for safety, love, esteem, and mastery in order to do *anything* else well. In other words, put your own oxygen mask on first, so that you can bring your full self (personal needs, interests, and all) to your purpose.

We have to truly respect our students' "inner core." We're like horticulturists who learn our students' tropisms—their leanings and preferences. We are about helping them grow in their own styles toward fulfilling their purposes. After all, the definition of purpose is an intention to do something meaningful for the self and of consequence in the world. It's not abandoning everything you care about to give to others. There is a balance between self-care and care of others. A balance between self-interest and interest in others. And nowhere in this definition is a measuring stick for determining how big or small your impact should be.

We're not competing in the Good Works Olympics. "Doing good" is *subjective. We* choose a way of contributing that is personally meaningful to *us*. It's not about satisfying other people's definitions of contribution. We are not subject to earthly judgments about the worthiness of our work or cause. Purposeful people realize that "meeting a need" is less about the tangibles of *what* they do and more about *why* they do it. This triggers a virtuous cycle; doing good makes us *feel* good. Feeling good compels us to do good.

"Job crafting" is the process of designing your job to make it meaningful and engaging.[75] Twenty years of research on hospital cleaners, employees in a manufacturing firm, a women's advocacy nonprofit, and tech workers undertaken by Jane E. Dutton and Amy Wrzesniewski converge on three strategies:

- *Task crafting* is shaping the types of tasks that make up your job.

- *Relationship crafting* is shaping who you interact with at work.

- *Cognitive crafting* is shaping the way you see the tasks and relationships involved in your work.

Candice Walker, a hospital housekeeper, cares deeply for patients and their families. She sees her work as much more than her cleaning responsibilities; she sees them as a form of healing and playing a key role "in the house of hope." Defining her role as a healer has meant that she pays special attention to the tasks that help patients to recover quickly, and deliberately forms relationships with them.

Rachel Heydlauff, a consultant for a firm specializing in organizational change, cares about sharing her expertise on positive organizational scholarship, a role that was not originally explicit in her job description. She increased this part of her role and pursued opportunities to deepen her expertise, to the point of developing a reputation for it. She intentionally builds deep, personal connections with her clients and colleagues to have influence on team morale and organizational climate.[76]

"Meeting a need" is subjective. People determine what is purposeful to them:

- A ticket salesperson sees their job as an essential part of providing people with entertainment, not just processing orders.

- An accountant provides economic peace of mind to their clients.

- The friendly waiter's service offers some respite to a construction worker who has been on their feet all day.

- The mobile phone sales representative helps a grandmother buy a service plan that lets her FaceTime with her grandchildren.

Virtually any job and every task can be carried out in a way that contributes to a need. We hold power to find the impact and purpose animating our daily and long-term efforts. And we can empower our students to do the same.

--- -- -- -- -- -- -- -- -- --

Bringing It All Together

Being of service is the lynchpin of the purpose mindset. It can stem from our adversities and advantages. Carving out space for intentional reflection on these experiences is the key to finding meaning in them. Before inviting students into a compassionate and imaginative space for processing their elements of purpose, please keep in mind these caveats:

- Support students in seeking professional help in dealing with mental health issues.

- Fortunately, human beings are amazingly resilient. Most recover from adversity on their own.

- Pushing people to talk about their feelings in the immediate aftermath of trauma may increase the likelihood of long-term emotional problems. Students will let you know when they are ready to talk.

- Different adversities can require different coping strategies. What may be beneficial for coping with one type of experience might not be helpful for another. Some people don't need to open up about their adversity at all.

- Given these different coping styles, ask your students what they need. Listen. Then do your best to provide that support.

Below, we make lessons from this chapter actionable for you and your students.

Self-Care

Here's the good news: you are reading this book because *you* want to be of service, to your students and beyond. Articulating the needs you want to meet in the world, and *why* they are important to you, is the best way to role-model being of service to young people. Reflect on the prompts below, and consider sharing them with your students.

Reflecting on Advantages

REFLECTION

a. What does being of service mean to you? Complete this sentence: My aim is to be of service by _____.

b. What does it mean to be of service as a parent, educator, or mentor?

c. What does it mean to be of service in your professional life?

d. Are the answers to a and b the same or different? Why?

MOTIVATION

a. What needs are you addressing when you are being of service? (Note—it can be more than one.)

b. Why is meeting this need important to you?

c. Does it stem from advantages or adversity you've experienced? If so, how did your adversity or advantages inform your motivation?

ACTION

a. How could you be more intentional about serving:

> Your students?
>
> Your community?
>
> Your workplace?

b. What's an act of service you could take in the next:

> Month:
>
> Week:
>
> Day:
>
> Hour:

Case Example:

During his college advising session with Marcus, Tim asked his standard initial question: "If you could do anything after high school knowing that you would be successful, financially secure, and your friends and family would support you, what would you do?" Marcus replied, "Become a YouTube gamer."

Tim asked his standard second question: "Why?" Marcus shared that he'd been viciously bullied during elementary and middle school. He fell into deep depression, with no one to turn to. To cope with his pain, he would lose himself in the world of online gaming on YouTube. There he discovered a popular YouTuber, with millions of followers and immense financial success. Marcus was drawn to him for one particular reason. He sprinkled throughout his videos personal stories about being bullied as a kid. Hearing his hero share experiences similar to his own had a profound effect on Marcus. He felt less alone and became hopeful that these challenges would not keep him from a brighter future. Marcus began posting his own videos to encourage his followers.

Through online gaming, Marcus was pursuing his purpose. Tim and Marcus researched colleges and universities with video production and editing majors and explored how Marcus might have a similar impact in other professions (e.g., as a psychologist, social worker, and middle school teacher).

Marcus went from disengaged in school to seeing it as an opportunity to achieve his personal goals and meet needs in the world.

What You Can Do for Your Student

Role-modeling service behaviors—helping others, contributing to your community, acting with integrity—is the best thing you can do to support your student to do the same. Once you've practiced self-care in the above section, reflect on the times you've seen your students exhibit these behaviors.

REFLECTION

a. When have you seen your student be of service? (Service can range from sharing a sandwich, a hug, or homework help with a peer.) Who have they helped, and how do they like to help?

MOTIVATION

a. Why do you think your student likes to be of service in this way? What needs do they enjoy meeting for others? Is this related to any advantages or adversity they've experienced?

ACTION

a. Talk with your student about their advantages or privileges, as well as an adversity they're ready to talk about. Students often struggle to articulate *why* their advantages have benefited them or *how* their adversity has impacted them.

b. *Ask about this adversity:* Explore with them how it impacted them. How did it make their lives harder? What did they realize about themselves and the world in facing this challenge?

c. *Ask for their expertise:* Give them this scenario: "If someone was going through something similar to your experience, how would you try to help them? What would you say to them? What actions would you take?" You may get very telling answers from these questions if your student has been well primed to open up. Ask them *how* they arrived at their responses.

PART TWO

RE:PURPOSE

6

Relationships

Create moments that matter.

Be the person you needed when you were younger.

—AYESHA SIDDIQI

Purpose is using your strengths and skills in a way that's of value to you and the world. Let's review the five purpose principles:

1. Commit to a *purpose mindset.*

2. Play *growth games* even when competing in *fixed games.*

3. Future-proof your skills as a *Creator, Facilitator,* and/or *Driver.*

4. Add your value as a *Trailblazer, Builder, Champion,* or *Guardian.*

5. Meet the *big five needs* in the world (physical, personal, community, societal, environmental).

To commit them to memory, use this mnemonic device:

- One **Mindset**

- Two **Games**

- Three **Skill Sets**

- Four **Value Types**

- Five **Big Needs**

We know that it's one thing to understand and remember these elements of purpose, but it's another to apply them in the messiness of life. The second half of this book will make clear how we use the elements of purpose to help students navigate their lives.

We call this work *Re:Purpose*.

To *repurpose* is to adapt the old and reappropriate it in new and creative ways. Turning the old into something new. It's transforming an old ladder into a chic bookcase, or a broken tennis racquet into a postmodern mirror. The next four chapters demonstrate how to repurpose the settings students live in. Just like the Apollo astronauts and scientists used the Hubble telescope to gain perspective on the bigger picture, we can use the five purpose principles to recast our settings. When we see the bigger picture, we have a clearer and wiser way to navigate each domain of life. We will take a deep dive into repurposing:

- Relationships (chapter 6)

- High school (chapter 7)

- College/postsecondary school (chapter 8)

- The workplace and beyond (chapter 9)

Let's Get It

Purpose work is not for the faint of heart. It's a long, slow game. It's full of fits and starts and is done in dribs and drabs . . . not in one sitting. And there is prep work involved. We'll talk about how to build a trusting relationship with your student that is primed for fruitful conversations. Our job is to cheer them toward discovering their own elements of purpose. We aren't the leaders, we're the followers in their journey. We trust that our students are going where they need to go. We are like tour guides on their bus. And we sort of point out, "On your left, there goes an example of you living your core values. Oh, look out to your right—it's a fight you're willing to fight." We're just pointing out what's happening as we go along, rather than designing it for them. We don't *teach* them their strengths, skills, core values, or service in the world. We whet their appetites for *their* self-discovery. Purpose can be learned, but it cannot be taught. We're going to share deep intel into how to create relationships that are open to and ripe for this learning.

Two essential ingredients for discovering purpose are *curiosity* and *space*. Students need an attitude of inquisitiveness about life, and the space and time to explore big questions. In a twenty-year study of the Harvard Business School class of 1974, the most successful graduates had two qualities in common.[1] One—*they believed they could do well,* and so they were driven and motivated. Two—*they were always asking questions.* Always wanting to learn more. The end of HBS wasn't the end of their education; they kept reading, talking to people, and asking questions of all those around them—their friends, family, and supervisors, and later their supervisees, life partners, and children. They remained in a perpetual state of curiosity, always wondering about themselves, others, and the world around them.

We cultivate curiosity in our students by *being curious about them*. By skillfully asking the right questions at the right time. Asking ourselves and our people, what makes you your best self? When you retire one day, what do you want people to stand up and say about you? What do you want to be remembered for? The timing and meaningfulness of your questions will determine the quality of your students' responses.

The stories we've shared about students' "aha moments" didn't come from our telling them what to think and believe. Their discoveries were *theirs*. We just asked the right questions at the right times. We learn to do this through close observation, by becoming students of our students. So while we offer you our flexible set of questions, it's up to *you* to learn *when* and *how* to ask them.

Typically, the right time is when your student feels it's the right time. They're open, relaxed, and trusting. Ready to share and be heard.

We know, gentle readers, that you may have just snorted, "When hell freezes over!" Maybe you can't recall more than three times a year when your monosyllabic, door-slamming, eye-rolling teenager was in this hypothetical "right space" to respond thoughtfully to your deep, meaningful questions about life. During elementary school, these times coincided with bedtime as a stalling tactic and, during high school, with softening you up to ask for money or the car keys. The rest of the time, your caring questions (like "How was your day?" and "Who drove you home?") were viewed as the Spanish Inquisition. You explained to your kids that you just wanted to be in the trenches with them during the ups and downs of adolescence, but were treated like a CIA operative using outdated Cold War interrogation strategies. They responded to your beautiful questions with side-eye. And accusations like "You ask a lot of questions" and "You seem like you always want to know what's going on with me." *Well . . . yes. Yes, I do want to know what's going on with you.*

How do you get beyond the suspicion, and the gulf between your turf and theirs . . . into the open, fertile fields for exploring life's biggest questions together? We know it seems like a huge leap in most households. It's time to bridge the gulf.

Calling BS

First, recognize that your students have finely tuned BS radars. Adults become desensitized to BS from years of exposure, but students are still allergic to it. And that's a good thing. The beauty of young people is earnestness and authenticity. BS is anything disingenuous, misleading, or unfair. It's the hidden agenda. Even when BS contains elements of truth, the slightest hint of a hidden agenda makes BS feel like "a greater enemy of truth than lies."[2]

People learn early in life that their parents have hidden agendas. Even when they mean well, parents get sucked into manipulating their kids out of fear and protectiveness. *Helicopter* parents fear that danger lurks around every corner ("I trust my kids, but not the world they live in"). *Snowplow* parents fear that if they don't beat down these threats, their kids will miss out ("I will blast away my kids' obstacles"). *Performance mindset* parents are thinking, if you can't beat 'em, join 'em—inject kids with winning attitudes ("I'll teach my kids to beat the system"). *Self-protective* parents cover their own assets more than their kids' for fear of being judged ("I must help my kids get into such-and-such university, to prove what a competent parent I am").

Students have a "fear detector," similar to their BS radar. When we're feeling anxious about their choices, they can smell it like sharks detect blood in the water. Questions that are veiled attempts to control or manipulate come across as exactly that. The result is instant tension and defensiveness. *Not* open, genuine curiosity that sparks self-discovery. This is why it's generally a good idea to calm down, meditate, pray, and hit your reset button before launching into a conversation driven by fear. Each fear-provoked conversation drives a little wedge into the relationship. That's why we coach parents to ask themselves one question before they intervene: "How would I parent right now if I weren't scared, worried, or anxious?" In other words, if you knew with certainty that regardless of the current situation, everything would work out fine for your student, how would you respond in this moment? What would you say or do?

When fear is not driving us, our parenting and listening improve dramatically. Suddenly the stage is set for real purpose discovery. We are present. We genuinely want to hear what our students have to say, and so we encourage them to speak freely. We listen carefully. We understand. We validate them.

Authenticity isn't just keeping it real with students, it's being honest with *ourselves*. We won't get too far if we don't get this part right. We have to ask ourselves: What do I really want for my student? Why? Am I imposing any of my own fears and needs on my student? We have to decouple *our* goals from *their* goals.

Even if we've spent our child's first fifteen years fearfully pushing our own agendas, it's not too late to come clean. Healthy relationships are fairly resilient and recoverable. They can bounce back quickly and often. There's still time for a fresh start.

So, what will it take for our students to trust us and want us on their team? In 2012, Project Aristotle explored the question: "What makes a Google team effective?"[3] Google had teams that were super-productive and high-performing. They built high-quality products on time and under budget. But there were plenty more teams that weren't doing as well. What made the difference? Was it team members' talents, years of expertise, productivity, gender or ethnic identities?

Nope. It wasn't the qualities of individual members. It was how they treated one another.[4] The most successful teams meshed well and felt *psychologically safe*. Psychological safety is the sense that interpersonal risks are safe to take here.[5] Success had more to do with safety than anything else. More even than individual talent, education, or experience.

When teams felt psychologically safe, they were more productive because people felt free to share ideas, admit and learn from mistakes, engage in learning, ask for help, speak up, and provide feedback to others.[6] They felt comfortable to be their *full* selves. Bottom line: people and relationships thrive when they feel safe to open up . . . when they can express ideas without fear of criticism or judgment, even when they disagree.

Safety is paramount when doing purpose work, because it means taking risks—to be open, vulnerable, and genuinely curious. We have to be open to uncertainty. We have to be vulnerable by sharing deep parts of ourselves. We have to lower our defenses and let people in. We have to feel protected from judgment, criticism, or embarrassment. So creating space for purpose exploration means creating *safe* space.

Psychological safety relies on *mutual trust* and *respect*.[7] Trust comes with a shared agenda—a sense that we're on the same team. And respect comes from the ability to follow through on this agenda.

On the Same Team

When deciding whether to trust people, we ask ourselves: *Are they trying to help, hurt, or use me?* There's a reason commissioned salespeople have a bad rap—we don't fully trust their intentions. We know it's likely that their hearts are divided between helping us reach our dreams and lining their own pockets, even if it means selling us lemons. Our kids pick up on our hidden agendas, too. They know when our awesome intentions for them are clouded by our own values, anxieties, or beliefs that we know what's best for them (because sometimes we do). To muddy the water further, often they *think* they know our misguided intentions and reject our earnest offers to support them.

In contrast, when people or organizations convince us that they're for us, with no opposite agenda—we trust them. When companies express this through warmth and connection, we buy in.[8] Think Amnesty International or Doctors Without Borders.

Conveying warmth is not necessarily about acting sweet, warm, and fuzzy with our students. It's building a *genuine* relationship. Warmth is earned by demonstrating the trustworthy intentions behind our actions. Oftentimes, it's the football coach who makes the team do hundreds of push-ups, the physics teacher who grades the hardest, the music teacher who won't let you rest until you get it right—who are seen by their students as the warmest, most trustworthy people. They prove that they push us *because* they care . . . sans hugs, feelings, or other fuzziness.

Our research shows that parents' high expectations make their students anxious only when they don't match students' own expectations.[9] Expectations hurt students only when they feel out of sync with them. But when students feel like you share their best interests and aren't driven by your ambitions or fears of failure—they can put up with a lot. They can tolerate honest feedback, being pushed out of their comfort zones, even firm correction. They'll trust you when you support them in the ways *they* want to get better.

Getting that very message across to our students pays huge dividends. In one study, middle school students were asked to write an essay about a personal hero.[10] Teachers gave them written feedback, and a chance to revise their essays to improve their grades. When handing back the essays, the teachers also attached a handwritten note. Half of the students received this neutral message: "I'm giving you these comments so that you'll have feedback on your paper." The other half received one that expressed personal intentions: "I'm giving you these comments because I have very high expectations and I know that you can reach them." The difference in outcomes was staggering. As a result of this simple handwritten message that conveyed a sense of personal connection, students were *ten times more likely* to revise their essay for a better grade.

Sadly, math motivation tends to drop as students get older. But not for those who felt their teachers cared for them.[11] Students who had strong relationships with their teachers were much more willing to lean in to calculus, algebra, and geometry. In general, when students believe you care and that you're in it with them, they're more willing to go all in. To listen, to receive feedback, and to push themselves toward their full potential.

Do you push your students? Do you ask them to go beyond their comfort zones and do hard things? Do they know *why* you push them? Have you clearly communicated it to them? Do they know that you care to support *their* dreams . . . not yours?

What Have You Done for Me Lately?

Besides being attracted to warmth and trustworthiness, we're also drawn to people, products, and companies that are highly competent.[12] Do they have the know-how? Do they appear efficient, capable, skillful, clever, and knowledgeable? Do they have the confidence and ability to carry out their intentions? Know-how is more than just intelligence—it's *special resources, skills,* and *creativity.* When people have the right abilities and skills to actually help us with something we can't easily do on our own, our respect and appreciation for them grow.

Our students do the same unconscious analysis when deciding who to trust. They're asking themselves: "Do I like working with this person?" (warmth and trust) and "Does this person know what they are doing?" (respect). So, to be let in, we have to show them a combination of *why* we want to help (we're *for* them) and *how* we can help. That we're approachable and able.

Students feel safe with adults they see as both warm *and* competent. Yes, we can outsource to others who can help guide our students. But this book is about putting tools in our own toolkits that will enable us to listen *more* skillfully and even join our students' team of trusted mentors.

So how can *you* uniquely help your people? By "helping" we're not talking about showing them you have strengths and skills in their fields of interest. What *you* have to offer is much more fundamental than knowing exactly how to guide them in becoming sports marketing managers, YouTubers, or ancient Egyptian art connoisseurs. *Your* competence is the ability to listen effectively when a young person reflects on a big life question. *Your* competence is the willingness to understand their perspective, to validate how they are feeling, and to do your best to help them based on what *they* are saying. We know there may be days when it's easy to feel like dinosaurs. Young people don't believe we can remember what it's like to be their age. They think we were born old and that social media has completely changed the way the world works. But truth be told, the deep needs for belonging and purpose that characterize the high school and college years remain the same.

So what *you* have to offer is what young people need most: a foundational relationship that will set them up for true and long-term success. Of everything we've discussed, your relationship with your people is hands down the most important influence on their ability to discover purpose.[13]

In one of our studies, students described feeling pressured into a performance mindset to survive at school despite it hurting their self-esteem and well-being.[14] But a follow-up study showed that those with good mentoring resisted the rat race and pursued purposeful goals.[15]

Relationships with parents and mentors are the blueprints for how students engage with the world and how they see themselves. It's humbling to realize that through their relationship with you, they can gain the self-acceptance, inspiration, and support needed to resist toxic societal expectations.[16]

What Good Mentoring Looks Like

Research on adolescents across demographics, in and out of the United States, suggests a few universal characteristics of "good" mentoring. It's a combination of "pushing," "pulling," and "partnering." Sometimes we have to pull our people in close to build relationships and show them we care. We do this by affirming them. Other times, we have to push them to step outside their comfort zones to become their best selves. We do this by challenging them. Still other times, we have to go to bat for them. We have to partner with them in addressing systemic barriers or injustices. We do this by advocating for and with them. Good mentoring is knowing the balance of when to push, when to pull, and when to step in and partner with them in changing unjust systems they swim in. In multiple studies, purposeful students had mentor figures (like great teachers or parents) who did all three.

Affirm Them

Affirming relationships are those in which students feel that they are valued and believed in and that their actions and decisions are understood. Affirmation is a lot like the parenting adage "catch them doing something right." It's not empty and general praise. It's expressing something specific that you see in them that's aligned with their elements of purpose. More often, parents are tempted to do the opposite—"catch them doing something wrong." Catch the things that aren't right, and critique and correct them (e.g., "I can understand what you did, but try doing X next time"). These are fear responses. We fear that our students might make mistakes, go off the rails, not be okay or good enough. We fear we will not have imparted all of our wisdom and warnings before they leave the nest. There's little to be gained in finding fault and fear reactions. They don't constructively help students grow and learn in the intended direction. (Think of the supervisor, friend, or family member who's constantly finding fault with you—how's that working out for you? For the relationship?) These comments instill fear, a sense of not being accepted or safe, because they're born from fear.

We recommend checking our inner critics before they speak. It's easy to overreact about what's needed right now or about the ultimate outcome. Take a deep breath and tell yourself, "My student is learning. Making mistakes is par for the course."

We always have a choice of how to react. We can mostly point out things that concern us, or we can tune in to things we admire about them. Students grow and change when they feel seen, accepted, appreciated, trusted, and respected. It inspires them to do more of the things that represent their best selves. So, if we want our students to be their best selves, and pursue their purpose, we have to catch them doing it. We're all works in progress. Notice progress in the right direction. Embrace who your student is right now ("I love watching you care for your friends that way" or "I love hearing you debate medical ethics with Aunt May") rather than constantly trying to improve them ("If you tweak this or that, it will go even better next time"). Say specifically what you appreciate about their *efforts* ("You worked so hard at linear equations, and now you're seeing the fruits of your labor") rather than evaluating their *personhood* ("You're a good student"). Find ways to cheer them on when the going gets tough ("I'm so proud of how you bounced back after getting knocked down . . . I see you working hard out here!").

Pro-Tips for Affirming Your People: Find creative ways of expressing to your people how much you value their purpose-related choices and actions. Notice whether there are ways they think, speak, do, act, believe, and so on that are in line with their purpose. Catch them in the act, and affirm what you see. Acknowledge sacrifices they may make for their core values, the strengths they're bringing to the things they do, the skills they're working at, and the positive impact they're having on others.

Affirmation Toolkit

Embracing Who They Are

- "I appreciate the way you role-modeled your values to your brother when you . . ."

- "You inspired me to be my best self today by the way you . . ."

- "I really admire your optimism [or other character strength]. It's so nice to be around your positive energy."

- "Thanks for making my life easier by using your skills in . . . to help me with . . ."

- "You helped me with . . . by putting your unique spin on it."

- "I am blessed to work/live/be with you, because . . ."

- "You made my day today by . . . [being of service in this way]."

Acknowledging Their Efforts

- "It impressed me when you [stayed true to your values, used your strengths, leaned into those skills, served others by . . .]."

- "Seeing you use your skills in . . . inspires me to do more with my skills."

- "You care so much about the quality of what you do. I love how you pay such close attention to . . ."

- "You're so brave for being so genuinely yourself, which isn't always easy. I admire the way you stayed true to yourself by . . ."

- "I noticed how hard you worked at [efforts related to purpose . . .]."

Cheering Them On

- "I am so proud of all that you've accomplished, such as [purpose-oriented choices] . . . and I know that you can [do whatever they are setting out to do]."

- "It makes me so happy to see you following your dreams to accomplish [their goals, not necessarily yours]."

- "I know you're capable of great things because . . . [evidence of living with purpose]."

- "I want you to go after that dream to . . . You need to know that you are already making a difference in the lives of others and in my life by [doing that thing related to your dream]."

Challenge Them

The truth is, the search for purpose is often stressful because it's hard to tolerate uncertainty.[17] Parents and mentors can play a huge role in emboldening students to face this challenge. We do this by instilling confidence students need to explore different avenues and make difficult choices. We can also help them to do what they didn't think was possible.

Another way to think about challenging students is to consider the expectations we place upon them. *Students always rise or fall to the expectations we set for them.* When we challenge them by setting high expectations, and articulate why we are setting them, it shows that we believe in them. If our students have high expectations of themselves, our high expectations can feel supportive, rather than stressful. Sometimes, challenging our students might feel in conflict with affirming them. Where affirmation is comforting, a challenge asks them to step *outside* their comfort zone. By definition, this doesn't feel great, and our gut reaction is to not upset the applecart. We might be tempted to take the path of least resistance in mentoring our students to keep the peace. Yet when we don't challenge young people, we inadvertently lower our expectations of them, denying them their full potential.

Challenging students is about inspiring them to take action toward their purpose—toward their agenda, not ours. It's drawing out their strengths and abilities. The ones needed to accomplish the goals they've set for themselves.

Our role is to provide support in an uncertain world. To let them know that, yes, they should pursue that goal because it's purposeful to them. We can help them to move beyond the doubt and uncertainty that may lead to inaction. We can instill in them the belief that they have the capacity to pursue their dreams and they are strong enough to bounce back from failure.

Challenging students is pushing them to pursue something that *you know* they are capable of *but that they don't think they are*. It's working toward something just outside their current skill set that *is* achievable with focus and determination. Education psychologists call this *the zone of proximal development*. To know when to challenge students, you have to realize when they are stuck, when they aren't moving forward or are dragging their feet. The next step is to understand *why*. If they aren't moving forward because they are scared of failure, *that's* when you challenge them. You challenge them *because* you believe in them. Challenging them instills your confidence in them when they lack it themselves.

Ultimately, good mentoring is the art of balancing affirmation and expectations. We affirm students to show them they have our unconditional support—no matter what they do or don't do, achieve or don't achieve. We will support and value them, *no matter what*. At the same time, we challenge them not because they need to prove themselves, but because *we believe in them*. Some will need more affirmation, while others will need to be challenged. The balance of the two is unique to each person, relationship, and circumstance.

Pro-Tips for Challenging Your People: Find creative ways of challenging your people to do things that stretch them but are still within reach. Notice whether there are ways that they can grow or new opportunities to offer them that are in line with their purpose.

Challenge Toolkit

Where do you challenge your students by holding high expectations of them?

- Is it academically? In sports? As a brother, sister, or other family member?

- In what areas do you hold higher expectations compared with other areas?

- If you don't have high expectations of them, are there opportunities where you *could* challenge them?

Now consider: *Why* do you set high expectations?

- Why is this important to you? Are the reasons you hold high expectations connected to *your* aspirations, or theirs? (You can be honest!)

- Reflect on core values or value archetypes; how do they influence your expectations? Use core values to explain why you (and they) share high expectations. "When you work hard at that goal, you're living out your values of growth, wisdom, and creativity . . . keep at it." "When you keep asking questions, that's the Trailblazer in you."

Why do you *know* that your students can meet these expectations?

- What specific examples from their past experiences prove they can meet these expectations?

- When have you seen them overcome challenges or meet high expectations?

- What's a step they can take in the right direction that's the right size? Challenging but not overwhelming?

Now, connect these three dots:

- "I'm challenging you to . . ."

- "I'm encouraging you to rise to these expectations because . . ."

- "I'm confident you can do it. I've seen you do it before when you . . ."

Advocate and Collaborate

Good mentoring doesn't exist in a vacuum. We have to recognize that we all coexist in larger systems that influence our ability to be successful. It's critical to equip students to do what they have to do. But also ask, *Are their settings designed to help or hold them back?* Sometimes it's not enough to affirm, challenge, and help students with their mindsets. It's the system—be it a school or other organization—that needs changing. Sometimes we need to *advocate* for our students. Knowing when to step in on their behalf is a tricky needle to thread. There's a fine line between being good advocates and being snowplow parents. How can we tell the difference between advocacy and snowplowing? Here are some key differences:

- *Snowplow parents remove any and all obstacles to make life easy for their students. Advocates step in when life becomes too difficult due to unfair obstacles.* Young people need opportunities to overcome challenges; snowplow parents clear away such opportunities. Snowplow parents fish for their kids and hand them the perch on the plate, rather than teach them how to fish. Advocates are judicious about only stepping in when the obstacles faced get too heavy for students to overcome.

- *Snowplow parents do the work for their students. Advocates work with their students.* Snowplow parents often remove obstacles without their students asking them to, or even knowing they've done so (e.g., Varsity Blues parents). Advocates are intentional in working *with* their students to overcome challenges. They collaborate and partner with them instead of taking power and agency away from them.

- *Snowplow parents use their privilege without regard or concern for equity. Advocates use their power with equity in mind.* When snowplow parents step in, they use their influence in a way that privileges their own students, often at the expense of other peers who aren't afforded the same power. This perpetuates systems of inequity. Advocates use their power to dismantle unjust systems. They combat rules of fixed games that disadvantage some, while privileging others. They do it to help their students, and any other person who may be disadvantaged by these "unfair rules."

When our students face obstacles or rules they're upset about, we can ask ourselves three questions to decide whether and how to step in:

- By intervening, am I supporting my student's growth or standing in the way of it? Can my student learn from struggling in the moment? Snowplowing deprives our students of opportunities for growth, especially outside of academics. A subtle form of snowplowing is not requiring any household responsibility beyond schoolwork from the student. Advocacy opens opportunities for growth that our students were deprived of due to injustice. Advocacy also role-models behavior that our students will learn positive lessons from.

- Is my student asking for my help? If so, have we discussed (and are we in agreement on) how I might best help? Snowplowing is stepping in without our students' consent, and usurping their power and agency. It's imposing help in unsolicited or unwelcome ways. Advocacy is providing the kind of support that our students request to navigate systems that place them at unfair and unacceptable disadvantage.

- Would intervening benefit my student at the expense of other people? If so, you might be combatting rules that were put in place to level the playing field.

We coach parents to do an honest heart-check on whether they're prone to advocate or to snowplow. Ultimately, snowplowing undermines our ability to affirm and challenge our students. It sends the message that we know best, and it makes students feel unseen, unheard, and unaffirmed. It also sends the message that *we don't believe in them,* lowering expectations and reinforcing self-limiting beliefs. Snowplow parenting, like the performance and passion mindsets, while well intentioned, is a strategy that ultimately backfires. Learning to handle obstacles, including frustrations and failures, is healthy for students. It teaches them skills needed to become competent adults. If we shield them from every little bump, they'll be ill-equipped to navigate the bigger potholes down the road.

In contrast, advocacy helps students gain access to opportunities that they would otherwise be blocked from due to inequalities or injustices. Partnering with them to address social barriers teaches them an invaluable set of skills for meeting needs in the world. This kind of mentoring builds students' sense of self-worth, vitality, validation, knowledge of self and others, and skills for branching out and building other such relationships.

Advocacy goes beyond equipping students for personal success; it equips them to serve as change agents who shape policies, cultural practices, and social norms that can benefit many others. Good advocacy and youth-led social change can go hand in hand. We help students build the capacity to do such important work through five mentoring practices: (1) sharing power, (2) amplifying voice, (3) mutual role-modeling, (4) collaborative doing, and (5) tackling system failures.[18]

By sharing power, we mean thinking of ourselves as co-leaders with our students. We encourage our students to get involved in organizations where they can lead or participate in democratic governance. If our students are getting exposure to this kind of governance, they're learning how to participate in a democratic society where they can make a difference.

Let's be clear, sharing power doesn't mean giving up our *authority as a wise elder.* There are benefits to relinquishing some *positional* power as the parent or adult mentor so students can learn to co-lead. For example, collaborating with students to create the family's rules for technology usage. This is different from giving up our *authority* that's found in our experience and wisdom. Sitting silently while our students make all the decisions isn't what we're talking about. Students want to hear what we have to say, and what we have to teach them. They appreciate our contributions to their efforts and success.

Amplifying our students' voices means getting the word out there about their views and values. Turning negative stereotypes of adolescents on their head. So while popular media refers to them as "immature," "impulsive," "self-centered," "naïve," "reckless," or "troubled," we can take opportunities to change that narrative. We can talk about their energy, enthusiasm, and the constructive aspects of youthful idealism and risk-taking. We can champion their expressions of identity, values, and needs that are often misunderstood or not heard by others. We can educate ourselves about the roots of many youth problems, including sociopolitical and historical forces, like racism, sexism, and adultism. And once we understand these facts well, we can share them with whoever will listen.

By respecting and amplifying students' voices, we're role-modeling the ways they themselves will communicate their ideas in the world. They'll learn to voice who they are and what they think and care about in ways that effectively create social change. By example, we can sow seeds of interest in civic engagement, activism, and social change. We do this by doing it: we step up by role-modeling the attitude and skills needed to do the work. Oftentimes it's a mentor who first introduces purpose and inspires students to take up a cause.

Mutual role-modeling is about seeing students as our role models, too. It's a two-way street. Students are sometimes bold in raising social justice and equity issues that we might avoid, or not even see. Students are the ones who notice and point out structural and classroom procedures that lead to discrimination and inequality. They can call out the ways that school policies worsen achievement gaps. They can research ways that school conditions harm students' well-being. When students see these problems, they also see solutions. They can play a key role in the strategic planning needed to transform organizations.

Together we can make some waves. Collaborative doing is also the best way to learn. Marching together for an important cause. Collecting food or toys and delivering them to a shelter. Reading books to patients in a children's hospital. Meeting with legislators and educating them on a need. Raising awareness about what students can contribute to organizations. Serving, protesting, and changing policies together teaches both mentors and students new skills, and doing it together ignites a sense of the excitement and immediacy of this work. These become mentoring moments.

Pro-Tips for Partnering With Your People: Consider how your student's interests and goals might intersect with an area of service that you also care about. Partnering with your people can be real (not forced) when you share some passion for the work. Encourage them to be the drivers in it through using their strengths and skills while you ride shotgun.

Advocacy Toolkit

Sharing Power and Amplifying Voice

- **AFFIRM YOUR STUDENTS' AUTONOMY AND AGENCY** ("That's interesting, tell me more about your idea" or "Congratulations on your good choices that led to winning the debate!"), rather than taking over or taking credit ("Aren't you glad I made you do debate team?").

- **INVOLVE YOUR STUDENTS IN GOVERNANCE.** Whenever possible, get your students involved in working with adults who use a democratic approach, rather than a top-down approach.

- **SHARE YOUR WISDOM.** Encouraging students to make their own decisions doesn't mean remaining silent—students desire your wisdom and validation of their choices.

Mutual Role-Modeling and Collaboration

- **BE A CO-LEARNER.** "I learn so much from you. I'm not the only expert here."

- **BE A GIVING ROLE MODEL.** Your example as a volunteer may inspire them to come up with other volunteer opportunities.

- **SCHEDULE IT INTO THE FAMILY CALENDAR.** Don't let the tyranny of the urgent derail the important things in life. Make collaborative doing a planned activity. Schedule time together to pursue your interests (a presentation by your favorite author), their interests (a concert by their favorite band), and shared interests (a Netflix documentary on artificial intelligence).

- **CREATE OPPORTUNITIES.** Check out existing opportunities among your friends, neighbors, schools, churches, and other local programs. Feel free to create your own.

- **MAKE IT FUN.** Working together to make a difference can be something memorable and enjoyable. The most important lessons are learned in play. Try to find a community service project that interests every person in the family.

- **LEARN ACROSS GENERATIONS.** Serve and learn from the oldest to the youngest. There are lessons to be learned from working at senior centers and at preschools.

- **ENLIST FAMILY AND FRIENDS.** Your students really see the value of service, social change, and social justice when everyone around you is on board.

- **NOTICE THE IMPACT.** Point it out when you see friends, family, and others making a contribution in the world.

Mentoring Moments

Having covered what good mentoring looks like in the broader strokes, we now zero in on what this looks like more specifically. The idea of affirming, challenging, and advocating for our students is probably not a tough sell, in theory. The struggle is imagining how to squeeze any of that into the chaotic, busy mess of everyday life.

Putting Moments in the Bank

Building meaningful relationships with young people takes time, but the actual building takes place in individual moments. Inch by inch, minute by minute, we earn the right with students to talk with them about things that matter. Every positive interaction we have together is an investment; it's money in the relationship bank. Negative interactions are a withdrawal from the bank. A removal of relational currency. The more we prioritize protecting our relationship with our students over sweating the small stuff, the more currency we acquire. Psychologists have evaluated the health of a relationship with the Gottman ratio—the number of positive to negative experiences. Stable and healthy relationships have a "magic ratio" of 5 to 1. Five positive feelings or interactions for every negative interaction or feeling.

The coin of the realm of purposeful mentoring is what we call "moments that matter." Moments that matter are those times that our students feel seen, heard, and validated. These can be big moments (a graduation, championship game, birthday celebration) or small ones (a passing remark, well-timed shoulder squeeze, or silly joke during a stressful time). There are two characteristics that make up any moment that matters. One, it causes our students to feel like *they* matter, because their ideas and opinions have been taken seriously, and they've been treated with respect. Two, it involves *talking about or doing something* that matters to them. Playing a video game together. Asking about a relationship of interest. Sharing memes or GIFs. Discussing their purpose.

Moments that matter are times when students share what matters to them with someone who makes them feel like *they* matter. This highlights the underrated power of *asking questions*. The conversation may have started with the simplest of questions:

- *What's on your mind lately?*

- *What are you excited about?*

- *What are you worried about?*

- *What's most important to you right now?*

When we ask questions out of genuine curiosity, we're sending the message to our students: "Your ideas and opinions matter." Just as importantly, their answers give us clues to what matters to them. The timing of these conversations is the true art. There are moments you make and moments you catch.

Moments You Make

The "moments we make" are those that we intentionally initiate and carve out time for. Easier said than done given our fast-paced lives, not to mention the shock to our students if we plopped down on the couch next to them and announced cheerily, "Here's an idea—let's have a conversation about your purpose!" Definitely not the way to go, unless you like when they look at you like you're a kook, roll their eyes, and hastily return to their phones and video games.

We can make meaningful moments, but we have to ease into them. That means transforming the time we already spend with them into meaningful moments. Our hectic lives are often a drain on us, and take us in such different directions from our students. Yet there is one time during the week that we can steal some regular time together. Mealtimes.

Research examined a slew of family, school, and neighborhood factors to see which ones were most related to good life outcomes for adolescents. Eating dinner together as a family was at the top of the list.[19] Even after accounting for the influences of family household income, race, and gender, students who did family dinner had the lowest rates of depression and risk/problem behaviors and highest levels of contribution and other positive youth development outcomes.

Research has also shown that eating together promotes psychological safety. It causes us to feel closer to one another, which makes us happier and more satisfied with our lives.[20] It fosters "culinary diplomacy" that promotes cross-cultural understanding and increased cooperation.[21] Sharing meals is a vulnerable act; we only break bread with people we trust. This is why holidays and socializing revolve around meals.

Setting the Table

Setting the table is about creating rituals and attitudes toward dinner conversation through practice. It's about facilitating a conversation that is inclusive *and* interesting for everyone involved. Pro-tip: Good topics for dinner conversation are non-divisive and yet they're ones where (1) everyone has a strong opinion and (2) everyone feels their opinion has merit. These criteria make for the most engaging and safe conversations. So, for example, dinner conversation may begin with a playful prompt or icebreaker, inspired by Neil Pasricha's *Book of Awesome*:

"What is better?":

- Peeling that thin plastic film off new electronics *or* sleeping with one leg under the covers and one leg out?

- Successfully moving all your clothes from the washer to the dryer without dropping anything *or* that one really good pen that never gets lost?

- Building an amazing couch-cushion fort *or* squeezing through a door as it's shutting without touching it?

The idea here is to create a practice where coming to the table feels easy and fun—not awkward and stressful. Everyone present feels welcome and dialed into the time together. We want questions that aren't about "winning" arguments. They're low-stakes ways to engage in playful, sometimes passionate, dialogue. The best part is that even the silliest questions can serve as prompts for purpose discovery, without anyone noticing. They're an opening salvo from which deeper meaningful conversations can emerge. Here are some different purpose prompts to try out:

- Which is better, X or Y?

- What's the best (show, game, song) of the last year?

- Top three best/worst (examples: top three colors, top three best foods, top three best cars, top three best meals Mom/Dad cooks).[22]

The goal of these prompts is to build community, so don't try to structure or formalize them too much. As long as people are having organic and engaging conversation, it's a win, no matter what's being talked about. Once a community and tradition of sharing is established, you can begin to incorporate more meaningful personalized prompts that get people to share about their sense of purpose. Think of the opening prompts as community-building appetizers. They whet your appetite for the collective meal. The main course prompts are personalizers; they are meant for everyone to share while each member of the family listens. Here are some questions that align with the elements of purpose. You could even choose a different personalized prompt for each day of the week, as below:

- Monday: What's something that happened over the weekend that you will remember one year from now? Why is that important to you? (Core values)

- Tuesday: What's a small win you've had recently? What did you do to make that happen? (Strengths)

- Wednesday: What's the best/worst/weirdest thing you learned this week? Why is it so great/bad/weird? (Skills)

- Thursday: What positive contribution have you made lately? Who did you help, and how did you help them? (Meeting a need)

- Friday: What made this week bad, good, or great? What was hard about it, and what got you through it? (Gratitude and adversity)

Adjust the questions as needed. These prompts work best when we role-model responses to them. To get the ball rolling, be prepared to answer first. So, if it was Monday, you might begin:

- "What's one thing that happened this week that you will remember a year from now? I'll start . . ."

A word of encouragement: even if such conversations start off a bit stiff and awkward, keep hope alive. Rituals and traditions can take hold if we give them time. When we stay the course, these conversations become soul food.

Moments You Catch

Moments we make are proactive, and moments we catch are reactive. Some of the best conversations with our students are unplanned. They occur in the car on the way to school. Or on a longer road trip. They occur while shopping or making dinner together or after watching a Netflix episode. Or when someone in the family gets some bad news or suffers a loss.

There are two types of moments we catch. Something happens *in the world*, and we draw out its meaning. Or something happens *to our student*, and we draw out its meaning. The first entails filtering events in the world through the lens and language of purpose. Imagine a conversation after watching the Golden State Warriors together.

You: Why do you like the Warriors so much?

Student: I dunno, they're good, they win a lot of championships.

[Beyond this no-brainer answer, they struggle to articulate why, so you use the language of purpose.]

You: Out of everything in the world, what do you think is most important to Steph Curry?

Student: Hmmm. Well, he does always talk about his family and faith a lot.

You: Draymond Green doesn't seem very fast, and he's a bad shooter—what makes him such a great player?

Student: Not sure . . . He seems really good at telling his teammates where to go on defense.

You: Yup, he seems to be a great facilitator and creator. He uses communication and critical thinking to his advantage.

You: What makes Steve Kerr such a great coach?

Student: He seems so calm and upbeat all the time, like a very Zen guy. Nothing ever seems to faze him.

You: Yup, and here's a guy who's seen a lot of trouble in his life. He lost his father to gun violence in Beirut, Lebanon, when he was just a college freshman. That tragedy inspired him to speak out on various issues, especially gun rights. *[Adversity shapes the contribution/impact we are motivated to make in the world.]*

As you can see, meaningful conversations don't have to be forced. Some of the most spontaneous and playful moments are where the magic happens. When we look through the lens of purpose, we find traces of it everywhere. We can capture little moments by putting words to these experiences.

We end with a story that demonstrates what a regular practice of affirming, challenging, and advocating during moments that matter does for students and relationships.

Tim's experiences as a school counselor in a large public high school often felt like barely contained chaos. School days were a constant stream of interruptions. Lockdown drills. Teachers who needed Tim's support. Students in distress. Parents seeking guidance.

There was only one predictable part of Tim's day. A senior we'll call Ben would come to Tim's office to "post up" during fourth period. Ben made himself at home, taking jump shots on the door-mounted basketball hoop, playing rap songs on his Bluetooth speaker, celebrating or lamenting the Boston Celtics' performance the night before. Rain or shine, Ben never missed a visit.

In Tim's office, Ben was charismatic, kind, with a wise and quick wit. Outside Tim's office was a different story. Ben was always in trouble, cutting classes, arguing with teachers, and coming late to school. He failed the majority of his high school classes and attended summer school every year. Graduation seemed unlikely.

Tim's colleagues wondered why he invested so much time in Ben. Why not focus his energies on the college-bound students who seemed more deserving of his attention?

Tim, however, recognized that this was no waste of time. He came to know a side of Ben that others had missed. Ben lived alone with his grandmother and worked thirty hours a week at a fast-food restaurant. He was remarkably independent, but didn't have a strong support network. Sometimes, in between jump shots, he would open up about his past and current struggles and his uncertain future. These conversations provided critical context to Ben's behavior at school.

Over time, Tim and Ben forged a rich and mutual relationship. While Ben had been defiant with most other adults out of distrust, he agreed to whatever Tim asked of him. In fact, Tim had a cadre of students like Ben—the ones not following school rules, serving detentions and suspensions, refusing to comply with assistant principals and deans. All of them were remarkably cooperative with Tim. All he had to do was ask, and it would be done.

These relationships demonstrated the power of trust and respect. These students could feel that Tim genuinely cared for and enjoyed them . . . and that he respected them. He saw in them their best selves. In return, they showed him mutual trust and respect.

What *Really* Matters

Of all the things we could possibly talk about, your students' relationship with you is their greatest asset in cultivating a purpose mindset. Deep down, we all know this, but the demands of everyday life, the academic and career pressures we experience, and the urgency of the to-do list can make our relationships fade to the background. We mistake the urgent for the important. We can focus so much on getting things done, to build for success, that we sacrifice our relational foundations to do so. We hope this chapter serves as a reminder of what's truly important in life, your *connection* with your people. When we put that at the center of our work with students, the things we hope for them—success, happiness, fulfillment—emerge as by-products in the long run. Relationship first and the rest will follow.

7

- - - - - - - -

School

Listen for your call, not someone else's.

If the path before you is clear, you're
probably on someone else's.

—JOSEPH CAMPBELL

The Call to Adventure

In 2006, a *New York Times Magazine* journalist, Rob Walker, conducted an experiment to test the power of storytelling.[1] He collated two hundred random objects on eBay that had no intrinsic value. He asked authors to come up with made-up stories about each object. Then he reposted these objects on eBay to see if the invented stories upped the value of the objects.

They sure did. A butterfly-embossed cigarette case that he had purchased for a dime resold for $33.77. A ceramic horse bust purchased for 99 cents was resold for $62.95. An old wooden mallet purchased for $1 was resold for $29. You get the idea.

All told, the two hundred objects he bought for a total of $197 were resold for $8,000. A markup of *3,900 percent!* Stories transform ordinary life and ordinary things into things of value. They help us make sense of life.

For centuries, stories have been used to pass on knowledge. A study in *Nature Communications* explains why—storytelling teaches social cooperation and social norms.[2] Stories help us explain every aspect of our experience, from relationships to memories to science to feelings. When we hear a good story, our mind makes cognitive and emotional connections that shape our understanding of the world around us. We learn deeply from a story because we remember the underlying emotions conveyed.

A Picture's Worth a Thousand Words

The most common stories we tell are in the form of figurative language. We use similes and metaphors *six times a minute* in conversation.[3] They help us to grasp abstract, complex topics quickly. They do this by comparing one kind of thing in terms of another.[4] They are especially good at using things in the physical world to illustrate abstract concepts.

Cool as a cucumber. Fiery temper. Sunny disposition. All are examples of using a more concrete and tangible reference (cucumber, fire, sun) to describe something abstract (emotions, attitudes, and mindsets). We use the metaphor of temperature to describe someone's emotional state: *She was cold to me.* We frame arguments as battles and wars: *They attacked me. I won the argument. They shot down my idea.* Money helps us conceptualize time: *I lost an hour. I can't give you the time. Time is money.*

A metaphor is a mental picture, and a picture says a thousand words. For instance, when we use "games" to describe the way we pursue our goals—you can picture what we're talking about. These mental representations give us a framework for how we receive information.[5] They're like coatracks for hanging ideas.

One metaphor that is prominent in the world of education is that of a *path.*[6] We say things like: *You're on the right path, you're headed in the right direction,* and *keep going!* We place students in "accelerated" courses or "pathways programs" to ensure they "pass" and don't "drop out." We give them "progress reports" that inform them if they are "on track." When COVID-19 forced schools to close, parents and educators worried that students would "fall behind."

The metaphor of a "path forward" is so embedded in the way we think about our students' journeys that we hardly notice it's there. Yet this metaphor insidiously permeates much of our advice and guidance for students. We imply that their journeys should be predictable and straightforward once they find the right path. The notion of a path brings to mind a continuous or linear road, with some alternative roads leading to the same destination.[7] This metaphor suggests that students will be all set for success once they find the right path. So simple. No more stress about uncertain futures.

A good path feels safe because it's well trodden and well marked. Nothing scarier than losing sight of the path and getting lost in the woods when the sun goes down. Nothing more comforting than suddenly finding the path in the same woods. Suddenly we're not lost anymore. We know how to get to where we're going. The promise of the path is a belief that we can predict the future. And if we can predict the future, *we can control it*. Hence the appealing allure of *pathway parenting*. In fact, most of K–12 education is designed around the premise of a path.

But here's the rub. The path metaphor is misleading. It gives students a false sense of how life actually works. It gets them fixated on reaching the end of the path, be it graduation, acceptance into college, or a specific profession. If you think you're on a path that leads somewhere special, you can't help but be anxious to get there. By using the path metaphor, we set the wrong expectations for students: that their school and career journeys are like lovely, well-marked trails. All they need to do is select the right one, and it'll lead them straight to the destination of their dreams.

The Gig Is Up

Pathway education may have made more sense in the "good old days" when people committed themselves to a company for thirty to forty years. The reward for climbing the corporate ladder (a nice straight path) was a fancy Rolex watch at retirement. In the 1960s, when the average worker held on to a job for twenty-one years, watches were flying out the door.[8]

This gig is over. Today, the more apt gift would be a stopwatch. In 2020, the median tenure in current jobs for all salaried employees was just four years, and for millennials less than three years.[9] Current college graduates can expect to have at least fifteen career-related jobs throughout their careers. That's a lot of change!

And it's not just employees who are shape-shifting, it's entire companies and industries. In the 1960s, spending your whole career as a "company" man or woman was possible because companies lasted that long. When a company made it onto the S&P 500, they could expect to last thirty to thirty-five years. That tenure will be cut in half in this decade, so many of today's S&P 500 companies will be gone in fifteen years.[10] Life spans of companies and tenures of employees are shrinking by the day. Nothing is set in stone.

The on-ramp into the workforce is just as precarious. Students are increasingly unlikely to enter fields related to their hard-earned degrees.

Signs You Are Stuck on the Path

- There is only one "right way" and several bad ones.

- You are mired in either/or thinking.

- You are more worried about making a wrong decision than excited about making the right one.

- You feel you are traveling on someone else's path.

- Everyone is expected to go the same way.

- You feel forced to choose from a set of mediocre options.

- Your choice is about running away from something, rather than toward something.

For example, nearly half of all computer science majors enter alternative fields, and over half of engineering majors don't become engineers.[11] And these are the majors where students are *most likely* to find a job related to their fields. In most other majors, nine of ten graduates don't land jobs directly related to their majors.[12]

These numbers, combined with alarming college dropout rates, suggest that the "straight path" from school to a stable and steady career is anything but. The notion of a "path" to financial stability is a relic of a golden era of work that no longer exists (if it ever did). Set paths are only set if you can predict the future. The only thing we can predict today is that we can't predict much. The future will bring increasing disruption and change.

Gone are the days of gold watches and retirement traditions for lifers—those who stay on the same path their whole careers. But new doors have opened. Where previous generations based their identities on their work and corporations, young people today see their identities more openly. They come from personal convictions. Abilities. Interests. Connections they make on their own. So, while predictable paths felt safe, identities today hold greater possibilities. The American entrepreneur Ping Fu said, "I believe that behind every closed door there is an open space."[13] It's time to step off the eroding path into those wide open fields. It's time to tell a new story.

The Seeker's Journey

Gone are the days when we could plan for a safe, predictable career path. But would we actually want it any other way? On a Friday night, who scans cable in search of a good ol' predictable show? Predictable is ho-hum. Give us some conflict, tension, throw in some unexpected twists and turns, and we might just have a story worth its salt. The most iconic stories—whether they're epic myths, fairy tales, or Hollywood block-busters—are about people who *reject* the path and blaze their own way forward. Analyses of thousands of stories across cultures reveal some universal themes in what's been called *the Hero's Journey*. Think about the great books and movies you've loved—the protagonists find the courage to step outside their comfort zones into the unknown. They are challenged and tested. They succeed and fail, and ultimately they're stretched in important ways.

Those who have written about the Heroine's Journey have added themes beyond those captured by the Hero's Journey.[14] Whereas the Hero's Journey paints a picture of events in the world that influence his behaviors and view of himself, the Heroine's Journey captures the battle within. The search to affirm and embody wholeness. This can mean integrating various kinds of wholeness. Success and failure. Perfection and imperfection. Joy and despair. It's a quest that emphasizes inclusiveness and persistence throughout the journey rather than a singular destination. We see what happens when people make choices that help them reclaim their authentic voices, values, and self-worth and take charge of writing their own story. We see the power of authorship for people and the world around them.

In this chapter, we introduce the Seeker's Journey. We've adapted relevant themes from heroes' *and* heroines' stories to capture the true stories of our students' journeys. Seekers are students. They're real-life hero/ines, navigating real-life experiences. Theirs is a voyage of true courage. One that requires resisting society's narrative of what success looks like. The Seeker's Journey is a cautionary tale for proponents of pathway parenting, pathway education, and career paths toward fame and fortune. In place of strolls down predictable paths, protagonists embrace exploration into new, unexplored territories. They are lightning bolts of bravery and nonconformity.

The Seeker's Journey unfolds in a series of acts, as in a play, that together offer a liberating metaphor for our students. One that frees them of set "paths" as they chart their own way.

Ordinary Person in an Ordinary World

Most stories begin with an ordinary person in an ordinary world. Luke Skywalker is a farm boy from the dusty planet of Tatooine. He rises from these humble beginnings to help save the galaxy. Katniss Everdeen is an ordinary sixteen-year-old from District 12—her ordinary world. She later

sparks the overturn of a totalitarian government. Moana lives on her island protected by the reef. Dorothy begins in the prairies of Kansas . . .

Stories take off when the hero/ines leave the safety and security of
familiar paths to fulfill their greater purpose. This is *the call to adventure.*
Luke's call to adventure is an urgent plea from Princess Leia delivered by
R2-D2. Katniss volunteers to take her sister's place in the Hunger Games
competition. Moana goes outside the reef to find Maui and restore the
heart of Te Fiti. Dorothy's call comes when Toto—representing her
intuition—is captured and escapes. Dorothy follows Toto (her instincts)
and runs away from home with him.

Hero/ines respond to the call to adventure by venturing out of the
comfort and predictability of their ordinary worlds. They step off their
predictable paths and take a leap of faith into the unknown to achieve a
dream, confront a challenge, change a life.

Seekers come to similar crossroads. They may become disillusioned
with the path they're on. They no longer see the status quo through rose-
colored glasses. Their call to adventure is not always a quest; sometimes
it's a need to find peace. To step outside their comfort zones to something
scarier but better. To discover who they truly are. Some question the path
when they are twelve years old, others twenty years old—for some, it may
not happen until they draw near retirement.

Most students start their educational journeys by following a well-
trodden path—the educational pathway that well-meaning adults forge
for them. They will follow the signs along the path and trust that they
will lead to a fulfilling destination. They will play by the rules and do
what is asked of them: competing in fixed games, working hard to get
good grades and test scores, applying to all the elite colleges in hopes of
later getting prestigious jobs, and on and on. They will buy into the idea
that "end destination = job" (teacher, scientist, electrician, lawyer, You-
Tuber, etc.). And so they will fixate on this end destination.

Inevitably they will come to a point—a crossroads—where they begin
to *question* the path. As they travel along, a sense of conflict and unset-
tlement will arise. Motivation will wane. They will start to realize: maybe
the path they're on isn't their own. Well-meaning adults will cajole and

coerce students to get back on the path. But in the Seeker's Journey, students will hear a different message that reassures them: "This internal conflict *is normal*. It opens the door to an enormous opportunity."

Good mentors point out that the urge to question is a sign that students are ready to explore. To seek answers to life's big questions when the destination may be unknown. In their ordinary world, their path will have them thinking too little and too small . . . only asking, "What's my end destination? What do I want to *be*?" The crossroads may in fact be the start of their call to adventure.

An adventure is different:

- It doesn't require you to know exactly where you'll end up.

- Uncertainty about the future may feel scary, but is expected.

- You embrace and savor the journey. You embrace the expedition.

- Every moment is to be honored (even the failures), because they tell you more about yourself, the world, and how you make your mark in it.

- Meaningful directions are more important than end destinations.

- We are guided by questions, rather than answers. Questions such as:

  - *What do I value?*

  - *What strengths make me my best self?*

  - *What am I capable of?*

  - *How can I contribute to the world?*

  - *How do I pursue my life, not anyone else's?*

  - *Who am I?*

These questions have to do with what you want to *do* (growth game), not just what you want to *be* (fixed game). These are the questions that precede the end destination question.

They respect the uniqueness of each traveler's journey: there are no cookie-cutter paths for hero/ines.

Hearing the call to adventure represents a departure from the ordinary world and an urge to see what the world has to offer. As Joseph Campbell notes, "destiny has summoned the hero and transferred his spiritual center of gravity from within the pale of his society to a zone unknown."[15] It's transferring your center of gravity from predefined paths to a zone unknown. *This* is where the adventure begins.

Reflect honestly on your own life. Have the most meaningful things you've done been leaps of faith or the result of traveling on a straight path? Has your journey been punctuated with twists and turns, dead ends and detours? So many of our most cherished experiences were not super-predictable. An unexpected opportunity came, and we took a chance! On a good day, we trusted ourselves and acted out of courage and authenticity.

Or sometimes we didn't take the leap but were catapulted into an adventure nonetheless. In the Hero's Journey, the call to adventure typically comes *to* the protagonist. Gandalf seeks out Frodo to take the ring out of the Shire. Peter Parker is bitten by a radioactive spider. Dorothy is swept up by a tornado.

In the Seeker's Journey, whether or not the call to adventure comes *to* you, it must surely come *from* you. Students must *choose to seek* the call. They must listen attentively for the call from within themselves. This is no passive listening. It's an *active* listening that involves search and research.

You have to listen inwardly to who *you* are, how *you* are wired, and where *you* thrive. There's nothing more exhausting than being pushed from the outside to reach higher and live bigger. Your calling is not imposed from the outside. It must be cultivated from the inside out. *To hear the call we first must learn how to listen for it.*

Ears Wide Open

When you're on a path, you aren't listening to yourself; you're on autopilot following external directions. Stepping off the path and listening inwardly is an intentional disruption of the script. How do you listen to and evaluate the things *you* gravitate to?

Ask yourself: How do you listen to and evaluate what music *you* like? If you were to listen to a new artist we recommend, what would you do? Most likely, the process would go something like this:

1. Open Apple Music, Spotify, or YouTube.

2. Find the artist's homepage and scroll through the list of albums, playlists, and songs.

3. Listen to the artist's most popular song. (It's probably representative of the rest of the artist's catalog, so if you don't like *this* song, chances are slim you'll like the rest.)

4. If you like this song, check out the artist's other most listened to tracks.

5. If you like these songs, listen to a full album.

6. If you can't get enough after listening to all the albums, check out the "fans also like" section to listen to artists similar to this one.

This is how students expand their self-knowledge about what music they like. They use a similar process for discovering all sorts of preferences, from cheeses to books to blockbuster movies.

Why not apply it to their vocational exploration? When we ask them about their life aspirations, cue the "deer in the headlights" responses. Cue the hemming, hawing, and struggling to say something that sounds true.

But when we ask them about music/movies/Netflix series/sports teams they like? Cue the clarity and confidence. Suddenly they know exactly what they like and why.

What's the difference? Students have a concrete decision-making process for evaluating music. They've learned to listen for what moves them.

They weren't born with good taste. They *developed* a sense of what they like and dislike through trial and error. After tasting enough ice cream flavors, they realized they like mint chocolate chip or raspberry sherbet the best.

The more we try things out while tuning in to how minds, bodies, and spirits respond to each thing, the better we understand ourselves. We come to know which flavors we love and which artists move us. This applies to everything from musical taste to what we want to do in life.

For more complicated decisions, we start to develop a system or categories of what to tune in to. When you've listened to your share of music, you learn to determine what you like by evaluating the artist's production, lyrics, and voice.

In the same way, when you listen to your life, you will learn to determine what it's authentically about by evaluating your values, your strengths, and the skills you're motivated to master. You will shift from listening to outside orders to inside intuitions. Because *they are who you are*. The more we listen, explore, and discover, the more likely we are to hear our call.

In sum, students can't know *what to do with their lives* before they understand *who they are*. So, when they notice something that piques their interest? We encourage them to *listen*. When there's a spark for photo editing, environmental justice, 3D animation, criminal law, food science? Fan the flames. Encourage them to follow their curiosity, even if you can't see where it may lead. Direction over destination. The more students tune in to what they're drawn to, the more they'll find their way.

Question to Consider:
What Are You Called to Do?

Fearing the Call

Hearing the call is not the same as heeding the call. When hero/ines hear the call, they do not bravely fly into action. No, sir—they initially say *no, thank you*. They run away or hide. When Luke Skywalker is asked to go to Alderaan to learn the way of the Force and help save the galaxy, he says:

"Alderaan? I'm not going to Alderaan. I've got to go home. It's late . . ."
When Moana's grandmother tells her the ocean chose her to voyage beyond the reef, she says: "But why would it choose me? I don't even know
how to make it past the reef . . . I can't . . ." Hero/ines resist their calls to
adventure out of doubt, insecurity, and fear of the unknown. And so do
our students. They self-sabotage, make excuses, procrastinate, or dodge
their call entirely. Accepting the call to adventure is embracing change.
Depending on one's risk tolerance, this may sound bold and exciting or
dangerous and terrifying. One thing is for sure, adventures are not for
the faint of heart.

We adopt performance and passion mindsets out of a desperation
for safety and certainty. The call to adventure means loosening this
death grip. The more important the call, the more scared we are to fail.
Seems safer to say no, thank you, and remain in Kansas with Aunt Em
and Uncle Henry. The devil you know seems better than the one you
don't.

When hero/ines refuse the call, mentors can guide them through this
impasse. Think Dumbledore from Harry Potter, Gandalf from *Lord of
the Rings,* Mary Poppins and, from *The Wizard of Oz,* Glinda the Good
Witch, Scarecrow, Tin Man, the Cowardly Lion, and the Wizard himself.

We can guide our students through their trepidation by recognizing
and reframing these critical crossroads ("Hey, this looks like a call to
adventure"). We can instill confidence that they have what it takes ("You
were *built* for this"). We can't do life for them, but we can talk them off
ledges and encourage them to fly.

One major way we support them is by validating that fearing the call
is universal. Most people aren't thrilled about stepping outside comfort
zones. Normalize and name it: "Fear of the unknown is what makes life
an adventure. It's tempting to just stay in our comfort zones. But what
you're doing—venturing out to try something new—is brave."

When our students are at an anxious crossroads, or struggling with
a momentous decision, invite them to air out their fears: "Of course
you're uneasy. This is a huge decision. Decisions like this are scary for
most people. What're you most nervous about?" This framing sends the

message that we understand the uneasiness and we're not afraid to look these feelings in the eye.

We can help them identify potential roadblocks to accepting the call. *What's the fear here? Is it impostor syndrome, fear of failure or the unknown? Or are you sensing that this isn't the right call for you?*

Question to Consider:
What's Holding You Back from Answering the Call?

Taking the Leap

Hero/ines eventually realize that some things about themselves or the status quo need to change. They may need to let go of some old scripts, habits, and ways of seeing themselves. They may need to challenge themselves. And so, after much ado, they commit to the journey. We call it *taking the leap*. Dorothy sets out on the yellow brick road. Luke leaves the safety of his planet. Moana ventures beyond the reef.

Taking a leap is committing to a direction, even when you don't know exactly where you'll end up. Leaps come at inflection points: choosing a college or a major, or deciding which job to take or city to move to. It's rejecting external pressure and making life decisions based on our intrinsic purpose. The term "leap" is instructive; when we sign that acceptance letter or job offer, it might feel like there is no going back. It's on this precipice that we can become terrorized by decision paralysis. How can we be sure this is the *right* decision? What if it's the *wrong* choice?

When we're on a path, it can feel like there is only one right way amid a sea of dead ends. But when we're on an adventure, the direction we head is far more important than where we end up. The journey *is* the destination. It means that the process of decision-making is far more valuable than a particular outcome. This shift in mindset, shedding the notion that we must have a clear destination mapped out, is profoundly liberating.

Viewing life as an adventurous journey, with no "right" path forward, takes the pressure off students. They will recognize that they don't have to have everything figured out. They don't need to know *exactly* what they want to do. In college, Belle was a chemistry major and Tim was a sports media and marketing major. They use little chemistry, sports media, or marketing in their current careers. Yet pursuing these majors was invaluable in discovering what careers *weren't* right for them. They had to head in a lot of "wrong" directions to get their bearings. Kind of like using your GPS to navigate in the city. You have to start walking in some direction, any direction, before the GPS gets calibrated and you can see whether you're headed in the right direction.

If we're honest, most of us have headed in "wrong" directions to find direction in our own lives. So why expect it to be any different for our students? Instead of constantly pushing them forward on the conveyor belt of education, let's support them to just start walking in some purposeful directions. When true exploration is happening, it's not a straight line. We zig and we zag. The guiding principles of purpose are like a compass for aiming us in purposeful directions. Using our compass means considering at various inflection points, "Which direction is the best way for me to . . ."

- *Use the strengths that I delight in?*

- *Invest in the skills I want to learn?*

- *Live my core values?*

- *Make my desired impact?*

Often we won't know the answers to these questions *until* we first take a leap of faith in this direction. The magic only happens when we start moving. Kind of like how a bike gets balanced once you start pedaling. A car can change direction once you step on the gas. And the Red Sea parted when people stepped into the water.

Even with the best intel, we can't predict the future. We'll *never* know for sure where a college, major, or career will lead us. Ultimately, outcomes in life are outside our control. But we do have control over the intentionality we bring to our decisions. While we won't always make the right choices, we can make them *for the right reasons*. When we lack information, intentionality becomes even more important. Are we intentionally making choices to use our strengths and skills to meet a need aligned with our core values? If yes, we're making the right choices, *regardless of the outcome.*

Placing intentions over outcomes frees Seekers to open their minds and get curious about their future. It transforms uncertainty into opportunity. Dread turns to wonder. It allows them to say: "I don't know what I want to do, but I'm excited to figure it out." They will recognize that even "wrong turns" are valuable learning opportunities. Good mentoring can draw out gems from even the most miserable experiences. *Why do you hate that class or job? Does it not align with your values? Are you not using strengths you delight in? Are you not learning the skills that matter to you? Are you feeling like what you're doing doesn't matter, that you can't make an impact?*

Question to Consider:
What Decision Will I Commit To and Why?

Passing the Test

Almost as soon as hero/ines take the leap and cross the threshold, they're tested. Luke struggles to wield his lightsaber and must go through many trials and tribulations to become a Jedi. Harry is tested by the sorting hat, on the Quidditch field, and throughout his time at Hogwarts. Katniss must risk her life while fighting many enemies.

Students *will* encounter setbacks and failure when they accept their call to adventure. That's the price of admission. And it's not necessarily a bad thing. Deep down, we all want to be pushed to our potential, to see what we're capable of. As discussed in chapter 5, if we run interference to keep students from facing any challenges, we rob them of the chance to grow and become their best selves.

Rather than helping students *avoid* inevitable setbacks, we can teach them how to *respond* well to adversity. This begins with us. Our attitude toward failure determines our response.

We tend to appraise obstacles in one of two ways—as a *challenge* or as a *threat*. When we believe we have the resources to cope with the adversity, we see it as a challenge to overcome. If we believe the problem is bigger than our resources, we see it as a threat. Feeling prepared turns a final exam into a challenge; it's an opportunity to demonstrate our mastery. Competing with three other teammates for the last spot on the varsity lacrosse team may feel like a threat—we could get cut from the team. It's not the obstacle itself, but *our perception* of the obstacle that determines whether it's a growth opportunity or a threat to our well-being.

Reframing Failure

Mentors play a key role in reframing setbacks as obstacles to overcome, instead of threats to be avoided. Imagine the following documentary following a first-gen student we'll call Ana.

Act 1, Scene 1. Ana is taking freshman English her fall semester. She's determined to do her best on her first essay assignment, worth 40 percent of her course grade. After hours of working at the library, she completes the essay and submits it online. She smiles to herself, self-satisfied: "Slam dunk. I got this."

Act 1, Scene 2. The next week, she's sitting in her dorm room, and gets a notification that essay grades have been posted. She feels a pang of nerves before opening the course website to check on her results. Ana quickly reassures herself. After all, she had mastered six AP courses, was the valedictorian, and one of only a handful of students from her high school to go on to college. She reminds herself of how happy her teachers were when she was accepted into Boston College. She has to do them all proud.

Ana clicks on her graded essay. Gut punch. It's covered with corrections and the professor's evaluation at the end reads: *This paper needs a lot of work. I am concerned with everything from grammatical structure to content. I recommend you go immediately to the academic support center on campus to get help with your writing . . . C-.*

Act 1, Scene 3, Take 1. That night she lies in bed sleepless, her mind racing. She asks herself the critical question:

Why?

I worked all week on that essay. I gave it all I've got. How could I have done so poorly?

The story Ana tells herself will make all the difference in her academic journey. For many underrepresented students like Ana, it's easy to see the grade as proof they aren't cut out for college. She's one of a handful of students of color at this university, and of these, even fewer are first-gen students from underresourced high schools. Recognizing they're different from their college peers makes them constantly question: "Do people like me succeed here?"

A common response among students from Ana's background is to interpret the poor result of their efforts as confirmation of their worst fear: *I don't belong here. Admissions made a mistake by accepting me. I can't handle the academics here.* "Belonging uncertainty," along with financial constraints, is one of the primary reasons people drop out of college.

When students interpret setbacks as failure, they disengage from the campus community and withdraw from peers and faculty. Rather than getting more help, they feel pressured to prove they belong by succeeding on their own. Asking for help becomes akin to waving the white flag. This isolation only perpetuates further failure. And ultimately, they succumb to their worst fears. They can give up on school, a direction that can get set from that first disappointing result on a paper.

At the end of the semester, Ana seriously questions whether she can ever fit in academically and socially at this college.

CUT!

This is not the only way for Ana to interpret her poor result.

Act 1, Scene 3, Take 2. After receiving her grade, Ana wakes up early the next morning from a restless night's sleep. She decides that her essay grade is a wake-up call: her writing strategy clearly didn't work. To get the results she wants, she has to double down. She starts by meeting with her professor to see what she can do to improve. They end up having a thirty-minute conversation that extends beyond concerns about the paper. She tells the professor that she is a first-generation student and that she came to college to become a secondary ed math teacher, but that she is doing poorly in her math courses as well. The professor encourages her to go to the academic support center to get her essay edited, and to get help with math. That she can get free tutoring from the center is news to Ana. The professor encourages her to keep dropping by for office hours so they can get to know each other. This also amazes Ana: she thought that office hours were for specific questions about the course. The professor discloses that she herself was a first-gen student who shifted career tracks because of academic difficulties in her original major. She reassures Ana that she has options—she can keep working at math or try other majors. The professor connects Ana with a senior from a similar background. Taking Ana under her wing, this older peer shares her own story of struggling during freshman year. She invites Ana to hang out with her friend group. She lets Ana in on a secret: fall semester of freshman year is tough for most everyone—sticking it out is the name of the game.

Act 1, Scene 4. Having explored other options, Ana returns to her original passion for secondary education and math. Despite the challenges, Ana graduates with honors and eventually enters the Donovan Urban Teaching Scholars Program, a one-year MA in education opportunity that provides a generous financial package and tuition support. She is developing a nonprofit organization focused on mentoring first-gen high school students in the college application process and transition to freshman year.

CUT!

Normalizing the experience of struggle as a common aspect of the college experience is one of the most helpful ways we can reframe challenges and difficulties for students. *Attributional reframing* is the act of helping students view failures as opportunities to adjust their strategies and levels of effort, rather than the result of factors they can't change. Reframing boosts students' motivation, resilience, emotional regulation, and academic outcomes in elementary, high school, and college students.

Compared with their peers, freshmen who watched video-recorded interviews of upperclassmen talking about overcoming their initial academic struggles had higher grade point averages and were much less likely to drop out after their first year.[16] Knowing that *being tested* is a common college experience (which can be conquered) makes students respond more adaptively. They see a test as a challenge, rather than a threat.

Students can benefit greatly from the reminder by trusted mentors that everyone faces challenges and failures. Failures do not mean *you* are a failure. Instead of thinking "am I the problem?" think "how can I be the solution?" Instead of wondering "am I a loser since I don't have many friends?" wonder "how can I open up to making more friends?" Instead of thinking "I failed the exam, I must be stupid" think "how can I do better next time?" It can help to remind students of the times they've overcome challenges—proof of their ability to overcome the next challenge. Finally, they can be reminded of *all the internal resources* they have at their disposal. They can tap into their authentic values. Use their strengths to address challenges at hand. Look for opportunities in the challenges to build universal skills. They can remind themselves of the positive impact they are striving to make.

When people are struggling, a simple question can turn the tides: Are you struggling because this is *important* or because it's *impossible*? If we're focused on the impossibilities or low odds of success, we want to give up. If we focus on the importance of the task, we want to double down. Important things take hard work. This reframing can increase both academic perseverance *and* performance.[17]

Question to Consider:
How Will I Respond to Obstacles?

The Turning Point

Even after overcoming various tests and challenges, the hero/ine's journey can still get harder when they arrive at the lowest point. It's that moment when we're held in suspense and tension, wondering if the hero/ine will make it out alive.[18] Harry's ordeal comes when he faces Voldemort for the first time, nearly dying in the process. Luke's ordeal is watching Obi-Wan sacrifice himself to Darth Vader. Sometimes it's an internal struggle. In the final showdown, Moana is faced with whether she can find the courage inside to answer the call of the ocean and persist in the quest to save her people.

The ordeal represents the existential crisis of the hero/ine's journey: the moment of facing one's greatest fear.[19] We call this *the turning point:* it's the moment in life when things aren't going well. No matter how well prepared we are, some life challenges will get the best of us. Not all obstacles can be overcome. We *will* fail.

Sometimes we don't have the ability to move forward, no matter how much we would like to. There will come a time when we all will wave the white flag, admit defeat, and move on. The challenge is in knowing *when* to do that.

The Road Less Traveled

Some vivid examples of people facing the ordeal come from the corporate world. *Twitter, Facebook, Amazon,* and *Netflix* have all faced near-death experiences. But they prevailed, rising to great heights of success . . . all because of how they responded to failure. When faced with their existential threat/near-death experience, here's what happened: they pivoted.

A business pivots when it keeps its vision but changes its core business strategy. The best businesses combine an ability to recognize when they are off course with the courage to drastically change direction. Twitter did not start as the media platform that has determined the results of presidential elections. It was initially a podcasting company called Odeo. Odeo pivoted when Apple introduced its own native podcast application in iTunes. Hence a side project of Jack Dorsey became Odeo's main business and Twitter was formed.

Amazon began as "only" an online bookstore before becoming the "everything" store. Today, 60 percent of its revenue comes from cloud computing services. Netflix wasn't always the one-stop shop for streaming TV shows and movies. In the mid-1990s, it was founded as a rent-by-mail DVD delivery service, a far cry from their current competition with Hollywood. In the early 2000s, Facebook was a glorified online "yearbook" where college students could rate whether their classmates were "hot or not."

None of these companies had a predefined grand plan for how to end up at the top of the food chain. Their successes were not due to the paths they initially chose. It was their ability to pivot: to understand their customers, to adapt to emerging technology, and to learn from their competitors. These companies weren't afraid to reorient themselves every step of their journey. Pivoting allowed them to adapt to new information and make informed decisions. Pivoting means having the courage to change when a strategy no longer works, all while having a clear vision for the new direction. In the same way, Seekers pivot onto a new course when it's time for a new strategy.

Reaping the Rewards

Taking up the call to adventure is not all threats, trials, and failures. There are definite payoffs for hero/ines. These range from saving the world to saving their own souls.[20] Katniss and Peeta survive the Hunger Games and claim victory. Luke acquires the blueprint of the Death Star and saves the galaxy. Harry acquires the Sorcerer's Stone, and House Gryffindor wins the cup.

For Seekers, the reward may be a new set of skills, strengths, and insights to keep for the ongoing journey. It may be an important epiphany about themselves or the world. These rewards may all be part of a newfound purpose. Not surprisingly, newfound purpose often comes with a sense of being enlivened, a sense of joy, a spark that has been lit.

This is the opposite of apathy, and yet it is not the kind of superficial and synthetic happiness so many people strive for. The spark that comes from purpose is different. It's an aliveness we feel to the core because we're into something deeply good, and bigger than ourselves. Something that connects us with others and with humanity. Something that grounds us in the awareness that we belong. We matter. We recognize that we live in a world of pain, and that pain doesn't necessarily dissipate in the presence of sparks. Sparks have the mysterious ability to be felt in the midst of suffering.

We intentionally use the term "spark" rather than "happiness" or "positive emotions," lest people think that meaningfulness has to feel light and airy. On the contrary, the purposeful work may be solemn, dignified, and filled with gravity. Hospice workers. Child oncologists. Search and rescue workers. And many, many other careers involve stress and stamina, both physical and emotional. For example, many of Belle's colleagues do clinical research, and policy work associated with trauma and injustice. Because humans tend to notice the things they persistently ask questions about, these colleagues often see more than their fair share of darkness, pain, and cruelty in the world. They can't unsee what they've seen. They have to work hard at self-care, lest they burn out. They do this work at great personal cost because they want to make the world a better place for future generations. That potential makes the work feel meaningful.

How do we know if work feels meaningful? What is the feeling of meaningfulness? In other words, if sparks aren't the same as the feelings of happiness the world chases after, what are they? And how do they enliven and enable us?

Type of spark	How does it enliven/enable us?
Joy	Lightens us up so we can play.
Gratitude	Gives us a sense of the blessings in our lives that we can give back to others.
Serenity	Calms us so we can savor the present moment.
Interest	Tunes us in to something in the world so we can learn with curiosity and fascination.
Hope	Helps us believe that things can and will change for the better so that we can trust in, wait for, long for something or someone.

Type of spark	How does it enliven/enable us?
Pride	Makes us conscious of our worth and dignity so we can do what matters to us rather than simply seek human approval.
Amusement	Opens our eyes to the humor in things, so we can take ourselves less seriously and enjoy the ride.
Inspiration	Enables us to draw energy from what's good in the world, and to add to it.
Awe	Gives us the sense we are part of something much larger than ourselves.
Love	Allows us to share all of the above sparks with others—individuals and communities.

Sparks don't just *feel* good. They have a physiological impact on our bodies that changes the way we think and act. They increase the scope of our visuospatial attention,[21] so we can literally *see* more of the world. They allow us to access more parts of our brain and memory, so that we can *understand* more of the world.[22] They reduce our inhibitions, fostering courage to venture forth in the world. They flush our bodies with oxytocin, improving our ability to connect with others. They make us more likely to trust other people,[23] which in turn makes them trust us. This is associated with forming stronger, longer-lasting bonds with individuals and support networks.[24] And yes, they can also make us feel better—bolstering sleep quality, immune systems, life satisfaction, and reducing mental and physical health symptoms.[25]

Different sparks enliven us in different ways. *Joy* opens us to creativity and play. *Interest* opens our ability to focus, remain curious, and seek out information and experiences. *Serenity* opens us to the present moment, slowing us down and allowing us to soak it all in. *Pride* opens our ambitions and gives us pleasure in the outcomes of our work. *Love* opens our hearts, so we are motivated by more than egos or selfish desires. It's the key spark that keeps us honest, lest we lose sight of our impetus for service and contribution in the world. Love is also the backpack that holds all the other types of sparks. It enables us to experience all other sparks in concert with those we love, making the journey all the more sweet.

Together these sparks perfectly equip us for the adventure that is the Seeker's Journey—opening our eyes to the world around us, our minds to possibility, and our hearts to other people. Interest, joy, and amusement provide the attention and creativity needed *to hear the call*. Pride and inspiration give us the courage we need to *accept the call* and *take the leap*. Hope and serenity make us resilient in the face of adversity, allowing us to overcome *tests and challenges*.

Finally, sparks can be signposts that inform and confirm we're going in the right direction. We can go down the list of sparks with students to identify which ones (if any) have been present on their journeys. Do they still experience joy and amusement sailing or playing basketball? Do they find computer programming inherently interesting? Are they inspired by the art they're creating? When there's been an absence of sparks for an extended period, that's a sign. It may be time to pivot.

To be clear, meaningfulness is not about feeling good *all the time*. The reality of life is that there are many moments that are boring and mundane. A study of professionals across various occupations found that people can't sustain a constant sense of meaningfulness in their work.[26] We'd flame out if we were burning cauldrons of sparks all day, *all the time*. Instead, meaningfulness is episodic. Work is punctuated by meaningful moments.

The magic number appears to be 20 percent. People who spent at least 20 percent of their time on "meaningful" activities were significantly less likely to suffer burnout than peers.[27] This finding is consistent with the Pareto principle, or the 80/20 rule.[28] According to this principle, 80 percent of outcomes are driven by 20 percent of actions.

- 80 percent of all traffic accidents are caused by 20 percent of drivers.

- 80 percent of a company's productivity is the result of 20 percent of employees.

- 80 percent of all pollution comes from 20 percent of factories.

- 80 percent of all U.S. wealth is held by 20 percent of Americans.

By extrapolating this rule of thumb, we propose the 80/20 *Purpose Ratio:* at least 20 percent of any given activity should spark you. If you have that, you're good. Some workplaces have put in place policies consistent with the 80/20 Purpose Ratio. Google allows employees to work on whatever they want to 20 percent of the time. This time has not gone wasted—it's inspired personal meaning and innovations like Google News, Gmail, and AdSense. What's good for employees is good for employers.

From time to time, we can consider whether the extracurriculars and work we choose to do meet this 80/20 threshold. If yes, consider your pursuits meaningful.

Using the Pivot Foot

An alum (whom we will call Liza) of our class and True North program (our college curriculum on purpose discovery) explained how she's used her elements of purpose to make decisions for her future:

> *Throughout my undergraduate and postgraduate experiences, True North has been a reminder to stay present. I have realized how easily life can fall into a routine, and I was constantly focused on the next step without checking in with where I was in the present. Each week I reminded myself to think through my job, my hobbies, and my relationships and question them. How was I cultivating my skills and developing my strengths? What parts of my job made me excited and passionate, and which parts felt draining? Working on a COVID research team this past year has been both challenging and rewarding. By taking the time to reflect on my elements of purpose, I could sense that while my passion for working with patients had stayed the same, I had found a new interest and strength in diagnostic medicine and research. These realizations gave me the courage to detour from my*

path into nursing programs, take some more classes, and now apply for training as a physician assistant. Essentially True North gave me the tools to be able to check in with myself and the confidence to be able to pivot in my career journey.

For a generation that over-worries about wasting time and losing a place on the game board, Liza's journey provides perspective about the importance of side trips. There is joy and benefit in trying things out. Explorations serve a great purpose. For Liza, it provided important clarification of what she wanted to do. And the language of purpose provided a way to understand what she did and did not like about a field.

Changing course doesn't have to be an about-face. In basketball, a pivot step is keeping one foot on the ground while moving the other foot. Pivoting provides navigational nuance; it helps us to recognize what should stay the same and what needs to change.

The End Is Just the Beginning

Oftentimes when we have found a direction that works for us or experienced some success, we cling to it. Stability feels good amid uncertainty. Yet the Seeker's Journey never proceeds in one direction forever. Humans are remarkably adaptable: the longer we are exposed to pain or pleasure, the more these sensations dissipate over time.[29] Biological habituation underpins the platitude "Good things don't last." It's why our favorite shoes eventually lose their appeal, the car we were so excited to drive is no longer thrilling, and the fifth piece of chocolate is not nearly as enjoyable as the first. It's why we get used to cleaning the dishes, raking the leaves, and making our beds. It's how that workout you used to not even finish now feels like a breeze. Thankfully, it's also why the heartbreaking pain of a loss eventually subsides.

We can only sustain intense joy or pain for so long until we return to equilibrium. Exposure breeds familiarity. Stability leads to comfort, and comfort leads to complacency. It's at moments like these, when we have overcome challenges and tasted real success, that we must *take the road back* and *recommit to the journey.* Change is not a bad thing, it's what makes life an adventure. Arthur Ashe put it this way: "Success is a journey, not a destination. The doing is often more important than the outcome."[30]

Hero/ines like Katniss, Luke, Dorothy, and Moana grow up to become adults as they traverse their respective journeys. They learn to harness their powers, become wiser and more battle-hardened. Our journey will change us, too. It will transform how we understand ourselves and the world.

The pathway model is problematic because it visualizes pushing students along a straight line: start at point A, travel to point B, and continue all the way through to Z. But the Seeker's Journey is more like a circle. Stories end and begin, end and begin. And while every so often we may return to our roots, *we* are not the same. We are wiser, more confident, and the better for it, battle scars and all.

This is the ultimate reward of the Seeker's Journey: transforming into the best versions of ourselves. And as we grow, so too does our purpose. The act of pursuing purpose evolves our purpose. And so we need to consistently conduct heart-checks, asking ourselves:

- *Have I changed over time for the better (and how)?*

- *Are these still my values, strengths, skills, and the needs I feel called to meet?*

- *Is the direction I'm headed still aligned with my purpose?*

If so, journey on. If not, you now have the tools to find your way. The more we embrace the recursive nature of life's journey, the better we come to understand ourselves.

Every Story Is Your Story

The Seeker's Journey is ubiquitous. Look for it in movies, books, and the real-life hero/ines around you. Refer to these stories for examples of hearing the call or refusing it, taking the leap and being challenged, or facing a turning point. Use the Seeker's Journey to share your own story with your students. The ups and downs, the good, bad, and ugly. Examples help students to expect and embrace these parts of their own journeys.

Below is a template to help you articulate your personal journey in dialogue with students:

Role-Modeling the Call to Adventure

- *Call to Adventure*

  — What did you feel called to do when you were younger? Did you accept the call to adventure? Why or why not? What happened as a result?

- *Refusal of the Call*

  — What held you back from accepting your call to adventure? What were the internal feelings that held you back? What were the external factors?

- *Meeting Mentors*

  — Who helped you on your Seeker's Journey? How did they help you?

- *Taking the Leap*

  — What's a big decision you made earlier in your life? Did you make the decision for the right reasons? Why or why not?

- *Being Tested*

  — What challenges and tests did you experience on your journey? How did you respond to them?

- *Facing the Turning Point*

  — When did you fail or have to pivot?

  — What happened once you pivoted?

  — When did you know it was time to quit?

- *Reaping the Rewards*
  - What did you enjoy most about your journey?
  - What aspects felt meaningful?
  - How did this sense of meaningfulness help you?

- *The End Is Just the Beginning*
  - How did your own Seeker's Journey change you over time?
  - How did it change your core elements of purpose?
  - What have you learned along the way?

Below is a template for drawing out your students' stories:

Students' Call to Adventure

- *Entering the Crossroads*
  - Are you resisting the path you're on?
  - Does the path you're on not feel like your own?

- *Call to Adventure*
  - What do you feel called to do? What big open-ended questions do you want to explore?

- *Refusal of the Call*
  - What are you afraid of?
  - How are you holding yourself back?
  - What would happen if you committed to a call?

- *Meeting Mentors*
  - Who can help you on your journey?

- *Taking the Leap*

  - What's a big decision that you will have to make?

  - Which directions in life align well with your values, strengths, skills, and the need you feel called to meet?

- *Being Tested*

  - What challenges or obstacles are you facing, or will you face on the journey?

  - How would you like to respond to these challenges?

  - How can you turn these tests into challenges instead of threats?

- *Facing the Turning Point*

  - When will you know if you have to quit?

  - How might you pivot if this direction doesn't work out?

- *Reaping the Rewards*

  - Do the things you've committed to feel meaningful at least 20 percent of the time? Why or why not?

  - What's been lost and what's been gained?

  - What could make your journey more meaningful?

- *The End Is Just the Beginning*

  - What will change if you reach your goals?

  - How will you change? How do you hope to grow further?

  - What do you hope stays the same?

The Seeker's Journey

- *Entering the Crossroads*
    - Are your students resisting the path they are currently on?
    - Is the current path they are on working for them?

- *Hearing the Call to Adventure*
    - Do your students feel empowered to listen for their own elements of purpose?
    - Do they have opportunities to listen for what moves them?

- *Resisting the Call*
    - What are your students afraid of?
    - How do they hold themselves back?

- *Taking the Leap*
    - What big decisions are they making?
    - How are they deciding what to do?

- *Passing the Test*
    - What obstacles could get in their way?
    - Are these obstacles challenges or threats?
    - What resources do they have to overcome challenges?

- *The Turning Point*
    - What sparks do they feel along their journey?
    - Do they experience enough sparks to make it feel meaningful?
    - If not, how could they pivot?

- *The End Is Just the Beginning*
    - How have they changed over time?

8

Higher Ed

Diversify your brand, social, and human capital.

Education is the passport to the future, for tomorrow
belongs to those who prepare for it today.

—MALCOLM X

The Million-Dollar Question

Should young people go to college? Conventional wisdom about whether
to go to college has gone around and around in circles. *Go at all costs.
Don't go, it costs too much. Go, but make it worth the cost.* The "go at all
costs" view emerged on the premise of a college degree as the golden ticket
to the American dream. Long ago, a college degree replaced a high school
diploma as the minimum qualification for entry into the skilled labor
market. And those with college degrees (compared with those without)
could earn more money over the course of their lives. The actual stories
of underprivileged and first-generation students provide insight into why
they fight for their college educations at all costs.

Belle's father, Chu-yu Liang, describes his life as a "miracle" . . .
because he made it to the United States to pursue the American
dream through higher education. It's an "against-all-odds" story
of a fatherless boy and his two sisters in China in the 1940s, when
widowed mothers had virtually no means of earning a paycheck and
ensuring basic survival. Poverty and food scarcity dictated his school
and work choices. When his grandmother suggested that he forgo
school to work as an apprentice at a local grocery store, he promised
himself he'd pursue his dreams of further education. This road came
to constant crossroads—relocations, school transitions, serious illnesses.
Each derailed (and spurred) his education. He never had a full year
in any one school until he moved to Taiwan and tested into a Chinese
Air Force Technical School—his best option for "free" education and
boarding. During two years of training to repair military aircraft,
he realized he was made for engineering. So he failed the graduation
exam on purpose to avoid being forced into the Chinese military.
(Unlike the U.S. military, from which one can retire in ten to twenty
years, there is no leaving the Chinese military.) Next, Chu took the
highly competitive exam for entry into one of only four colleges at the
time. He ranked the engineering program first, but was admitted
into agricultural college. After two years of majoring in this unrelated
field, he attempted again to test into engineering school, this time
with success.

He started his entire college degree over as an engineering major
in order to pursue this field that would pave the way to higher
education in the United States. He was admitted into Oklahoma
State University for graduate school. He arrived in the States with a
$500 airplane ticket bought by his aunt, a $200 traveler's check from
his mother, and $2,400—the exact amount required for immediate
deposit in order to secure a student visa. Two years later, he graduated
with an MS in mechanical engineering.

Today, Chu's children and grandchildren are Americans pursuing
their purpose. They are beneficiaries of his Seeker's Journey—his
courage to step off the path again and again to answer the call to

adventure. It was not easy. It involved wrong turns, failures, pivots. It involved persistence and sacrifice. It involved great blessings and rewards for generations.

To this day, there continues to be a steady stream of underrepresented college students giving the shirts off their backs for a college degree. But a combination of rising costs and student loan debt, decreased acceptance rates, and stagnant wages has contributed to buyer's ambivalence and re-morse. Lower-cost alternatives have popped up everywhere. Income share agreements. Coding bootcamps. Online credentialing programs. One such program, Make School, is a combination of a short-term coding bootcamp and traditional college whose goal is to get students hired as software engineers. Google's Career Certificates promise "high-paying high-growth job fields—no college degree required." Meanwhile, doubts about higher education continue to inch up each time we hear about a college dropout building a fortune in Silicon Valley.

- Mark Zuckerberg: *Dropped out at nineteen, net worth $73.7 billion.*

- Steve Jobs: *Dropped out at twenty-one, net worth $8.3 billion at the time of his death.*

- Michael Dell: *Dropped out at nineteen, net worth $21.8 billion.*

- Bill Gates: *Dropped out at nineteen, net worth $95.8 billion.*

And the list goes on.

Just when we thought ambivalence about going to college couldn't get worse, it's gotten worse since COVID-19.[1] College enrollment num-bers dropped another 5 percent a year after the start of the pandemic. It dropped nearly 10 percent for community colleges. And low-income students were 2.3 times less likely to enroll than higher-income peers. The percentage of Americans ages eighteen to twenty-nine who view college as "very important" dropped 33 percent from 2013 to 2019.[2] Forty-six percent of parents said they would prefer that their children not go to a four-year college after high school, even if there were no financial or other barriers.[3] A 2021 New America/Third Way survey found that almost two out of every three college students said college "is not worth cost anymore."[4] This says an awful lot about people's current confidence in the value of higher education.

Not Black or White

What's contributed to doubts about college are strong disputes in the popular press. Pundits often cherry-pick statistics representing one side of the debate:

A. Everyone should go to college because it always pays dividends and carries little risk,

or

B. Only those with substantial family wealth can afford it.

Yes, It Pays Off

Nine out of ten jobs created are going to people with college degrees.[5] Compared to high school grads, typical college graduates will earn about $900,000 more over their working lives.[6] For the average person, the net present value of a college degree is $344,000. In other words, this is the amount of money that a college degree is worth today. And its value increases exponentially over one's career. Estimates put the forty-year net present value of a bachelor's degree from Boston College at nearly $1.5 million.[7]

Recent history suggests that a college degree will be more important than ever in the aftermath of COVID-19. In the great recession of 2008, the United States lost 7.2 million jobs. Eighty percent of jobs lost did not require a college degree.[8] And when the economy rebounded, an astonishing 95 percent of jobs created during the recovery required education beyond high school.[9] We're already seeing similar trends from the fallout of COVID-19. American workers with only a high school diploma are twice as likely to be unemployed as those with a bachelor's degree.[10] What was true in 2008 is proving to be true today; the worse things get, the more important a degree becomes.

Yes, There Are Risks

That said, it's too simplistic to think that college is a good financial investment for *all* students. The data shows that the payoff is variable: high *if you graduate,* low if you don't make it all the way through. It's estimated that six in ten who start college *never* finish. It's especially disturbing that the ones most likely to drop out are underprivileged students.

To add to these disincentives for low-income students, they're also four times less likely to go to a selective college compared with those from wealthy families who have similar grades and test scores.[11] This is the result of undermatching—a well-documented phenomenon where poor students are steered toward programs with low completion rates at the front end of the application process, rather than during admissions.[12] Given the risk and hardship, it's no shock that even those with a lot to gain from a college degree are hedging their bets. After all, only some get into selective institutions, and only some make it to the finish. Even fewer land a meaningful job that can stave off crushing student debt. It's a pipe dream to think that everyone can enjoy what's offered at the country's richest, most prestigious colleges. So shouldn't we be encouraging students (especially underprivileged ones) to forgo college and focus instead on getting good jobs with fair wages, decent unions, healthcare, and transportation? Why waste time and money when there are entrepreneurs out there making millions without a degree? Entrepreneur Neil Patel lamented that "college was a waste of time, a waste of energy, a waste of money, and a waste of potential."[13]

A More Nuanced Picture

These may seem like compelling arguments. But the true value of college is a little bit more complicated. College is immensely valuable and worth the price of admission when we use it wisely. It's not enough to just go to college—we need to be intentional about investing in higher education in a way that will pay off in the future.

This brings us to several questions: What should you get out of college? What's the true value of higher education? When making college decisions, young people should consider three types of value: brand capital, social capital, and human capital.

Brand Capital

How people choose a college reveals much about what they *think* the value of college is. Out of four thousand institutes of higher education in the United States alone, how do people pick one? A quick Google search would tell us there are at least thirty metrics one should consider when choosing a college (e.g., quality of faculty, curriculum, study abroad, etc.).[14] But, in reality, students and families (except those driven by affordability) overwhelmingly pick their school based on reputation.[15] We look at the list of schools we've been accepted to and pick the most exclusive college we can afford. We want to go to the most prestigious school possible. We want the school with the most respected reputation or brand, so that *we* will be respected. Respect by association.

In marketing, *brand equity* refers to the social value of a well-respected name. In college selection, we call this *brand capital*. Brand capital suggests that the value of higher education results from social signaling. A college degree from a "name-brand" institution sends a signal to prospective employers that students are ambitious, talented, and hardworking. This is called the *halo effect*—if a person has one positive attribute (the college they attended), people assume they have other positive attributes (they are hardworking, ambitious, conscientious, etc.).

Economists explain how a college's reputation (or brand) signals the value of the college's people and programs.[16] Consumers rely on reputation to evaluate a product's quality when it's hard to judge it another way. For example, "experience" products, like a bottle of wine, a healthcare provider, or a college education, are hard to assess without experiencing them first. So we make decisions based on reviews or word of mouth. It's why people will pay a lot for a bottle of wine that's been highly rated by a wine connoisseur. And why people want a referral for a doctor. And why people choose a college that's highly ranked in *U.S. News & World Report*.

It's not just students and parents who buy into name-brand schools. It's employers as well. Elite firms, like Wall Street's leading investment banks, consulting firms, and law offices, prefer graduates from prestigious colleges.[17] They use college reputation as a "quick and dirty" way to infer individual ability. You got into a top-notch college, so you must be top-notch. Halo effect.

A sprinkling of firms, like Deloitte, BBC, and Virgin Money, have switched to a "college-blind" hiring process because they realize that brand name isn't a perfect measure of student ability. One study showed that when exit exams are available, employers rely less on college reputation and more on individual student ability to set earnings.[18] Hopefully, one day these practices will be more widespread so that employers can spot great candidates at lower-ranked schools. In the meantime, make no mistake—brand capital is real. It's part of why a Mercedes-Benz can cost ten times that of a Hyundai. It's part of why a Patek watch costs a hundred times more than a Seiko. And it's often why graduates of prestigious schools get first dibs on interviews for prestigious firms and programs.

Brand capital *is* important, but its value is exaggerated.

We'll be talking about two types of capital that *far eclipse* brand capital's impact on graduates' *long-term success*. The first is the value of *relationships* people can build while in college. Relationships can be the biggest factor in whether students graduate from college or not. Decades of research have found that formative relationships serve as the foundation for learning, belonging, and thriving.[19] Students learn more and fail less when they have close relationships with their professors.[20] Even *perceptions* of relationships drive student outcomes. When students see their professors as helpful, encouraging, and approachable, they're more likely to build relationships with them and thrive in college. When they view their professors as cold, uncaring, and unapproachable, they're more likely to disengage academically.[21] The more students interact with faculty, the more likely they are to be successful.[22] Simply put, when students have relationships with caring adults on campus, they are more satisfied with college, and more successful upon graduation.[23]

The benefits of these college relationships spill into life beyond college. Students' networks help them connect to job leads: over 50 percent of all job applicants rely on formal and informal networks during their employment search.[24] And networks help students successfully land their jobs. Over half of all job *placements* are the result of a personal connection. Your network is your net worth. Relationships don't just help students get through college, they set them up for long-term success.

By long-term success, we're talking about more than prestige or decent pay. So often people who chose a job for only these reasons admit that they don't love or even like their work. They work to live, rather than live to work. Since jobs will make up so much of their waking hours and self-identity,[25] let's hold higher hopes for graduates than just barely tolerable jobs. Good jobs have been defined by "work engagement"—doing work you love that uses your strengths and skills and aligns with your values.[26] Research reveals that one of the most important things in life is a purposeful job[27] and that finding one is the primary reason Americans go to college.[28] Unfortunately, Gallup's State of the American Workplace survey revealed that 70 percent of full-time employees are *not* engaged at work.[29] Only 30 percent are doing work they love.

A survey of thirty thousand graduates was done to see what about a college education prepared them for good jobs and good lives.[30] The two factors that were clearly tied to these outcomes were *people* and *experiences*.[31] What mattered in students' future work engagement was not how prestigious their college was, but whether they had people on campus who had cared about them as a whole person, got them excited about learning, and encouraged them to pursue their purpose. Supportive relationships during college more than *doubled* their odds of being engaged in their later work lives.

Hands-on experiences during college also doubled their odds of being engaged in their later work lives. These include internships where students could apply what they were learning in the classroom, extracurricular activities, and working on projects that took at least a semester to complete.

And what's good for students is also good for colleges. A poll of thousands of alumni found that those who had significant relationships with even one or two professors were twice as likely to find their college experience very rewarding.[32] Alumni with seven to ten strong relationships were three times as likely to have an extremely rewarding college experience. Having three friends and taking just one class with one great professor can be the difference between a bad college experience and a great one.[33] The true value of education is not the logo on the hood, *it's what's under the hood*. It's the relationships that students build and the opportunity for experiential, hands-on learning.

Social Capital

The research makes it clear: relationships formed in college are incredibly valuable. Yet it's not just relationships themselves, but the *social capital* they provide students.[34] Social capital is your access to connections that can promote your potential and purpose.[35] The power of social capital happens through four actions: a flow of knowledge, access to opportunity, social credentialing, and reinforcement of identity or position.

Imagine that you're a graduating senior trying to get your foot in the door of the aviation industry. Your roommate's aunt is a pilot with Delta Airlines and holds social capital in this competitive field. You ask her for an informational interview and she shares tips she has gleaned through her career (flow of knowledge). She lets you know of a position in her department that hasn't been posted yet (access to opportunity). She offers to connect you with the hiring manager, to whom she recommends you send your résumé and cover letter directly. It works in your favor to be associated with this aunt, since she is in excellent standing at Delta (halo effect, social credentialing, and reinforcement of identity).

A college campus can dramatically boost your access to social capital. It's a hotbed of people who have connections to programs, internships, and resources that may be aligned with your vocational aspirations and purpose. Whenever you build a relationship you are expanding your world and the opportunities you have access to.

The day we were completing this chapter, Belle received this letter from a graduate describing their relationship this way:

> *The further I get in life, the more I realize that I could not have done it without the mentorship and support I was lucky to cultivate throughout my lifetime. Throughout college, I was introduced to so many different interests and new ideas, and I felt like I was standing at a crossroads with a million decisions to make. While sometimes I would try to answer my questions with my own experiences and internet searches, the truth is there was nothing more valuable than the insight of those who had walked the path before me. There was one professor in college that I was able to go to for anything—to talk about my college experiences and my career interests and everything in between. She was able to provide emotional support when I was stressed and guidance from her own career experiences that were relevant to my explorations. She was always honest with me and encouraged me to discover what would make me truly happy. It is because I have had mentors like her in my corner that I have been able to learn and grow based on not only my experiences alone, but also*

the world of knowledge and experiences that exist in the people around me.

Below are types of social capital you can tap into by asking people in your network questions like these.

Types of Social Capital

- **INFORMATION CAPITAL:** Do you have any wisdom or guidance that would be helpful for me on my journey?

- **OPPORTUNITY CAPITAL:** Do you know of any internships, jobs, or programs that may align with what I am looking to do?

- **REFERRAL CAPITAL:** Could you connect me to another person who could help me on my journey?

- **RECOMMENDATION CAPITAL:** Would you be willing to put in a good word for me and speak to my ability and potential?

These elements of social capital are listed in order from lowest cost to highest. Providing information is easy and relatively painless. Providing a recommendation is potentially more time-intensive and risks the recommender's reputation. The strength of your relationships with people in your network should factor into the type of social capital you can request from them.

When Tim's principal asked him to create a job description for himself as director of community engagement, he decided his purpose would be building the social capital of his school. He created a partnership project that formed "official" collaborations with local institutions of higher ed, as well as local employers. Arborists, EMT companies, real estate agencies, and local credit unions all came on board. He sought out workforce development programs and nonprofit organizations.

The benefits of these partnerships were bidirectional. Tim held social capital that organizations valued—access to students they could potentially recruit. The partners all pitched their programs to students, encouraging them to apply. Students who were interested would then meet with their guidance counselors to discuss the fit with their purpose and get help with the application. Although students could've applied to these programs on their own, the partnership project *reduced the friction of accessing social capital*. Social capital came to students' doorsteps. This project resulted in a 30 percent increase in students matriculating to a high-quality postsecondary program.

Human Capital

The third major asset of a college education is *human capital*. This is the value *you* bring to the world. It's what you have to show for your college experience. Human capital represents all the knowledge and skills you've gained. One of the best opportunities to grow human capital is by having *formative experiences* during college.

In a large study of graduates, there were three key college experiences aligned with finding purposeful work: (1) a mentor who encouraged them to pursue their dreams; (2) an internship or job that helped them apply what they were learning in the classroom; and (3) a class focused on making meaning of their work. In other words, *formative experiences* led to purposeful work after college.[36] And great jobs and great lives go hand in hand. Graduates who have purposeful work are *ten times* more likely to be happy and healthy.

Employers agree that the value of higher education is driven by formative experience. Over 90 percent of managers and executives said they were more likely to hire a recent graduate who's had an internship or apprenticeship with an organization.[37] In a large study asking employers what they looked for when hiring recent graduates, at the top of their list were internships, employment during college, and volunteer experiences.[38] At the bottom of the list? College reputation, grades, and coursework. Employers place more weight on students' experiences than on academic credentials. They care more about what you've done than what you know.

The Association of American Colleges & Universities refers to *high-impact practices* (HIPs) as college experiences most linked to student engagement, well-being, and career preparation.[39] These include first-year seminars, service learning, learning communities, research fellowships, and internships. HIPs provide opportunities to gain hands-on learning and community. HIPs are linked to improved grades, classroom engagement, and course completion and decreased absenteeism.[40] They improve students' critical thinking skills and deepen classroom learning.[41]

There are two overarching benefits of hands-on experiences: to test and to show. Formative experiences are how we test out our elements of purpose. They provide an opportunity to listen for the call. Liza thought her core values and strengths were best applied in the nursing field, but experience proved otherwise. Experiences are opportunities to listen and hear your call. To build on your technical and universal skills. To try to make a positive impact in the world.

The second benefit is a chance to show your human capital. Experiences are tangible evidence of our capabilities. Saying you're good at computer programming is not as convincing as actually cracking the code in your data science internship. More and more, the value of higher education is dependent on your ability to communicate it. You have to *show your work*. Experiences are how we signal to the world our commitment to our values, strengths, skills, and contribution. Experiences allow you to *self-credential*.

Get Your Money's Worth

The term "capital" usually refers to money. So often money is the metric used to determine the value of higher education. How much will it cost? What's the return on investment? It's time to expand the scope of college capital to include brand, social, and human capital. A college's benefits for you can go way beyond the *U.S. News & World Report* ranking, status, and prestige level. While going on a college tour may help you evaluate a college, basing your decision on the beauty of the campus and social skills of the tour guide is equivalent to judging a book by its cover. Yes, meal plans, social life, and location may be side perks to college life, but these factors should not be the bases for choosing a college.

When you're considering whether a college is for you, use the lens of social capital. Investigate what kinds of relationships you can build at this school, using the four elements of purpose.

- Are there professors or student groups who have similar core values and areas of interest or passion?

- Are there people who have technical and universal skills that I'm motivated to learn?

- Is this a place my strengths will be valued?

- What impact in the world are people here trying to make? Is this the type of impact that I'd like to be a part of?

- Would joining this college community open up networks and resources that I can benefit from?

Next, critically consider the opportunities for formative experiences.

- What are the hands-on opportunities available where I can use my strengths, develop skills, and make a positive impact?

- Are there particular programs I'm interested in? Work-study programs? Internship opportunities? Travel abroad programs? Service learning? Formative education opportunities?

- What are the opportunities for developing my human capital? More and more institutions, like Northeastern University, Drexel, Georgia Tech, MIT, and the University of Massachusetts Lowell, are offering "co-operative" programs, where students take on career-oriented jobs *while* earning credit.

- Which colleges combine hands-on experiences with reflective practices that help students identify their calling in life? Leaders in formative education, like Boston College, engage students in mentorship programs, retreats, leadership opportunities, and service learning where they discover themselves intellectually, socially, psychologically, and spiritually. All this so they can contribute as whole people in the world.

Formative relationships (social capital) and formative experiences (human capital) are the engines that drive us toward purpose. They're the key ingredients for living a successful, meaningful life. So we need to advance beyond asking "Should I go to college?" and "Where should I go?" to tackle more pointed questions:

- Where can I gain the most capital?

- How can I build meaningful relationships?

- How can I access formative experiences that shape my purpose?

- How can I design my college experience to be transformational?

Don't Talk About It, *Be* About It

Leveraging social and human capital from the college experience might seem like common sense. But only one in four graduates form caring relationships with faculty members.[42] Less than half of all students report engaging in an internship or apprenticeship, even though hiring managers and executives say these are the most important qualifications for employment.[43] Marginalized and underrepresented students are faring even worse. Low-income students report even fewer relationships with teachers, nonfamily adults, friends of family, and coaches.[44] First-generation college students are nearly three times more likely than peers to report having *zero* close college relationships.[45]

What's going on? Why are students struggling to build relationships and take advantage of hands-on opportunities in college? Unfortunately, they are part of a growing epidemic sweeping across the country.

They feel alone.

Alone, Together

A recent survey of twenty thousand people showed that loneliness in the United States is on the rise.[46] A majority feel that no one knows them well (58 percent) and often or always feel alone (52 percent). Almost two-thirds of respondents feel that their interests and ideas are not shared by those around them. Of all demographics, Gen Z (those age eighteen to twenty-two), were most likely to report feeling chronically lonely (79 percent), compared with millennials (71 percent) and boomers (50 percent).[47] Loneliness is their number one fear, ranking ahead of losing a home or a job.[48]

They have cause for worry. Lonely people are at greater risk for premature mortality. The physical health fallout of loneliness is on par with substance abuse, obesity, injury, and violence.[49] U.S. Surgeon General Vivek Murthy describes loneliness as "the subjective feeling that you're lacking the social connections you need. It can feel like being stranded, abandoned, or cut off from the people with whom you belong—even if you're surrounded by other people. What's missing when you're lonely is the feeling of closeness, trust, and the affection of genuine friends, loved ones, and community."[50]

Despite the deeply felt pain associated with loneliness, we don't do ourselves any favors in order to get out of it. Eighty-five percent of American adults prefer to rely on themselves as opposed to other people, and four out of five agree that they rely solely on themselves.[51] Asking for help seems somehow antithetical to the "pull yourself up by your bootstraps" mentality of Americans. People fear that asking for help will make them seem incompetent, inferior, and dependent on others.[52] There's a fear that asking for help signals that you need it.

Ironically, the *opposite* is true: seeking help makes individuals seem more competent to others, not less.[53] And it shows you are willing to take risks. Asking for advice actually conveys confidence and wisdom (you know what you don't know, and you know when to ask).[54] Employees who ask for help are happier and more successful in their roles.[55]

Another challenge is that even when students *want* help, most don't know how to ask for it. People aren't taught to identify the type of help they need and when. And if you don't know what you need, you can't make an effective ask. Below is a guide for growing your capital. We'll walk you through exactly what you need to know about what type of support to look for and how to find it, as well as strategies for recruiting people to be on your team. We'll show you how to use the language of purpose to build transformative relationships and ace any job interview.

- - - - - - - - - - - - - - - - -

Guide to Growing Your Capital

The first step to growing your capital is making room for it. We are often so busy that we can't add another thing. Our lives are spread two miles wide and half an inch deep. Growing capital requires time and going deeper in a few manageable directions. It doesn't mean running in a million new directions. It means spring cleaning to remove some distractions and clutter, so that the most valued things can be discovered. We realize that for the overscheduled students of today, this may seem like an impossible feat. Below we provide some practical tips, but it's essentially prioritizing relationships we care about and pursuing experiences that are meaningful to us, and not being afraid to say no to "opportunities" that fall outside these descriptions.

In our homes, college dorm rooms, and work computers, many of us have what's called a junk drawer (or closet). It's a place where we throw everything that *might* be of use. It becomes a big, unorganized mess. Some of the things might have been worth keeping, but now everything is inaccessible. And we didn't put the things of value in their rightful places, so we could find them when we needed them. Now, as a result, we have no clue what's even in the drawer.

Often we live life like this. Accepting *all* offers for friendship, a good time, or a résumé line item. We jam-pack them all into our overflowing drawer. Maybe some of these taught us important lessons that can be used to make future decisions. But since we didn't have a good filter for curating our college (or other) experiences, now we don't know what to make of it all.

We need some smaller bins for organizing these experiences, so that we can use them to help us make future choices. To borrow a few tips from the organizing expert Marie Kondo, we need to simplify our lives. We need a filter for making these daily choices about which things are life-giving and aligned with our purpose. And which are not. This is not to say we can never do anything that's a waste of time. Take time to rest, play, hang out with friends and family, binge Netflix, and do nothing. We need breaks, after all.

But since your time is precious, be selective about the relationships and experiences you deeply invest in. Sometimes this means that opportunities that come your way are not for this season of your life. (Trust us when we say that so many of the opportunities that we think are "once in a lifetime" will come around again. So be patient.) Sometimes it means it's time to let go of the ones that are no longer serving you well. Maybe they once were, but are not anymore. Thank them for the role they once played—then let them go.

In the next sections, we're going to give you some bins and tips for organizing your capital so that you can make a plan to pursue them selectively.

Three Fellow Travelers

As mentioned, Seekers, just like hero/ines, have mentors and other companions with them on their adventures. As the saying goes, no person is an island. On your purpose journey, there are three different types of people who help you navigate. But if you don't know to look for them, they might just pass you by. So who are they?

Anchors

Sometimes we need companions, confidants, sidekicks who are there for us when we hit a bump in the road. Anchors are the people we feel comfortable reaching out to at four in the morning to share our troubles. They inherently get us. They're good at knowing what we need, when we need it. We call them Anchors for a reason: in times of uncertainty, they ground us. They're trustworthy and there for us even when the whole world has left us. Anchors make us feel psychologically safe being our authentic selves. They have our back. They are like Sherpas who carry our backpacks and tell us what to bring in order to climb to the summit.

Also, don't forget your sidekick groups. Sometimes they're a support group, your safe haven for clearing out some mental baggage. Often it's the people who say, "Come on over." The three words that promise relief or fun is on the way. Game nights and Netflix binges with besties. Shooting hoops with roomies. Being together is your reset button even when not a word is spoken. In any shape and form, Anchors are people you do life with.

Who's your person(s)? Do you have people on your team who unconditionally support you through thick and thin?

Guides

Other times, what we most need is *guidance*. While Anchors break our fall, Guides move us forward. They've been where we are heading. Life is a steep climb, and it's encouraging to have those ahead of us on the journey "call back." Guides tell us which mountain to climb, where the rocks are, the bumps, and how to navigate the climb. They may even order us the food and equipment. When we're at an inflection point in our journey, and we're unsure of what to do next, Guides are the people who can best help us. We turn to them for *advice* or *information*. They are practical and clear-minded. The organizational psychologist Herminia Ibarra refers to Guides as "strategizers" who share insider information that can be used to move forward or get ahead.[56]

Do you have access to people who help you make decisions? Whom do you turn to for wisdom and direction?

Bridges

When we know where to go, we may need help getting there. Bridges can connect us to opportunities and resources. They can help us *access* other formative relationships or experiences as we pursue our purpose. Bridges are at a point in their journeys where we would like to be. They're farther along on the very type of journey that motivates and inspires us. They can throw us a line, or serve as a bridge from where we are to where they are. Their lived experiences serve as road maps. They've gained insights or significant achievements that we could benefit from. Bridges are the people who can introduce us to a person whom we need to hear a "yes" from. They help get our foot in the door or over the transom, so that we can make the magic happen. Our world is flatter than ever, and so new Bridges are often just a LinkedIn connection away. Ibarra refers to them as opportunity givers who provide introductions to other influential people.[57]

You may already have more Anchors, Guides, and Bridges than you realize. How many people do you think you know? Hazard a guess. The average American knows *six hundred* people.[58] We drastically underestimate the number of people we know. It's because there's a cognitive limit to the number of people we can have a stable relationship with—for most, that number hovers between one hundred and two hundred.[59] Our brains can't easily recall everyone we've had a relationship with. Our networks are way bigger and more valuable than we give them credit for.

Eco-Mapping

So, let's create a visual of your latent networks. In the center of a large piece of paper, write your name. Put the names of all the people you know around your name. Include your family members, your friends, your coworkers, your neighbors. Cast a wide net. Write down everyone you know. Include people you're currently close to, as well as old acquaintances and classmates. As you begin writing names down, consider the connections each of these people have. Write down those names as well. An interesting thing happens. The more names we write down, the more people keep coming to mind. This is called activating our latent network. Try to write down all of your first- and second-degree network members. That is, you know them directly (first degree) or the person you know has direct connections with them (second degree). Those closest to you should be placed closest to your name, while mild acquaintances should be positioned farther from the center of your network.

Once you've finished your eco-map, step back and take a look. Not bad! This is your social capital.

Knowing What to Ask For

The next step is knowing what to ask for from your social network. Organize the names of your supports into these three categories (it's fine to put the same names in more than one category):

Anchors	Guides	Bridges
Emotional support and sounding boards	Information, advice, and guidance	Access to opportunities and other people

The type of support we need often depends on our stage of the Seeker's Journey, and it would be helpful to use the chart above to think through who we might reach out to. If we're still considering *all* possible life directions, we're in the exploration stage. We can reach out to Anchors for *emotional support* and to act as *sounding boards* for generating ideas. If we've narrowed our options down, we're in the deciding stage. We can reach out to Guides for *advice* and *guidance*. If we've made a decision and are pursuing a specific goal, we can reach out to Bridges for *recommendations* and *referrals*.

Guiding Question	Stage	Support Needed	Support Person
Open-ended and broad: What are my options?	Learning and exploring	Emotional support, sounding board, and ideas	Anchors
Close-ended and specific: Should I do X or Y?	Deciding	Guidance and advice	Guides
"How" questions: How do I achieve my goal?	Pursuing	Recommendations and referrals	Bridges

Making the Ask

We're aware that most people despise networking. What comes to mind are awkward, transactional conversations. We don't like acting fake and superficial. We don't like asking for help, burdening people, or feeling indebted. We don't like using people like props.

Fortunately, the networking we're talking about is different. Traditional networking is about gaining things from others; we are talking about *building* a relationship. It's about making a genuine connection. It's powered by interest, enjoyment, and a sense of awe that we're all part of a giant tapestry, each playing our part in the world and connected by tiny threads. This invisible web of connections holds us all together. The connections are always there. Always ready for us to tighten them.

And we do this simply by approaching people with sincere curiosity. Dale Carnegie put it this way: "You can make more friends in two months by becoming interested in other people than you can in two years by trying to get other people interested in you."[60] Social networking involves an open heart and mind toward people. An enthusiasm for trying to understand and learn from the people we meet. We want to know what makes them tick, and what gets them up in the morning.

We see our shared core humanity with the person in front of us, so we're not intimidated or put off by the surface differences between us. We delight in the differences. We seek to diversify our networks. It's a little like diversifying our portfolios. This is one of the most important principles of investing. It means ensuring that you spread your capital among different investments so that you're not relying on just one investment for all your returns.

Networking is the opposite of "finding our people," which is code for going through life looking to meet others just like us. It's stepping out of that comfort zone into the unknown. Networking is one of the best parts of our call to adventure. People are interesting, and there are souls out there worth knowing. When we meet people different from us we're stretched. We learn new things. We go deeper in our convictions and understandings.

Every interaction can be mutually beneficial. According to self-determination theory, everyone has three psychological needs: *autonomy, competence,* and *relatedness.* And a fourth one may be added: *beneficence.* "Beneficence" is defined as "the sheer pleasure of having contributed to others."[61] In other words, helping others is a pleasure.[62]

Keep this in mind when reaching out to those in your network. You're not just asking for a handout. You're not thinking, "What can I get from this person?" Instead, you're giving someone an opportunity to make a positive impact on someone else. That someone else is you. Yes, it's a favor, but it's also a *gift.* If someone reached out to you because they saw you as an expert in the field and believed you could help them move forward in their lives, how would you feel? Important and needed? Requests like this meet the needs of both the helpee and the helper. Asking for help from people brings out the best in them. The hard part is knowing *what type of help you need and how to ask for it.*

The more specific your ask, the more likely you are to get a favorable response. Here's an ask that's too vague: *I was hoping you could talk to me to help me figure out my future.*

Much better ask: *I am a recent college graduate interested in product management, because my internship in application support made me realize I love working with customers. Would you be willing to talk with me for fifteen minutes about what skills and certification I would need to be marketable for product management positions?*

In the first ask, it wasn't clear *how* the expert could be helpful. If people don't think they can be helpful, they won't accept the offer. The second ask provided a brief reason for the interest in the field and explained how the expert could be helpful: by talking about the skills and training needed to be marketable in the expert's field. A clear ask reassures people that *they can be helpful* and their time is well spent. The clear ask should be followed by a clear thank-you that is very specific about how the expert was helpful and how much the time spent was appreciated.

On the next page we provide a template for how to ask for help at different stages of your Seeker's Journey.

Return the Favor

Invest in your social network members. Pay it forward. Ask them, "How can I help you?" Before requesting anything from them, offer to help first. Express encouragement and affirmation. If someone asks for something like an informational interview, say yes when your schedule allows. Connect people who you think would be interested in each other. Offer advice when solicited. Answer inquiries in a timely manner.

In a recent example, a former student of Belle's took the time to write to her on LinkedIn: *"I was fondly telling a coworker about the awesome applied psych practicum I took in college and was reminded how grateful I am to have had that opportunity . . . I truly would not be as happy or excited about where I am today without it. So thank you for all that you did and I hope all is well!"* Belle responded by inviting her to come to the current practicum class and share her career story. She immediately responded

ANCHORS	**GUIDES**	**BRIDGES**
Emotional support and sounding boards	Information, advice, and guidance	Access to opportunities and other people
I'm considering options after high school. I have no idea what I want to do for a career, so I would love to learn from as many different perspectives as possible. Would you be willing to chat for fifteen minutes about your college experience and how it was helpful (or not) in your career decisions?	I'm going to college next year and majoring in education. I think I want to become either a teacher or a school counselor, but don't know how to decide. Would you be willing to chat for fifteen minutes about your experience as an educator and give me some insights or advice?	I'm graduating from college this year and looking to start my career as a data analyst at a large financial firm. Since you work at Morgan Stanley, your wisdom would be invaluable to me. Would you be willing to chat for fifteen minutes about tips and strategies I could use to land my first job? If not, are there other people in your field you recommend I talk to?

affirmatively: *"Absolutely, I would love to! I was able to connect with Alannah while she was in your class last semester and I was thrilled to hear she was in BC HR just like I was. Please feel free to reach out now or in the future through LinkedIn or my email. So great to reconnect!"* She came and did a beautiful job presenting in Belle's class. You can bet that Belle will be eager to write letters of recommendation for her in the future.

Making the Connection

The more we reflect on our network members, the more we realize how abundant our connections are. The more specific our ask for help, the more likely we are to receive it. Now comes the real challenge . . . actually having that sit-down conversation and making it count.

Here's a big tip. We build relationships with people by finding commonalities. The more we share in common with someone, the more we like them. The more we get to know anyone, the more we realize we have in common. The challenge is keeping a conversation going long enough to make these connections.

Here's a way to prepare for rich conversations. Ask yourself: *What are five things you would want to know about anyone you meet?* Write them down and then create questions to ask for each one. This simple exercise will help you invite people to share genuinely about themselves.

A variant of the same exercise helps you to prepare to do the same. Ask yourself: *What are five things I would want someone to know about me?*

In case you're wondering what you have in common with a network member who seems very different from yourself (e.g., age, race, gender, etc.), we'll let you in on a secret. You both have some sense of purpose. Here's how to get people talking about these deeper parts of themselves en route to discovering commonalities.

- Core values

  - *What do you value most about your career? In the world of work, what's most important to you?*

  - *What should I value in college/career/life?*

- Character strengths

  - *What are some things someone needs to be good at in order to succeed in your profession?*

  - *What makes you good at your job? What's been the secret to your success?*

- Skills

  - *What skills have you learned over your career? What skills are you focused on mastering now?*

  - *What are some skills you think I should invest in? Why?*

- Being of service

  - *What positive impact are you trying to make in your position? Who are you helping? Why is making this impact important to you?*

  - *What problems are most pressing for your organization/clients?*

Inevitably, in answering these questions, commonalities will surface. And as we point out the shared values, strengths, skills, or impact, meaningful connections will form.

In the process of talking about purpose, there will be opportunities for you to ask for information, advice, and wisdom:

- Asking for information

  - *What does your company do? Do they make a product or provide a service?*

  - *What other organizations focus in this area?*

- Asking for advice

  - *What would you recommend I do in my situation?*

  - *If you were in my shoes, what would you do?*

- Asking for wisdom

  - *What life lessons have you learned throughout your own career?*

  - *What's some advice you would go back and give to yourself at my age?*

- Recommendations

  - *Are there other companies/organizations I should look into?*

  - *Are there any opportunities or resources that I should check out?*

  - *Are there books I should read or podcasts I should listen to?*

— *Are there other people in this space I should be talking to? Would you mind connecting us?*

The more conversations we have like this, the more knowledge and wisdom we will acquire. We'll build on opportunities and understanding of the job landscape. We'll walk away each time with insights to help us navigate our journeys. And we may gain our most valued relationships of our lifetime.

Closing with Gratitude

After connecting with our network members, we should always express appreciation by explaining the help and value they provided. A gratitude letter can follow this template:

1. Thank them for the *action* they took ("thanks for sitting down with me," "thanks for responding to my email," etc.).

2. Explain specifically how they helped you. What valuable information, advice, wisdom, or recommendations did they provide ("your insights on the difference between a PhD in counseling psychology and MA in social work provided me a much clearer picture of the two professions")?

3. Share with them the action you will now take as a result ("thanks to this conversation, I am more excited than ever to apply for such-and-such program at University College").

4. Promise to keep them updated on your journey ("I will let you know when I hear back from schools!").

5. Thank them again.

Closing the loop like this not only makes *them* feel good by letting them know how they were *of service* to you, but it also signals that they're now on your team. Keep them updated on your journey and thank them for their contributions. Beneficence in action. The people who help you often become your greatest cheerleaders, if you give them the chance. You also benefit from sending this letter. Gratitude letter writers experience increased life satisfaction and decreased depressive symptoms.[63] Recent top Twitter trends show that despite overarching anxiety and sadness during the COVID-19 year, tweets that express gratitude have increased 20 percent.[64] People look for something to be grateful for in the midst of difficult times.

In for the Win

Once we've explored and discovered our direction, how do we get accepted into the school, program, or job? In other words, how do we convince an employer or admissions committee to give us a shot? Here's another secret. Selection committees and interviewers need to be convinced of three things:

- Will you work hard?

- Do you have the skills to be successful?

- Will you work well with others?

Answering these (sometimes unspoken) questions well can seal the deal.

Will You Work Hard?

The admissions committee wants to know if you will invest in your classes, take advantage of all the resources available to you, and be "all in" at their institution. Employers want to know if you will meet deadlines and go the extra mile to be successful. Whether they directly ask or not, they're looking for evidence of your motivation to invest in their position.

An effective and genuine way to show them your motivation is to share with them your fifth purpose principle—the need you want to meet in the world. Share the story of your calling and why it's important to you. Show them how you can pursue this aspiration by joining their organization. Show them how the position you're applying for will help you pursue your aspiration to make a particular contribution. When colleges or employers understand the impact you want to make, and how it's connected to their position or organization, they'll appreciate the depth of your intrinsic motivation.

Can You Be Successful?

Besides the motivation to work hard, organizations want to know if you have the competencies to do the job. You can address this question (whether or not they ask you directly) by communicating your strengths and the skills you want to master. Study the list of strengths and skills listed in their job posting. Then show your work. In other words, use specific examples to show them how your strengths align with the strengths they're looking for. Tell stories of times you've leveraged these strengths in and out of school. List some skills you've committed to mastering over time, and describe how their organization provides you an opportunity to do so. If you don't have a specific skill they are looking for, you can turn this into your advantage; as a lifelong learner, you're most interested in this college or position because it provides an opportunity to build skills you're eager to develop. Express your ambition, motivation, and long-term commitment.

Can You Play Nicely with Others?

The third thing organizations want to know is what you'll add to their community. Will you be a good team player? Will you be a positive addition to the organizational culture? Are you someone people in their community will like and want to work with? Maintaining a positive and healthy culture is a top priority in most organizations. You can have all the motivation and skills in the world, but if no one wants to be around you, it's a nonstarter. To give them a sense of your kindred spirit and character, show them how your core values align with the organization's core values.

9

Work (and the World)

Cultivate an inner world that ripples into the outer world.

You never change things by fighting the existing reality. To change something, build a new model that makes the existing model obsolete.

—BUCKMINSTER FULLER

Create, Don't Conform

A famous commencement speech begins:

> *There are these two young fish swimming along and they happen to meet an older fish swimming the other way, who nods at them and says "Morning, boys. How's the water?" And the two young fish swim on for a bit, and then eventually one of them looks over at the other and goes "What the hell is water?"*[1]

As we rush through our days, overworked and underresourced, we often don't notice the most important realities that shape our lives. We think we're calling all the shots, but we don't see how our environments influence the choices we make. In the last three chapters, we've brought to light how three key environments shape our purpose: relationships, high school, and higher ed. This last chapter zooms out further to look at the workplace and larger society as settings that also shape purpose. We are like fish—and our homes, schools, and workplaces are the waters we swim in.

Business Is Booming

The US economy has been on an incredible run in the twenty-first century. Despite two recessions, the GDP has doubled from 10.3 to 20.9 trillion since 2000.[2] In the last decade, 22.6 million jobs have been created.[3] In 2020, the unemployment rate of 3.5 percent matched a low from half a century ago and was only a third of the level at the start of the decade.[4] Judging by these metrics, the United States is clearly winning.

Unfortunately the same can't be said of the average American household. Average household wealth has only grown 0.3 percent[5] and wages have remained stagnant.[6] Meanwhile, costs of living have risen dramatically. In the last decade, the cost of attending universities has jumped 144 percent for private universities and 211 percent for public universities.[7] In the same span of time, rent prices have increased an average of 8.86 percent every year, significantly outpacing wage inflation,[8] and average family health premiums have increased 55 percent, twice as fast as wages and inflation.[9]

So where has that $10 trillion in generated wealth gone? In his book *Winners Take All*, Anand Giridharadas notes that "the average pretax income of the top tenth of Americans has doubled since 1980, that of the top 1 percent has more than tripled, and that of the top 0.001 percent has risen more than sevenfold—even as the average pretax income of the bottom half of Americans has stayed almost precisely the same."[10] The twenty richest Americans own more wealth than the bottom half of all Americans—a total of 152 million people.[11]

When Winning Makes Us Lose

Whether or not you experience income inequality directly, you are probably *feeling* its impact. As we noted in the beginning of this book, over the last twenty years, rates of depression have risen across the board in the United States. Young people have been hit especially hard; between 2009 and 2017, rates of depression rose by more than 60 percent among those age fourteen to seventeen, and 47 percent among those age twelve to thirteen.[12] What's especially surprising is *who* is at risk for behavioral and mental health problems; research suggests that adolescent health risks come from *both* ends of the economic spectrum, and may be driven by school contexts.[13] It's understandable that people struggling with poverty and income insecurity would suffer from such health risks. Yet those who are "winning" the economic race are also clearly struggling.[14]

The psychological effects of inequality affect *everyone*. Consider this: Do you feel like *you* are winning? Do you feel stable, safe, or secure with your position in life? Are you satisfied with what you have? Are you navigating life with a sense of ease, fulfillment, and contentment?

Or do you feel the need to prove yourself? Do you feel an urgency to keep hustling and striving just to maintain? If yes, you're experiencing the psychological effects of *scarcity* generated from a society shaped by inequality.

Not Enough

As described in chapter 1, scarcity is the feeling of "not enough."

Not *having* enough.

Not *being* enough.

Not having enough education, work experience, or expertise. Not having enough healthcare, savings, or days off. Not having enough time, attention, or energy.

Not being smart, funny, creative, skinny, good-looking, rich enough . . .

and on and on. Scarcity comes in all shapes and sizes and is the respecter of none. No matter how much we have going for us, few escape the tentacles of scarcity thinking.

When Americans were asked how much money would be "enough" to get by, people who made less than $30,000 a year said they needed $43,000 to get by.[15] People who made $40,000 said they needed $55,100. People making $60,000 said $69,400.

We tend to think that "enough" is more than what we have. Also notice that everyone's definition of enough is different. In other words, we tend to feel like we don't have enough, even though we don't know what "enough" *is*. Is it affordable rent? Owning our own house? A job with a dignified title? How much *is enough,* really?

Is Enough-ness Absolute or Relative?

From a money perspective, there are two ways to gauge *enough-ness.* One focuses on whether you have enough money to meet your material needs. This is called *absolute income.* The other focuses on whether you have enough based on how you measure up to others. This is called *relative income.*

Research has shown that an increase in *absolute income* does indeed make our lives better. The increase gives us an opportunity to buy material goods, experiences, and a sense of security. Money *does* buy happiness . . . but not for everyone.

Increased absolute income is most helpful to people who don't have enough to meet their material needs. If you're homeless and hungry, your neighbor's salary is not your concern. You just want enough money to put a roof over your head and food on the table. And having the amount you need to cover this will be a huge boon to your well-being. In countries with greater levels of poverty and lack of access to education, absolute income is positively correlated with life satisfaction.[16]

What about for everyone else? How important is absolute income *once your material needs are met*? Research shows that there are diminishing returns to the happiness we feel from absolute income.[17] Contrary to what we think, buying more and more material things beyond those actually needed will not satisfy us. The more our basic needs are met, the less absolute income impacts us. The link between happiness and absolute income is *weakest* in more materially rich, educated countries.[18]

Keeping Up with the Joneses

That said, why do so many of us strive to death over increasing our incomes even when our material needs are met? Seems as if the *more* money we make, the more we want. This brings us to the second way we gauge enough-ness.

Once our basic needs are met we shift from worrying about our absolute income to worrying about our relative income. Perceived relative income is an invisible yet powerful motivator. In *The Broken Ladder*, Keith Payne notes:

> When a neighbor pulls up in a new car, we don't typically say to ourselves, "They have an Audi, so I need one, too." We are more sophisticated and mature than that. We might tell ourselves that our neighbor's good fortune is none of our business, or that she deserves the new car because of her hard work. If we do have an immediate impulse to keep pace with her, we might banish the thought as soon as it appears. And yet, the next time we get in our own car, we notice just a little more than yesterday how worn the seat is getting. Social comparison is inevitable.[19]

Which amount would you choose to earn, A or B:

A. $82,000 per year while everyone else made $41,000?

B. $164,000 per year while everyone else made $328,000?

In one study, a majority of people chose option A.[20] It felt more important to make more money than others, even if it was half of what could be earned.[21] People tend to prioritize *relative income* over *absolute income*.

Seems absurd, but it's real. This built-in drive we have toward social comparison consumes people. Feeling like we have less than other people makes us miserable. People who live in wealthier neighborhoods report *lower* levels of well-being than those with comparable incomes who live in poorer neighborhoods.[22] Having rich neighbors makes us *more* unhappy.[23] Why is this? Because it causes relative deprivation: the more we feel that people around us are doing better than us, the worse we feel about how *we* are doing. Relative deprivation makes us feel like *we're* not enough. And our relative standing makes a huge difference in our happiness and health. Compared with *actual* social status, *perceptions* of oneself as lower than others in social status were more consistently correlated with psychological and physical health problems.[24] In other words, we gauge whether we are enough by how we compare with others more than by whether our needs are actually met. Even if we're perfectly well-off, we feel like we might not be if our neighbors have more than us.

Our sense of "not enough" keeps growing, in part because of the growing hole in our social safety net. Sixty percent of millennials don't have enough money to cover a $1,000 emergency.[25] Two out of three Americans live paycheck to paycheck, especially millennials.[26] And two out of three worry that they won't be able to afford healthcare in the coming year.[27] These numbers tell the story: a majority of people feel they don't have the absolute income they need to just get by. Is it any wonder that the poorest Americans are getting depressed? They are getting left behind, even as the United States boasts the highest gross domestic product ever generated by a country (over $22 trillion in 2021).

Mountains and Molehills

Income inequality isn't just a problem for absolute income. Relative income is also becoming an increasing sore spot. Especially for more affluent people. Imagine that income was akin to levels in a pyramid. For every dollar of income earned, you can add an inch to your location in a pyramid. One in five Americans have zero or negative wealth[28]—they are on the ground level of the pyramid . . . maybe even the basement. Fifty percent of workers make $18,000 a year, so their location in the pyramid is roughly equivalent to the height of the Empire State Building. The median household income is around $68,000, making an average family's location in the pyramid a mile high.[29] That's twice as tall as the tallest building in the world. Seems like a pretty sweet view until you consider that your *distant* neighbors in the top 1 percent income bracket are eight and a half miles above you, in the penthouse.[30] Their view level is nearly *twice the height of Mount Everest*. But wait, there's another level to the pyramid. The top .01 percent are 110 miles high in the clouds,[31] over *ten times* the height of Mount Everest and well above the Kármán line, which serves as the border between earth and *outer space*. Their wealth is literally out of this world. Speaking of which, Jeff Bezos's real estate is on another planet. His earnings in 2020 would place him in the loft of the pyramid, so high up that it is the equivalent of going to the moon and back.

Twice.

The average American has it much better than a poor American, and someone in the top 1 percent has seven times more money than an average American. But someone in the .01 percent has *thirteen times* more absolute income than someone in the top 1 percent. It's clear that 99.99 percent of all Americans will never be at the top of the game. Not even close. So if our well-being is riding on how we compare with others, we're not going to feel good anytime soon.

Pyramids Are Tough Places to Live

Because our larger society is one giant pyramid system—birthed from inequality, scarcity, and the performance mindset—many of the organizations within it follow suit. Most schools, colleges, and organizations are designed like mini-pyramids. And the people within these pyramids are the fish who don't notice the waters they swim in. The students and employees who work and learn in pyramids are perpetually dissatisfied with their status. They are constantly swimming upriver, fighting for limited resources, trying to do the breaststroke past others to get out front.

Swimming in these waters for long enough eventually influences how we view the world, and ourselves. Pyramids are designed to make us conform to three central beliefs and behaviors:

- *I have to be the best (so I need to constantly maximize).*

- *I am not enough (I compare myself with others, many of whom have more than me).*

- *Only the strong survive (so I act out of a scarcity mentality).*

Pyramids

Belief	Behavior
"I want to be the best."	Maximize.
"I am not enough."	Compare myself with others.
"Only the strong survive."	Act out of scarcity.

"I Want to Be the Best"

The sense of not being enough drives us to want to do more, be more, get more. We need to be the *best* to be enough. When our self-worth is defined by being the best, we become *maximizers*.[32] Maximizers obsess over external outcomes, rather than their internal purpose. We focus on the *ceiling*—whatever is the biggest, fastest, best. Maximizing can permeate every aspect of our lives. If you have ever spent hours researching the very *best* smartphone, read countless reviews merely to decide whether to watch a movie, or obsessively scoured Yelp for the *best* restaurant while on vacation, you've had a brush with maximizer thinking.

Maximizing isn't bad in itself—sometimes you want to get the best deal. When college graduates try to maximize the salary of their first job out of college, they make 20 percent more than their peers.[33]

But here's the rub. We can get sucked into thinking we need to maximize *every* decision and outcome in life. Maximizing causes us to relentlessly search and strive, and second-guess the value of what we have: *Do I have the best smartphone? The best house? The best wife? The best life?*

It makes us ambivalent: *Maybe I should replace them all.*

It causes us to obsess over future decisions: *What's the best path forward?*

It fills us with regret: *If I had only done my best in college, I wouldn't be stuck in this dead-end job.*

People who maximize are more depressed and less happy, optimistic, and satisfied with life and themselves.[34] Those college students who got 20 percent higher salaries because they were so worried about getting to the top weren't happier than their peers—they ended up more dissatisfied with their jobs.[35]

"I Am Not Enough"

One high school student in our study described it this way:

> *I've been dealing with insecurities . . . like everyone I know. I've had all the thoughts. Am I good enough? Smart enough? Popular enough? Do I look nice enough in this outfit? And I've always been such a people-pleaser. I've always felt the need to cater to everyone around me, and live up to how they see me. Being a teenager, growing up in a pandemic, with such high standards being set by social media, magazine covers, whatever you look at—it's just hard for me to hold on to the fact that those opinions of me don't matter. How do I get to that point?*

Most of us growing up in a pyramid society have experienced these thoughts. Looking to the left and the right, and *up,* and comparing ourselves with other people. What's unique about this student is that she recognizes it, and isn't willing to settle for it. This is rare because so many students just assume that this is how everyone feels, and so we should just accept it. But as you'll see, that's not true. It's possible to look beyond pyramids to see our value and truth from other sources.

The more a setting emphasizes position, rank, seniority, or any other comparison metric, the more the people in the setting are prone to a sense of inadequacy. We stake our self-worth on how we stack up to the competition. We constantly feel not enough because our eyes are on the people around us and above us. We can see that we aren't measuring up.

Often we think the best strategy to deal with this problem is to win the race to the top. But the truth is, the race never ends. There's always another ladder to climb or another foe to vanquish. It's exhausting. You strive to be the biggest fish in your high school. When you arrive, it feels fantastic for a flicker, and then you're off to college to compete with even bigger fish. Then off to the job market. Then off to climb each rung of the corporate ladder. And on and on. It's not the urge to better oneself that's the problem. It's the sense that you are not enough because of how you compare with others. The relative deprivation created by social comparison takes a tremendous toll on minds, bodies, and spirits. College students who focus most on status and self-image have the highest rates of depression and anxiety, learn less in their classes, get worse grades, have the poorest relationships, and feel like they don't belong.[36]

The "big-fish-little-pond" effect explains that students' views of themselves depend on the size of other fish in the pond. The bigger the other fish and the more comparative the setting (for example, the degree of emphasis on grades, test scores, accolades, etc.), the worse students feel about themselves. A large-scale study of secondary school students from thirty-three countries demonstrates a direct link between highly competitive programs and students' negative self-concepts.[37] Students in high-achieving schools (compared with the ones with the same ability in low-achieving schools) felt worse about their talents, abilities, and, ultimately, themselves.

"Only the Strong Survive"

The structure of a pyramid creates a feeling of scarcity. While there is plenty of surface area on the bottom, the higher we ascend, the harder it is to get to the next level, and the fewer goodies there are to go around. There's a small number of coveted spots in selective colleges. Only a handful of people are promoted to the top of an organization. And there is one valedictorian. To be the best, to reach the top, we have to battle for limited opportunities and resources. This sense of scarcity contributes to zero-sum thinking. If someone else gets the spot, there won't be a spot for me. Remember the game of musical chairs? Do you see kids standing politely to the side so that others can take their first grab of chairs? No one wants to be left standing.

Heather McGhee argues that this type of thinking, that others will profit only at our expense, has been a foundational belief that has stoked racial tensions and aggression toward others throughout the history of the United States.[38] The same ideas that have created racial inequality have created economic inequality; there just isn't enough to go around. We can't afford to give anything up, to extend more opportunity to more people, because it will come at our expense. The taller the pyramid, the bigger the gap between the haves and the have-nots, the *harder* we have to fight for our slice.

Masters of the Universe

In February 2021, a group of junior analysts at Goldman Sachs made headlines when results of their internal survey went viral. The survey detailed the working conditions and overall well-being of the analysts. They were making around $80,000 a year, which is a great salary for someone right out of college. However, they were also working almost one hundred hours a week, sleeping five hours a night, and suffering from plummeting mental and physical health since their arrival. On a scale from 1 to 10 (with 10 being the best, and 1 the worst), they scored their happiness at work a 2. And their personal life as a 1. Each analyst was miserable and none expected to last six months at the company.

A junior analyst position at Goldman Sachs is highly coveted and competitive. Only 4 percent of applicants earn this spot.[39] So the young professionals surveyed were the elite of the elite. They were the winners. Top of their pyramid. What did they have to show for it? Sleep deprivation. Crippling anxiety. A growing sense that their days in this workplace were numbered.

We are not commenting on whether to pursue careers in finance. Just that when students are driven from a place of scarcity, insecurity, and comparison with others, we know where this road will lead.

Signs You Are Suffering in a Pyramid

- You are a perfectionist and overachiever who needs to maximize/optimize everything.

- You constantly compare yourself with other people and struggle with feeling like you are not good enough.

- You never feel like you *have* enough (time, energy, opportunity, attention).

- You feel bad when you see other people succeeding.

- You always feel the need to prove yourself.

- You are never *satisfied*. You are always looking up: you want to do more and be better.

- Good never feels good enough.

- You are relentlessly focused on the future or second-guessing your past—never in the present.

- If you are not always hustling, you will be left behind.

- When you take a break from email, you turn on your automatic out-of-office reply . . . even though it's a weekend.

Made for More

Maybe we've convinced you that the pyramids that humans have built *stink*. They're exhausting. Maybe you're a manager or policy-maker and you recognize the ways *you* contribute to sustaining pyramids every day.

But a nagging voice in the back of your head reminds you that *this* is the reality of the world you live in. You might not like it, but you best stay in the game. Sure, pyramids aren't fair, but that's not your problem. *You* didn't create the system. Besides, playing the game well is what's gotten you admission to top colleges, top jobs, and all manner of success and accolades. Perhaps it's why you're reading this book—anything to give you an edge. By gosh, you're certainly not going to be the dope who stops playing and gives up your chair.

We get it. We get the fear that pyramids are all we have. That it seems like we don't have a choice. And yet we also know that we were made for more. We can live a different life. In one of two ways. First, we can change ourselves. We start by resisting the urge to play into the rules of the pyramid. And we take responsibility for our part in it.

Maybe we remain working in pyramids but initiate small decisions that begin to shift culture there, or maybe we hatch new systems altogether. Indeed, it's possible to create *ecosystems:* groups of people who work together toward a shared purpose.

Ecosystems support people to have three freeing beliefs:

- *I want to be my best self: instead of trying to maximize everything, I am fulfilled when I have what I need to live my calling.*

- *I am enough: instead of comparing myself with others, I look inward for wholeness.*

- *Everyone can win: I act out of a sense of abundance and gratitude.*

Ecosystems

Belief	Behavior
"I want to be my best self."	Fulfill.
"I am enough."	Fix eyes inward.
"Everyone can win."	Act out of abundance.

"I Want to Be My Best Self"

Recall that people in pyramids relentlessly reach higher toward the ceiling, because what they've done and what they've got is simply not enough. People in ecosystems, on the other hand, are freed up to embrace the present. Rather than reaching for ceilings, they find *floors*. Finding a floor is creating a line in the sand that says *this* is enough to make me happy. It's saying that *this* is enough money, enough prestige, enough status. It's standing comfortably in that place. They feel grounded once they've found the floor and they're standing on it. They've moved away from the maximizer's impulse to seek excess in everything. They've become *fulfillers*. Rather than forever striving for ceilings to prove themselves worthy, they remain grounded once their needs are fulfilled. This is not the same as underachieving or lacking ambition. These people are constantly growing, motivated to be their best selves, rather than someone else.

Research shows that there are immense benefits in becoming a fulfiller. Fulfillers are less depressed and anxious, more optimistic and happy, and more satisfied with their decisions and lives.[40] No longer a slave to perceived relative needs, they fulfill absolute needs. Instead of constantly pushing toward more than they need, they marvel at what they have. They feel grounded and content.

"I Am Enough"

Recall that people in pyramids struggle with never feeling satisfied for long. It just seems that they're not as good as the people they've got their eyes on. People in ecosystems are valued for who they are. Right here, right now. They're not looking outward for approval or for a reference point to compare themselves with. Instead they are listening to their inward call. It may not even be a call for any power or prestige. And that is just fine, because they know that who they are is enough. Their self-image is not solely based on what others think of them. No person (or societal measuring stick) gets to tell them who they are or what they are worth. Instead they attune inward for who they are and who they're called to be. They recognize their own inherent value. No one needs to prove their self-worth.

"Everyone Can Win"

This is not the same as "everyone gets a trophy," which is still a pyramid goal. Where pyramid cultures promote a feeling of scarcity, ecosystems foster a sense of abundance. And profound gratitude. A fundamental belief of a thriving ecosystem is that what goes around comes around. When we are for each other, committed to meeting the needs of the community, individual needs will be met as well. Since people are contributing to one another, a sense of trust grows that *there will be enough for everyone*. And since there is enough to go around, we don't need to be stingy and tight-fisted. We can be generous and openhanded.

To be clear, it's not that ecosystems are perfect because they're filled with perfect people. And it's not that there's no competition in an ecosystem. It's possible to cooperate and compete at the same time. However, our motivations for competition differ in pyramids versus ecosystems. In pyramids, we compete to outperform others. Our self-worth feels dependent on how we stack up. In ecosystems, we compete to become the best versions of ourselves. Our self-worth doesn't depend on the results of the competition. Tom Brady described cooperative competition this way: "You do your job so everyone around you can do *their* job."[41] Similarly, Bill Russell said: "My ego demands, for myself, the success of my team."[42] This is the opposite of zero-sum thinking; true communities create win-win situations. Success isn't defined by how you compare with others, but by how you contribute to them.

Survival of the Fittest

"Survival of the fittest" is the phrase that people tend to associate with Darwin's theory of evolution. And it fits with the pyramid rule of thumb—that "the best person wins." Yet individual selection was just one small part of Darwin's theory. He pointed out that groups that cooperate with one another win out over groups that strictly compete against one another.[43] Think of prairie dogs using systems of predatory warning and elephants raising their young cooperatively.[44] Thousands of honeybees cooperate in building their nest, collecting their food, and rearing their brood. Each member makes a valuable contribution to the brood.

Darwin's theory applied to pyramids might predict that individuals climbing the pyramid may beat out other individual competitors, but a group of people who work as a team will rule the day. David Sloan Wilson put it this way: "Selfishness beats altruism within groups. Altruistic groups beat selfish groups."[45] Effective groups overcome individual self-interest to advance the well-being of the entire group; this is the great unlock of the human race. Humans haven't advanced due to any special physical strength, speed, or the sharpness of their teeth. Whether it was hunter-gatherers, agrarian farmers, or the twentieth-century social state, humans have prevailed when we cooperated with one another.

The scientist William Muir provided a powerful illustration of pyramids.[46] He created two groups of chickens and bred them to see which group could produce the most eggs. In the first group he selected the chickens who produced the most eggs and mated them with other super-successful chickens. He did this for several generations to create a group of superstar chickens. At the same time, he selected a group of run-of-the-mill chickens to compete against the superstars. Some of these average chickens were great producers; some barely produced any eggs at all. After seven generations, what happened?

The superstar chickens got *crushed* by the average chickens. Muir actually had to stop the experiment early because only three superstar chickens were still alive—the rest killed each other off in the effort to become the alpha chicken. The average chickens ultimately produced 160 percent more eggs than their superstar compatriots.

Muir attributed the average chicken's overwhelming success to one thing—*they didn't care about the pecking order*. Instead of a pyramid that fostered intra-group competition, theirs was an ecosystem where every chicken could contribute. A cooperative group defeated a group of selfish chickens.

It's not only chickens who suffer from pecking orders. In pyramids, our worth is defined by our position in the pecking order. When humans obsess over where we stand, live, or work relative to others, resentment reigns and teamwork deteriorates. NFL and MLB teams with greater degrees of pay inequality (that is, members of the same team living on very different floors of the pyramid) perform worse on the field and lose more games.[47] In factories with greater pay inequality, employees are less productive, and are more likely to miss work.[48] Companies with greater pay inequity make poorer-quality consumer products.[49] College professors who work at institutions with greater pay inequality are less productive, less likely to work together, and less satisfied with their jobs.[50] The more organizations are structured as pyramids marked by inequity, the worse the morale of their members, the worse that organization performs.

The Glue

Sports journalist Sam Walker spent eleven years trying to find the secret ingredient that made the best teams thrive. He analyzed more than twelve hundred teams in thirty-seven different sports over the past 150 years.[51] He then identified the top 0.1 percent of teams that had garnered the most success over time. Dynasties. His list included the 1960s Celtics, the 1990s US women's soccer team, the New Zealand All Blacks rugby team, and the Cuban women's volleyball team, among others. He was looking for evidence of any similarities across these uber-successful teams.

One common characteristic surfaced. Was it a "once-in-a-generation" talent? A collection of superhumans? The amount of time spent practicing? A legendary coach? Well, many of the teams in the study had these characteristics, but there was only *one* thing that *every* single great team had.

A captain who rallied the team.

Walker's research found that the beginning of a successful run always coincided with a captain taking on team leadership, and the end of that run concluded with a captain vacating their role. This held true across all teams. What's even more interesting is the type of captain who led the team. These captains were rarely the best players. They weren't necessarily giving impassioned locker room speeches. It wasn't their talents that made them effective, it was their *character*. These captains—including the likes of Yogi Berra, Tim Duncan, Bill Russell, and Carla Overbeck—all had three character qualities.

Unwavering commitment to the group's purpose. They had what Walker describes as "extreme doggedness and focus on competition." They would do anything needed, including testing the limits of the rules combined with aggressive play. They made clear that the *team's* success was the most noble and supreme goal.

Glue that holds the team together. While they may have played loudly on the field, these captains were never the center of attention off the field. They led by example; they were willing to get their hands dirty and do the thankless jobs, and they motivated others with "passionate nonverbal displays." When they communicated, they did so with understated, practical, and democratic communication styles. Not to put themselves at the center of the group, but to draw the members to the center.

Leadership aligned with personal purpose. These captains were not perfect. Sometimes they clashed with coaches, owners, and people outside the team. Yet they were respected for their courage in standing up for strong, personal convictions, especially to protect the team. So, while they were all about team outcomes, they were intentional about leading and playing in a way that aligned with their own clear sense of self.

In sum, creating harmonious ecosystems was at the heart of team success. These ecosystems were marked by collective individualism. The entire team valued what each individual brought to the table. And each player fully bought into what the team was trying to accomplish. Win-win relationships.

Harmonious ecosystems understand that helping members become their best selves is good for the community, too. After all, individuals make up the ecosystem. The ecosystem needs them to survive and thrive.

Where a pyramid causes members to all dive for the biggest piece of pie, an ecosystem inspires members to contribute to making the *pie bigger* for all to enjoy.

Is Change Possible?

Can we really influence the water we swim in? As it turns out, fish can make a difference. Researchers have shown that fish contribute more nutrients to their marine ecosystem than any other source.[52] The impact they make is enough to cause changes in the growth of the organisms they live with. We, too, can influence the waters we swim in with the daily choices we make about how we spend our time there.

Take a Temperature Check

There is a popular urban myth that if you put a frog in boiling water, it will jump right out. But if you put it in lukewarm water and slowly increase the temperature over time, the frog will stay put until it boils to death. Rising income inequality has heated the waters we swim in, slowly. Insidiously turning our world into a pyramid. If we want to change the waters we swim in, start with this temperature check:

What type of systems do you and your students live in?

Critically reflect on your high school, college, or organization. What's its mission or purpose? In other words, why does it exist? Is there a shared mission that everyone in the organization would agree on? *Stated* purpose is not the same as *lived purpose*. What are the most important or tracked outcomes? What metrics are held in highest regard?

If the school's ulterior motive is to get its students into as many prestigious universities as possible, you'll see evidence of this in its structures, rules, processes, and people. GPAs will be a top indicator of success. Same with Advanced Placement courses. Students will feel pressured to take the hardest classes they can, not because they love to learn, but because it will strengthen their college applications. As will service and volunteer work. It's important to do that, too, for the sake of looking good (rather than doing good). And even after working their fingers to the bone at great personal cost, they're still likely to believe: *I am not enough (there are people better than me). I have to be the best (I must try harder). Only the strong survive (there aren't enough resources for everyone).*

How do we change persistent outcomes like these? This process begins when leaders and members reflect honestly on whether their mission or purpose promotes pyramid thinking. Does the purpose or mission create:

- Zero-sum attitudes and performance mindsets?

- A sense of scarcity and artificial core values?

- Comparison between members and an obsession with fixed games?

- Inequity so that only an elite few benefit?

Does the purpose or mission cause people:

- To constantly feel "not enough"?

- To feel the need to be the best in everything?

- To protect and fight for their share, since only the strongest survive?

If you answered yes to the questions above, chances are you're stuck in a pyramid. Another sign of a pyramid is you have trouble articulating the organization's purpose. Without a clearly defined shared mission, any organization's goal defaults to *fighting for the biggest slice of the pie*, be it grades, college admissions, or market capitalization. Thankfully, there's a simple first step toward changing organizational culture, one that you're now fully aware of: *purposeful reflection*. Bring your community together and consider:

- What do we value most as a community? What are we willing to sacrifice for?

- What strengths do we want our members to use?

- What skills do we want people to learn and master?

- What needs are we trying to meet for ourselves, our community, and the world?

Redesigning pyramids starts by giving people the space to reflect on the organizational purpose and their own purpose. This simple and small act can have outsized results, especially in the world of work. When it comes down to it, people from all walks of life experience fulfillment at work and general well-being when their workplaces help them meet five needs: survival, contribution, mastery, connection with others, and purpose. "Decent" work meets these five needs.[53] When people are given the autonomy to change and design their work so that it aligns better with their purpose, they experience improved well-being, work engagement, and performance. In contrast to a top-down approach that forces the same changes on everyone in an organization, the benefits of this bottom-up approach demonstrate the importance of giving workers the freedom to reflect on personally meaningful aspirations and skills. And when workers are given this freedom and choice to shape their work accordingly, it makes them more satisfied and more productive.[54] And interventions at work aimed at building a sense of belonging and community improve well-being, job satisfaction, and organizational commitment while lowering absenteeism and turnover intent.[55] The only way we can break down pyramids is by getting intentional about the ecosystems we want to inhabit.

To What End?

Once when Belle was in graduate school, her significant other, David, asked her what she wanted to do with her life. She answered, "To be a professor." And to her surprise, he responded, "Your dreams are too small." What was he talking about? As a first-generation doctoral student, she thought most would agree that she was shooting pretty high. She was baffled by this response, and has never forgotten it. Today she understands her humble (now) husband's meaning so much better. His words were not a condemnation of professors. Nor a criticism that she wasn't shooting high, or maximizing enough. He was asking, "So, you want to be a professor . . . but to what end?" His words were a charge to dream bigger. To set her sights on more than what she could be (an end destination), to the reason *behind* becoming a professor. Toward the more expansive calling that's not fenced in by a particular role or job. What work was she longing to do? What contribution and change did she envision she could make by becoming a professor? This book on the work she and Tim are doing is about this bigger dream and purpose.

Dear friends, we wish the same for you. There is so much adventure that awaits you.

Conclusion

The soul [authentic self] grows by subtraction, not addition.

—HENRY DAVID THOREAU

Less Is More

Michelangelo's *David* is considered one of the most beautiful sculptures in the history of art. The sculptor's description of how he created the angel went something like this: *I came across a big, ugly block of marble, and in it, I saw David. All I had to do was chip away the excess stone.*

Like Michelangelo, all we have to do is chip away the excess stone—our insecurities, fears, biases, distractions—to set our authentic selves free. Good editors do the same with a rough draft. They see the essence of a beautiful story buried under authorial insecurities, fears, biases, and distractions, clearing them away to expose the story's greater truths.

Once your authentic self comes into view, it becomes a powerful compass for navigating life. *With greater ease and joy.* We hope this book has inspired you to see your life, and the young people in it, with a fresh perspective. Use it to carve away what doesn't serve you: the siren's call of wealth, power, and prestige. An obsession with fixed games. A myopic, self-serving definition of achievement. The unattainable expectations of others. We live in a world that insists that the only way to succeed is through the power of *more:* do more, get more, be more. We are inundated with articles, podcasts, and books promising to tell us the exact things every person needs to do to be successful and happy. It's always *more.* If you take away one lesson from this book, let it be this: you have everything you need. You don't need more. You don't have to bend yourself into a pretzel to fit someone else's definition of success. You don't have to be all things to all people.

But whatever you choose to be, let it be purposeful.

ACKNOWLEDGMENTS

As an authorship team, we deeply appreciate:

Our agent, Gail Ross. You've been our bridge from the ivory tower to Main Street. You've shown us how to translate scientific findings into language real people get so they can benefit from them. You've been our greatest champion and mentor, preparing us as first-time authors to present our ideas to the top publishers in NYC. Ultimately guiding us to the best—St. Martin's Press. Making us able to take our work into the world.

Our dream editor, Elizabeth Beier. You are a muse, drawing out the creative artistry of your charges. Beyond your brilliance, you are just the loveliest human being. We scored the winning lottery ticket when you entered our lives. Thanks also to Laura Clark for bringing out the best in us during our first book pitch in NYC and taking a chance on us; Danielle Prielipp for expertly leading our marketing strategy; Gabrielle Gantz for your savvy in directing our publicity campaign; Soleil Paz, our talented jacket designer; Brigitte Dale and Hannah Phillips for shepherding the manuscript through the finest details of the editing process; and the rest of our gifted collaborators at St. Martin's Press for your creativity, invaluable guidance, and support of us.

Our students (past and present). B. L.'s research assistants, mentees, and those in her classes at Boston College. And T. K.'s students from the Boys and Girls Club, Summer Search, Medford High School, and beyond. For anyone who wonders why we have this unwavering belief in the resilience and awesomeness of the next generation, they can just take one look at *you*. The sparks who keep society moving forward.

Our research and direct service collaborators and colleagues. This book would not have been possible without years of research and direct service to understand how people grow into agents of change and contribution in the world. And this research and service would not have been possible without people like Lauren Melkus—thank you for investing in us, and partnering so faithfully as we together create tools and curricula and cultivate purpose at Boston College. It's been an immense privilege and joy to collaborate with such generous educators, researchers, philanthropists, and research participants throughout the decades, and your stories and legacies are sprinkled throughout this book.

I (B. L.) am so grateful to:

My family, for delighting in my journey. Chu-Yu, Catharine, Philip, and Ruth, for your selfless love. Eli, for cheering me on when I was first considering becoming a psychologist. David L., for cheering me on and up, period. Chach, for being my heart-shaped rock. Zoe and Toby, for being the radiant lights in my life—I love being your mom. You, along with Desiree, Evie, Marina, Connor, Ben, and Max, give me hope that the future is in good hands. Most of all, thank you David T.—you are simply my best human. You remind me how good God is.

My dearest friends and life mentors—you know who you are. Whether we are listening closely to one another, solving problems, talking one another off a ledge, praying, or celebrating life—we are *for* each other. You are my happy place. As is obvious from my research and this book, I think a lot about what makes good relationships good—you bring out the best in one another. And I learned a lot about this from you.

My coauthor, T.—working with you is so fun and interesting every day. You constantly amaze me with your out-of-the-box thinking. You are 75 percent Trailblazer and 75 percent Builder. They don't add up to 100 percent because you're so good at multitasking. Beyond these skills and strengths, it's a gift to work with someone so honorable and trustworthy. You are the real deal.

Where it all started—Lisa Damour. You planted the first seeds with your encouragement to write a book and willingness to share your own learnings as an author. Watching you use your platform to do such good has been my fuel and inspiration.

I (T. K.) am so grateful to:

My family, and especially my wife, Emily. You have always seen the best in me and pushed me to become my best self (even when I don't want to!).

This book wouldn't have been possible without your support. I'm forever grateful for Max and Theo for providing me with my purpose. A huge thank you to Tony and Jennifer for being the best parents a guy could ask for. I'm grateful for my sister, Jesse, for being the caring, thoughtful, empathetic parent every kid needs. Linda, for being the most committed and caring grandparent. Kate, who has shown me what living out your purpose really means.

I'm also hugely grateful for my Vermont people: You can't navigate life without the right crew, and I've been blessed with the best. Nate, thanks for being my sounding board on our long runs, and pretending to find my ideas interesting (even when hearing them on repeat for the thousandth time). Emily M., thank you for sharing your design talents to bring our ideas to life. Thank you to all my Boston parents. Parenting is the hardest thing in the world, and it helps to brave the journey with fellow travelers.

I also want to thank all my colleagues on this journey. I greatly appreciate your stamina and willingness to endure my endless stream of ideas and questions and my constant efforts to push the envelope and innovate the way things are done. I've been lucky enough to have people who empower me in every step of my professional journey.

And to Belle: Meeting you changed the trajectory of my career and my life for the better. I couldn't have asked for a better mentor and partner on this wild adventure of ours. Thanks for always believing in me, balancing my strengths with your incredible talents, and being such a consistent, authentic force for good. Every day, I'm grateful to be able to call you a coauthor and friend.

NOTES

1. Mindset

1. Guynn, J., Snider, M., & Tyko, K. (2020). Coronavirus fears spark "panic buying" of toilet paper, water, hand sanitizer. Here's why we all need to calm down. Retrieved from https://www.usatoday.com/story/money/2020/03/02/coronavirus -toilet-paper-shortage-stores-selling-out/4930420002/.

2. Inglehart, R., & Abramson, P.R. (1994). Economic security and value change. *American Political Science Review, 88*(2), 336–354.

3. Parker, K., & Horowitz, J.M. (2015). Parenting in America: Outlook, worries, aspirations are strongly linked to financial situation. Retrieved from https://www .pewresearch.org/social-trends/2015/12/17/parenting-in-america/.

4. Twenge, J.M. (2017). *iGen: Why Today's Super-Connected Kids Are Growing Up Less Rebellious, More Tolerant, Less Happy—and Completely Unprepared for Adulthood—and What That Means for the Rest of Us.* Simon & Schuster.

5. U.S. Bureau of Labor Statistics. (2020, May). Learn more, earn more: Education leads to higher wages, lower unemployment. *Career Outlook.* Retrieved from https:// www.bls.gov/careeroutlook/2020/data-on-display/education-pays.htm.

6. Lowrey, A. (2020). The college wealth premium has collapsed. Retrieved from https://www.theatlantic.com/ideas/archive/2020/01/college-wealth-premium -collapsed/604579/.

7. CEW Georgetown. (2021). America's divided recovery: College haves and have-nots. Retrieved from https://cew.georgetown.edu/cew-reports/americas-divided -recovery/.

8. Ibid.

9. Taras, V., Shah, G., Gunkel, M., & Tavoletti, E. (2020). Graduates of elite universities get paid more. Do they perform better? Retrieved from https://hbr. org/2020/09/graduates-of-elite-universities-get-paid-more-do-they-perform-better.

10. Lou, M., & Griggs, B. (2021). Acceptance rates at top colleges are dropping, raising pressure on high school students. Retrieved from https://www.cnn .com/2019/04/03/us/ivy-league-college-admissions-trnd/index.html.

11. National Center for Education Statistics. (2015). Postsecondary attainment: Differences by socioeconomic status. *The Condition of Education,* 1–7.

12. Maldonado, C. (2021). Price of college increasing almost 8 times faster than wages. Retrieved from https://www.forbes.com/sites/camilomaldonado/2018/07/24 /price-of-college-increasing-almost-8-times-faster-than-wages/.

13. Hanson, M. (2021). Student loan debt statistics. Retrieved from https://educationdata.org/student-loan-debt-statistics.

14. Ibid.

15. Reeves, R.V. (2018). *Dream Hoarders: How the American Upper Middle Class Is Leaving Everyone Else in the Dust, Why That Is a Problem, and What to Do About It.* Brookings Institution Press.

16. Arcidiacono, P., Kinsler, J., & Ransom, T. (2019). Legacy and athlete preferences at Harvard. Retrieved from https://www.nber.org/papers/w26316.

17. Thompson, D. (2019). The cult of rich-kid sports. Retrieved from https://www.theatlantic.com/ideas/archive/2019/10/harvard-university-and-scandal-sports-recruitment/599248/.

18. Thompson, D. (2018). American meritocracy is killing youth sports. Retrieved from https://www.theatlantic.com/ideas/archive/2018/11/income-inequality-explains-decline-youth-sports/574975/.

19. Railton, P. (2021). Moral camouflage or moral monkeys? Retrieved from https://nationalhumanitiescenter.org/on-the-human/2010/07/moral-camouflage-or-moral-monkeys.

20. Gatti, R.C. (2016). A conceptual model of new hypothesis on the evolution of biodiversity. *Biologia, 71*(3).

21. Solnit, R. (2010). *A Paradise Built in Hell: The Extraordinary Communities That Arise in Disaster.* Penguin Books.

22. Margulis, L. (2008). *Symbiotic Planet: A New Look at Evolution.* Basic Books.

23. Steinberg, L., Graham, S., O'Brien, L., Woolard, J., Cauffman, E., & Banich, M. (2009). Age differences in future orientation and delay discounting. *Child Development, 80*(1), 28–44.

24. Gardner, M., & Steinberg, L. (2005). Peer influence on risk taking, risk preference, and risky decision making in adolescence and adulthood: An experimental study. *Developmental Psychology, 41*(4), 625–635.

25. Lepper, M.R., Greene, D., & Nisbett, R.E. (1973). Undermining children's intrinsic interest with extrinsic reward: A test of the "overjustification" hypothesis. *Journal of Personality and Social Psychology, 28*(1), 129–137.

26. Aronson, E., & Carlsmith, J.M. (1963). Effect of the severity of threat on the devaluation of forbidden behavior. *Journal of Abnormal and Social Psychology, 66*(6), 584–588.

27. Dittmar, H., Bond, R., Hurst, M., & Kasser, T. (2014). The relationship between materialism and personal well-being: A meta-analysis. *Journal of Personality and Social Psychology, 107*(5), 879–924.

28. Kasser, T., & Ryan, R.M. (1993). A dark side of the American dream: Correlates of financial success as a central life aspiration. *Journal of Personality and Social Psychology, 65*(2), 410–422.

29. Kasser, T., & Ryan, R.M. (1996). Further examining the American dream: Differential correlates of intrinsic and extrinsic goals. *Personality and Social Psychology Bulletin, 22*(3), 280–287.

30. Luthar, S.S., & Latendresse, S.J. (2005). Children of the affluent: Challenges to well-being. *Current Directions in Psychological Science, 14*(1), 49–53.

31. Luthar, S.S., Suh, B.C., Ebbert, A.M., & Kumar, N.L. (2020). Students in high-achieving schools: Perils of pressures to be "standouts." *Adversity and Resilience Science, 1*(2), 135–147.

32. Spencer, R., Walks, J., Liang, B., Mousseau, A.M.D., & Lund, T.J. (2018). Having it all? A qualitative examination of affluent adolescent girls' perceptions of stress and their quests for success. *Journal of Adolescent Research, 33*(1), 3–33.

33. Kasser, T. (2002). *The High Price of Materialism.* MIT Press.

34. Ibid.

35. Spencer, K. (2017). It takes a suburb: A town struggles to ease student stress. Retrieved from https://www.nytimes.com/2017/04/05/education/edlife/over achievers-student-stress-in-high-school-.html.

36. Brackett, M. (2019). *Permission to Feel.* Celadon Books.

37. Howard, J.C. (2021). What happens in a mother's brain when her baby cries. Retrieved from https://www.cnn.com/2017/10/23/health/moms-babies-crying -response-universal-study/index.html.

38. Marlin, B.J., Mitre, M., D'Amour, J.A., Chao, M.V., & Froemke, R.C. (2015). Oxytocin enables maternal behaviour by balancing cortical inhibition. *Nature, 520*(7548), 499–504.

39. Stern, R. (2019). Mr. Rogers and the importance of social and emotional learning. Retrieved from https://thehill.com/opinion/healthcare/476163-mr-rogers -and-the-importance-of-social-and-emotional-learning.

40. Mauss, I.B., Tamir, M., Anderson, C.L., & Savino, N.S. (2011). Can seeking happiness make people unhappy? Paradoxical effects of valuing happiness. *Emotion, 11*(4), 807–815.

41. Segran, E. (2018). Zola's plan to take on the $72 billion wedding industry. Retrieved from https://www.fastcompany.com/90212949/zolas-plan-to-take-on -the-72-billion-wedding-industry.

42. Ford, B., & Mauss, I. (2014). The paradoxical effects of pursuing positive emotion. In J. Gruber & J. T. Moskowitz (Eds.), *Positive Emotion: Integrating the Light Sides and Dark Sides* (pp. 363–382). Oxford University Press.

43. Gentzler, A.L., Palmer, C.A., Ford, B.Q., Moran, K.M., & Mauss, I.B. (2019). Valuing happiness in youth: Associations with depressive symptoms and well-being. *Journal of Applied Developmental Psychology, 62,* 220–230.

44. Cyders, M.A., & Smith, G.T. (2008). Emotion-based dispositions to rash action: Positive and negative urgency. *Psychological Bulletin, 134*(6), 807–828.

45. Mauss, I.B., Tamir, M., Anderson, C.L., & Savino, N.S. (2011). Can seeking happiness make people unhappy? Paradoxical effects of valuing happiness. *Emotion, 11*(4), 807–815.

46. Damon, W. (2008). *The Path to Purpose: How Young People Find Their Calling in Life.* Simon & Schuster.

47. Bronk, K.C., Hill, P., Lapsley, D., Talib, T., & Finch, W.H. (2009). Purpose, hope, and life satisfaction in three age groups. *Journal of Positive Psychology, 4,* 500–510.

48. Crocker, J., & Canevello, A. (2008). Creating and undermining social support in communal relationships: The role of compassionate and self-image goals. *Journal of Personality and Social Psychology, 95*(3), 555–575.

49. Gallup. (2021). Forging pathways to purposeful work: The role of higher education. Retrieved from https://www.gallup.com/education/248222/gallup-bates -purposeful-work-2019.aspx.

50. *People*'s Staff. (2021). Edgar Mitchell's strange voyage. Retrieved from https://people.com/archive/edgar-mitchells-strange-voyage-vol-1-no-6/.

51. Blattner, M.C., Liang, B., Lund, T., & Spencer, R. (2013). Searching for a sense of purpose: The role of parents and effects on self-esteem among female adolescents. *Journal of Adolescence, 36,* 839–848.

52. Koren, M. (2020). Galaxy brain is real. Retrieved from https://www.the atlantic.com/science/archive/2020/12/hubble-pictures/617251/.

53. Ibid.

54. Gibran, K. (2020). *The Prophet.* Alma Classics.

55. Gallup. (2021). Forging pathways to purposeful work: The role of higher education. Retrieved from https://www.gallup.com/education/248222/gallup-bates -purposeful-work-2019.aspx.

2. Games

1. National Center for Education Statistics. (2015). Postsecondary attainment: Differences by socioeconomic status. Retrieved from https://nces.ed.gov/programs /coe/pdf/coe_tva.pdf.

2. Takahashi, D. (2020). Newzoo: 2.7 billion gamers will spend $159.3 billion on games in 2020. Retrieved from https://venturebeat.com/2020/05/08/newzoo -2-7-billion-gamers-will-spend-159-3-billion-on-games-in-2020/.

3. Chase. (2020). State of the stream December and 2020 year in review. Retrieved from https://blog.streamelements.com/state-of-the-stream-december-and -2020-year-in-review-aa4146f074be.

4. The concept is inspired by the 2013 book *Finite and Infinite Games,* by James P. Carse (Simon & Schuster). See also *The Infinite Game,* by Simon Sinek (Portfolio/ Penguin, 2019), for how this concept is adapted to a business setting.

5. Dweck, C.S., & Yeager, D.S. (2019). Mindsets: A view from two eras. *Perspectives on Psychological Science, 14*(3), 481–496.

6. McGonigal, J. (2011). *Reality Is Broken: Why Games Make Us Better and How They Can Change the World.* Penguin.

7. Spencer, R., Walsh, J., Liang, B., Mousseau, A., & Lund, T. (2016). Having it all?: A qualitative examination of affluent adolescent girls' perceptions of stress and their quests for success. *Journal of Adolescent Research, 33*(1), 3–33.

8. Cowen, T. (2012). What percentage of 7-footers are in the NBA? Retrieved from https://marginalrevolution.com/marginalrevolution/2012/05/what-percentage-of-7-footers-are-in-the-nba.html.

9. U.S. Department of Education. (2016). Advancing diversity and inclusion in higher education. Retrieved from https://www2.ed.gov/rschstat/research/pubs/advancing-diversity-inclusion.pdf.

10. Wilson, V., & Rogers III, W.M. (2016). Black-white wage gaps expand with rising wage inequality. Retrieved from https://www.epi.org/publication/black-white-wage-gaps-expand-with-rising-wage-inequality/.

11. Wilkerson, I. (2020). *Caste: The Origins of Our Discontents*, 19, 71. Random House.

12. Twenge, J.M. (2017). *iGen: Why Today's Super-Connected Kids Are Growing Up Less Rebellious, More Tolerant, Less Happy—and Completely Unprepared for Adulthood—and What That Means for the Rest of Us*. Simon & Schuster.

13. Ryan, R.M., & Deci, E.L. (2020). Intrinsic and extrinsic motivation from a self-determination theory perspective: Definitions, theory, practices, and future directions. *Contemporary Educational Psychology, 61*, Article 101860.

14. Klapp, A. (2015). Does grading affect educational attainment? A longitudinal study. *Assessment in Education: Principles, Policy & Practice, 22*(3), 302–323.

15. Kaplan, A., & Maehr, M.L. (2007). The contributions and prospects of goal orientation theory. *Educational Psychology Review, 19*(2), 141–184.

16. Deci, E.L., & Ryan, R.M. (Eds.). (2004). *Handbook of Self-Determination Research*. University of Rochester Press.

17. Sheldon, K.M., & Krieger, L.S. (2014). Service job lawyers are happier than money job lawyers, despite their lower income. *Journal of Positive Psychology, 9*(3), 219–226.

18. Landry, A.T., Kindlein, J., Trépanier, S.-G., Forest, J., Zigarmi, D., Houson, D., & Brodbeck, F.C. (2016). Why individuals want money is what matters: Using self-determination theory to explain the differential relationship between motives for making money and employee psychological health. *Motivation and Emotion, 40*(2), 226–242.

19. Tang, X., Li, Y., Duan, W., Mu, W., & Cheng, X. (2019). Character strengths lead to satisfactory educational outcomes through strength use: A longitudinal analysis. *Frontiers in Psychology, 10*, Article 1829.

20. Sorenson, S. (2014). How employee's strengths make your company stronger. Retrieved from https://www.gallup.com/workplace/231605/employees-strengths-company-stronger.aspx.

21. Wooden, J., & Carty, J. (2005). *Coach Wooden's Pyramid of Success Playbook*. Revell.

22. Liang, B., White, A., Rhodes, H., Strodel, R., Gutowski, E., Mousseau, A., & Lund, T. (2017). Pathways to purpose among impoverished youth from the Guatemala City dump community. *Community Psychology in Global Perspective, 3*, 1–21.

23. Niemiec, R.M., & McGrath, R.E. (2019). *The Power of Character Strengths: Appreciate and Ignite Your Positive Personality.* VIA Institute on Character.

24. Smeding, A., Darnon, C., Souchal, C., Toczek-Capelle, M.-C., & Butera, F. (2013). Reducing the socio-economic status achievement gap at university by promoting mastery-oriented assessment. *PLOS One, 8*(8), Article e71678.

25. Deci, E.L., & Ryan, R.M. (Eds.). (2004). *Handbook of Self-Determination Research.* University of Rochester Press.

26. Vasquez, A.C., Patall, E.A., Fong, C.J., Corrigan, A.S., & Pine, L. (2016). Parent autonomy support, academic achievement, and psychosocial functioning: A meta-analysis of research. *Educational Psychology Review, 28*(3), 605–644.

3. Skill Sets

1. Palmer, P. (2004). *A Hidden Wholeness: The Journey Toward an Undivided Life.* John Wiley & Sons.

2. Berthene, A. (2019). 82 percent of US households have an Amazon Prime membership. Retrieved from https://www.digitalcommerce360.com/2019/07/11/82-of-us-households-have-a-amazon-prime-membership/.

3. Johnson, J. (2021). Global market share of search engines 2010–2021. Retrieved from https://www.statista.com/statistics/216573/worldwide-market-share-of-search-engines/#:~:text=Ever%20since%20the%20introduction%20of,share%20as%20of%20July%202020.

4. Mohsin, M. (2020). 10 Google search statistics you need to know in 2021. Retrieved from https://www.oberlo.com/blog/google-search-statistics.

5. Statista Research Department. (2021). Facebook: Number of monthly active users worldwide 2008–2021. Retrieved from https://www.statista.com/statistics/264810/number-of-monthly-active-facebook-users-worldwide/.

6. Roser, M., Ortiz-Ospina, E., & Ritchie, H. (2019). Life expectancy. Retrieved from https://ourworldindata.org/life-expectancy.

7. Federal Reserve Economic Data. (2020). Infant mortality rate for the United States. Retrieved from https://fred.stlouisfed.org/series/SPDYNIMRTINUSA.

8. Madrigal, A. (2019). Your smart toaster can't hold a candle to the Apollo computer. Retrieved from https://www.theatlantic.com/science/archive/2019/07/underappreciated-power-apollo-computer/594121/.

9. Schumpeter, J.A. (1942). Creative Destruction. In *Capitalism, Socialism, and Democracy.* 3d ed. New York: Harper and Brothers.

10. Muro, M., Maxim, R., & Whiton, J. (2019). Automation and artificial intelligence: How machines are affecting people and places. Retrieved from https://www.brookings.edu/research/automation-and-artificial-intelligence-how-machines-affect-people-and-places/.

11. Cone, E., & Lambert, J. (2021). How robots change the world: What automation really means for jobs, productivity and regions. Retrieved from https://www.oxfordeconomics.com/recent-releases/how-robots-change-the-world.

12. Zahidi, S. (2021). We need a global reskilling revolution—here's why. Retrieved from https://www.weforum.org/agenda/2020/01/reskilling-revolution-jobs-future-skills/.

13. Goos, M., Manning, A., & Salomons, A. (2014). Explaining job polarization: Routine-biased technological change and offshoring. *American Economic Review, 104*(8), 2509–2526.

14. Stack Exchange. (2019). What is the purpose of this "red room" in Stranger Things? Retrieved from https://movies.stackexchange.com/questions/102266/what-is-the-purpose-of-this-red-room-in-stranger-things.

15. Roser, M. (2013, updated daily). Employment in agriculture. Retrieved from https://ourworldindata.org/employment-in-agriculture.

16. Muro, M., Whiton, J. & Maxim, R. (2019). What jobs are affected by AI?: Better-paid, better-educated workers face the most exposure. Retrieved from https://www.brookings.edu/research/what-jobs-are-affected-by-ai-better-paid-better-educated-workers-face-the-most-exposure/.

17. Haggerty, J. (2021). Objections overruled: The case for disruptive technology in the legal profession. Retrieved from https://www2.deloitte.com/content/dam/Deloitte/uk/Documents/corporate-finance/deloitte-uk-technology-in-law-firms.pdf.

18. Gruetzemacher, R., Paradice, D., & Bok, L.K. (2020). Forecasting extreme labor displacement: A survey of AI practitioners. *Technological Forecasting and Social Change, 161,* Article 120323.

19. Grant, A.M. (2016). *Originals: How Non-Conformists Move the World.* Penguin Books.

20. Brekelmans, S., & Petropoulos, G. (2020). Occupational change, artificial intelligence and the geography of EU labour markets [Working paper]. *Bruegel, 3,* 1–32.

21. Deming, D.J., & Noray, K. (2020). Earnings dynamics, changing job skills, and STEM careers. *Quarterly Journal of Economics, 135*(4), 1965–2005.

22. Nietzel, M.T. (2020). New report: The size of the college earnings premium depends on where you live. Retrieved from https://www.forbes.com/sites/michaeltnietzel/2020/05/19/new-report-the-size-of-the-college-earnings-premium-depends-on-where-you-live/?sh=653649dd2dc3.

23. Altonji, J.G., Arcidiacono, P.S., & Maurel, A. (2015). The analysis of field choice in college and graduate school: Determinants and wage effects. National Bureau of Economic Research. Retrieved from http://www.nber.org/papers/w21655.

24. Schmidt, B. (2018). The humanities are in crisis. Retrieved from https://www.theatlantic.com./ideas/archive/2018/08/the-humanities-face-a-crisisof-confidence/567565/.

25. Harris Interactive. (2011). STEM perceptions: Student & parent study: Parents and students weigh in on how to inspire the next generation of doctors, scientists, software developers and engineers. Retrieved from https://news.microsoft

.com/download/archived/presskits/citizenship/docs/STEMPerceptionsReport
.pdf.

26. Deming, D.J., & Noray, K. (2020). Earnings dynamics, changing job skills, and STEM careers. *Quarterly Journal of Economics, 135*(4), 1965–2005.

27. Ferguson, R.W., & McPherson, M.S. (2017). Strengthen the student educational experience. Retrieved from https://www.amacad.org/publication/future-undergraduate-education/section/3.

28. Roberts, A. (2021). Driving? The kids are so over it. Retrieved from https://www.wsj.com/articles/driving-the-kids-are-so-over-it-11555732810.

29. World Economic Forum. (2021). Skills stability. (2021). Retrieved from https://reports.weforum.org/future-of-jobs-2016/skills-stability/.

30. Deming, D.J., & Noray, K. (2020). Earnings dynamics, changing job skills, and STEM careers. *Quarterly Journal of Economics, 135*(4), 1965–2005.

31. Kelly, K. (2010). *What Technology Wants.* Penguin Books.

32. Versus. (2021). Sony PlayStation 4 vs Sony PlayStation 5: What is the difference? Retrieved from https://versus.com/en/sony-playstation-4-vs-sony-play station-5.

33. Klein, Ezra. (2020). "We're in the climax of a movie": Tim Urban on humanity's wild future. Retrieved from https://www.vox.com/podcasts/2020/2/10/21131219/tim-urban-wait-but-why-ezra-klein-show-future-of-humanity-technology-ai-climate-change.

34. Hershbein, B., & Kahn, L.B. (2018). Do recessions accelerate routine-biased technological change? Evidence from vacancy postings. *American Economic Review, 108*(7), 1737–1772.

35. Manyika, J., Lund, S., Chui, M., Bughin, J., Woetzel, J., Batra, P., Ko, R., & Sanghvi, S. (2017). Jobs lost, job gained: What the future of work will mean for jobs, skills, and wages. Retrieved from https://www.mckinsey.com/featured-insights/future-of-work/jobs-lost-jobs-gained-what-the-future-of-work-will-mean-for-jobs-skills-and-wages.

36. Burning Glass Technologies. (2019). The power of transportable skills: Assessing the demand and value of the skills of the future. Retrieved from https://www.burning-glass.com/research-project/transportable-skills/.

37. Ibid.

38. IBM Newsroom. (2010). IBM 2010 global CEO study: Creativity selected as most crucial factor for future success. Retrieved from https://www.ibm.com/news/ca/en/2010/05/20/v384864m81427w34.html.

39. Burning Glass Technologies. (2019). The power of transportable skills: Assessing the demand and value of the skills of the future. Retrieved from https://www.burning-glass.com/research-project/transportable-skills/.

40. Ibid.

41. Heckman, J.J., & Kautz, T. (2012). Hard evidence on soft skills. *Journal of Labour Economics, 19*(4), 451–4.

42. Ibid.

43. National Research Council. (2012). *Education for Life and Work: Developing Transferable Knowledge and Skills in the 21st Century.* Washington, DC: The National Academies Press.

44. Duhigg, C. (2016). What Google learned from its quest to build the perfect team. *The New York Times.*

45. National Research Council. (2012). *Education for Life and Work: Developing Transferable Knowledge and Skills in the 21st Century.* Washington, DC: The National Academies Press.

46. Dyer, J., Gregersen, H., & Christensen, C.M. (2019). *Innovator's DNA: Mastering the Five Skills of Disruptive Innovators.* Harvard Business Publishing.

47. Ibid.

48. Santora, J. (2021). Patreon statistics: Users, revenue, top categories and more. https://influencermarketinghub.com/patreon-stats/#toc-1.

49. Leskin, P. (2019). American kids want to be famous on YouTube, and kids in China want to go to space: Survey. Retrieved from https://www.businessinsider.com/american-kids-youtube-star-astronauts-survey-2019-7.

50. Buffer. (2019). State of social: 2019 report. Retrieved from https://buffer.com/state-of-social-2019.

51. Slabakova, B. (2021). 23 gig economy statistics that prove it's not just a trend. Retrieved from https://capitalcounselor.com/gig-economy-statistics/.

52. Porter, T., Molina, D.C., Blackwell, L., Roberts, S., Quirk, A., Duckworth, A.L., & Trzesniewski, K. (2020). Measuring mastery behaviors at scale: The persistence, effort, resilience and challenge-seeking task (PERC). *Journal of Learning Analytics, 7*(1), 5–18.

4. Value Archetypes

1. Lahey, J. (2014). Why kids care more about achievement than helping others. Retrieved from https://www.theatlantic.com/education/archive/2014/06/most-kids-believe-that-achievement-trumps-empathy/373378/.

2. Sagiv, L., & Roccas, S. (2017). What personal values are and what they are not: Taking a cross-cultural perspective. In S. Roccas & L. Sagiv (Eds.), *Values and Behavior* (pp. 3–13). Springer.

3. Schwartz, S.H., & Cieciuch, J. (2021). Measuring the refined theory of individual values in 49 cultural groups: Psychometrics of the Revised Portrait Value Questionnaire. *Assessment.*

4. SI Staff. (2021). SI Exclusive: LeBron James explains his return to Cleveland Cavaliers. Retrieved from https://www.si.com/nba/2014/07/11/lebron-james-cleveland-cavaliers.

5. Patagonia. (2021). Environmental activism: Patagonia. Retrieved from https://www.patagonia.com/activism/.

6. Decoder with Nilay Patel. (2021). Recode decode: Rose Marcario [Podcast]. Retrieved from https://overcast.fm/+QLdtRp3a4.

7. Wyche, S. (2021). Colin Kaepernick explains why he sat during National Anthem. Retrieved from https://www.nfl.com/news/colin-kaepernick-explains -why-he-sat-during-national-anthem-0ap3000000691077.

8. Kasser, T. (2014). Teaching about values and goals: Applications of the circumplex model to motivation, well-being, and prosocial behavior. *Teaching of Psychology, 41*(4), 365–371.

9. Sherman, D.K., & Cohen, G.L. (2006). The psychology of self-defense: Self-affirmation theory. *Advances in Experimental Social Psychology, 38,* 183–242.

10. Crocker, J., Niiya, Y., & Mischkowski, D. (2008). Why does writing about important values reduce defensiveness? Self-affirmation and the role of positive other-directed feelings. *Psychological Science, 19*(7), 740–747.

11. Kasser, T., & Sheldon, K.M. (1995). Coherence and congruence: Two aspects of personality integration. *Journal of Personality and Social Psychology, 68*(3), 531–543.

12. Cohen, G.L., Garcia, J., Apfel, N., & Master, A. (2006). Reducing the racial achievement gap: A social-psychological intervention. *Science, 313*(5791), 1307–1310.

13. Cohen, G.L., & Sherman, D.K. (2014). The psychology of change: Self-affirmation and social psychological intervention. *Annual Review of Psychology, 65,* 333–371.

14. Cohen, G.L., Garcia, J., Apfel, N., & Master, A. (2006). Reducing the racial achievement gap: A social-psychological intervention. *Science, 313*(5791), 1307–1310.

15. Cohen, G.L., Garcia, J., Purdie-Vaughns, V., Apfel, N., & Brzustoski, P. (2009). Recursive processes in self-affirmation: Intervening to close the minority achievement gap. *Science, 324*(5925), 400–403.

16. Miyake, A., Kost-Smith, L.E., Finkelstein, N.D., Pollock, S.J., Cohen, G.L., & Ito, T.A. (2010). Reducing the gender achievement gap in college science: A classroom study of values affirmation. *Science, 330*(6008), 1234–1237.

17. Cohen, G.L., & Sherman, D.K. (2014). The psychology of change: Self-affirmation and social psychological intervention. *Annual Review of Psychology, 65,* 333–371.

18. Kasser, T., Rosenblum, K., Sameroff, A., Deci, E., Niemiec, C., Ryan, R., Árnadóttir, O., Bond, R., Dittmar, H., Dungan, N., & Hawks, S. (2014). Changes in materialism, changes in psychological well-being: Evidence from three longitudinal studies and an intervention experiment. *Motivation and Emotion, 38,* 1–22.

19. Cohen, G.L., Aronson, J., & Steele, C.M. (2000). When beliefs yield to evidence: Reducing biased evaluation by affirming the self. *Personality and Social Psychology Bulletin, 26*(9), 1151–1164.

5. Needs in the World

1. Liang, B., White, A., Rhodes, H., Strodel, R., Gutowski, E., Mousseau, A.M., & Lund, T.J. (2017). Pathways to purpose among impoverished youth from the Guatemala City dump community. *Community Psychology in Global Perspective, 3*(2), 1–21.

2. Ballard, P.J., Malin, H., Porter, T.J., Colby, A., & Damon, W. (2015). Motivations for civic participation among diverse youth: More similarities than differences. *Research in Human Development, 12*(1–2), 63–83.

3. Liang, B., Spencer, R., West, J., & Rappaport, N. (2013). Expanding the reach of youth mentoring: Partnering with youth for personal growth and social change. *Journal of Adolescence, 36*(2), 257–267.

4. Carlo, G., White, R.M., Streit, C., Knight, G.P., & Zeiders, K.H. (2018). Longitudinal relations among parenting styles, prosocial behaviors, and academic outcomes in US Mexican adolescents. *Child Development, 89*(2), 577–592.

5. Yeager, D.S., Henderson, M.D., Paunesku, D., Walton, G.M., D'Mello, S., Spitzer, B.J., & Duckworth, A.L. (2014). Boring but important: A self-transcendent purpose for learning fosters academic self-regulation. *Journal of Personality and Social Psychology, 107*(4), 559–580.

6. Grant, A.M. (2013). *Give and Take: A Revolutionary Approach to Success.* Viking.

7. Ibid.

8. Lum, T.Y., & Lightfoot, E. (2005). The effects of volunteering on the physical and mental health of older people. *Research on Aging, 27*(1), 31–55.

9. Stengel, J. (2011). *Grow: How Ideals Power Growth and Profit at the World's Greatest Companies.* Currency.

10. Schreier, H.M., Schonert-Reichl, K.A., & Chen, E. (2013). Effect of volunteering on risk factors for cardiovascular disease in adolescents: A randomized controlled trial. *JAMA Pediatrics, 167*(4), 327–332.

11. Magen, Z., & Aharoni, R. (1991). Adolescents' contributing toward others: Relationship to positive experiences and transpersonal commitment. *Journal of Humanistic Psychology, 31*(2), 126–143.

12. McLaughlin, K.A., & Sheridan, M.A. (2016). Beyond cumulative risk: A dimensional approach to childhood adversity. *Current Directions in Psychological Science, 25*(4), 239–245.

13. Lukianoff, G., & Haidt, J. (2019). *The Coddling of the American Mind: How Good Intentions and Bad Ideas Are Setting Up a Generation for Failure.* Penguin Books.

14. Freud, S. (2015). *Civilization and Its Discontents.* Broadview Press.

15. This does not include people who suffer from complex trauma, which is defined as ongoing and/or sustained trauma.

16. Ungar, M. (2018). Systemic resilience. *Ecology and Society, 23*(4), Article 34.

17. Lim, D., & DeSteno, D. (2016). Suffering and compassion: The links among adverse life experiences, empathy, compassion, and pro-social behavior. *Emotion, 16,* 175–182.

18. Klimecki, O.M., Mayer, S.V., Jusyte, A., Scheeff, J., & Schönenberg, M. (2016). Empathy promotes altruistic behavior in economic interactions. *Scientific Reports, 6*(1), Article 31961.

19. Von Dawans, B., Fischbacher, U., Kirschbaum, C., Fehr, E., & Heinrichs, M. (2012). The social dimension of stress reactivity: Acute stress increases prosocial behavior in humans. *Psychological Science, 23*(6), 651–660.

20. Lifton, R.J. (2012). *Death in Life: Survivors of Hiroshima.* University of North Carolina Press.

21. Tedeschi, R.G., & Calhoun, L.G. (2004). Posttraumatic growth: Conceptual foundations and empirical evidence. *Psychological Inquiry, 15*(1), 1–18.

22. Kübler-Ross, E. (1997). *Death: The Final Stage of Life.* Scribner.

23. Tedeschi, R.G., & Calhoun, L.G. (2004). Posttraumatic growth: Conceptual foundations and empirical evidence. *Psychological Inquiry, 15*(1), 1–18.

24. Stellar, J.E., Manzo, V.M., Kraus, M.W., Keltner, D. (2012). Class and compassion: socioeconomic factors predict responses to suffering. *Emotion, 12*(3), 449–59.

25. Baumeister, R.F. (2013). What is better—a happy life or a meaningful one? Retrieved from https://aeon.co/essays/what-is-better-a-happy-life-or-a-meaningful -one.

26. Strecher, V.J. (2016). *Life on Purpose: How Living for What Matters Most Changes Everything.* HarperCollins.

27. Ibid.

28. McGonigal, K. (2016). *The Upside of Stress: Why Stress Is Good for You, and How to Get Good at It.* Avery.

29. Gilbert, D. (2009). *Stumbling on Happiness.* Vintage Books.

30. Vohs, K.D., Aaker, J.L., & Catapano, R. (2018). It's not going to be that fun: Negative experiences can add meaning to life. *Current Opinion in Psychology, 26,* 11–14.

31. Tedeschi, R.G., Calhoun, L.G., & Groleau, J.M. (2015). Clinical applications of posttraumatic growth. *Positive Psychology in Practice: Promoting Human Flourishing in Work, Health, Education, and Everyday Life, 2,* 503–518.

32. Tedeschi, R. & Moore, B. A. (2016). *Posttraumatic Growth Workbook.* Oakland, CA: New Harbinger Press.

33. Sommer, K. L., & Baumeister, R. F. (1998). The construction of meaning from life events: Empirical studies of personal narratives. In P. T. P. Wong & P. S. Fry (Eds.), *The human quest for meaning: A handbook of psychological research and clinical applications* (pp. 143–161). Lawrence Erlbaum Associates Publishers.

34. Ibid.

35. Weissbourd, R., Batanova, M., McIntyre, J., & Torres, E. (2020). How the pandemic is strengthening fathers' relationships with their children. Retrieved from

https://mcc.gse.harvard.edu/reports/how-the-pandemic-is-strengthening
-fathers-relationships-with-their-children.

36. Hunter, I., McLeod, A., Valentine, D., Low, T., Ward, J., & Hager, R. (2019). Running economy, mechanics, and marathon racing shoes. *Journal of Sports Sciences, 37*(20), 2367–2373.

37. Pederson, E., & Lieberman, D. (2017). How gratitude helps your friendships grow. Retrieved from https://greatergood.berkeley.edu/article/item/how_gratitude_helps _your_friendships_grow.

38. Smith, A., Pedersen, E.J., Forster, D.E., McCullough, M F., & Lieberman, D. (2017). Cooperation: The roles of interpersonal value and gratitude. *Evolution and Human Behavior, 38*(6), 695–703.

39. DeSteno, D. (2018). *Emotional Success: The Power of Gratitude, Compassion, and Pride.* Houghton Mifflin Harcourt.

40. Feeding America. (2021). Hunger in America. Retrieved from https://www .feedingamerica.org/hunger-in-america#:~:text=In%202018%2C%2014.3%20 million%20American,live%20in%20food%2Dinsecure%20households.

41. United Nations Sustainable Development. (2021). Water and sanitation. Retrieved from https://www.un.org/sustainabledevelopment/water-and-sanitation/.

42. 2020 state of the nation's housing report: 4 key takeaways for 2021. (2021). Retrieved from https://www.habitat.org/costofhome/2020-state-nations-housing -report-lack-affordable-housing.

43. Gallup. (2019). More Americans delaying medical treatment due to cost. Retrieved from https://news.gallup.com/poll/269138/americans-delaying-medical -treatment-due-cost.aspx.

44. Mental Health America. (2021). The state of mental health in America. Retrieved from https://www.mhanational.org/issues/state-mental-health-america.

45. Anxiety and Depression Association of America. (2021). Facts & statistics. Retrieved from https://adaa.org/understanding-anxiety/facts-statistics.

46. Academies of Sciences, Engineering, and Medicine. (2020.) *Social isolation and loneliness in older adults: Opportunities for the health care system.* National Academies Press.

47. NORC at the University of Chicago. (2020). Historic shift in Americans' happiness amid pandemic. Retrieved from https://www.norc.org/PDFs/COVID %20Response%20Tracking%20Study/Historic%20Shift%20in%20Americans %20Happiness%20Amid%20Pandemic.pdf.

48. Bateman, M. (2019). Low-wage work is more pervasive than you think, and there aren't enough "good jobs" to go around. Retrieved from https://www .brookings.edu/blog/the-avenue/2019/11/21/low-wage-work-is-more-pervasive -than-you-think-and-there-arent-enough-good-jobs-to-go-around/.

49. Engle, J., & Tinto, V. (2008). Moving beyond access: College success for low-income, first-generation students. Retrieved from http://www.pellinstitute.org /publications-Moving_Beyond_Access_2008.shtml.

50. International Labor Organization (2020). ILO/SIDA Partnership on

Employment; Young People Not in Employment, Education, or Training. Retrieved from https://sustainabledevelopment.un.org/content/documents/26634 NEET_Sida_brief.pdf.

51. Pulliam, I. (2019). Six facts about wealth in the United States. Retrieved from https://www.brookings.edu/blog/up-front/2019/06/25/six-facts-about-wealth-in -the-united-states/.

52. Harvard T.H. Chan School of Public Health. (2020). Black people more than three times as likely as white people to be killed during a police encounter. Retrieved from https://www.hsph.harvard.edu/news/hsph-in-the-news/blacks-whites -police-deaths-disparity/.

53. Payscale. (2021). Racial and gender pay gap statistics for 2021. Retrieved from https://www.payscale.com/data/gender-pay-gap.

54. American Civil Liberties Union. (2021). ACLU news & commentary. Retrieved from https://www.aclu.org/news/civil-liberties/block-the-vote-voter-suppres sion-in-2020/.

55. International, WWF. (2021). Living planet report 2020. Retrieved from https://livingplanet.panda.org/en-us/.

56. The Guardian. (2019). "Worrying" rise in global CO2 forecast for 2019. Retrieved from https://www.theguardian.com/environment/2019/jan/25/worrying -rise-in-global-co2-forecast-for-2019.

57. World Economic Forum. (2021). The global risks report 2020. Retrieved from https://www.weforum.org/reports/the-global-risks-report-2020.

58. Climate Central. (2021). Top 10 warmest years on record. Retrieved from https://www.climatecentral.org/gallery/graphics/top-10-warmest-years-on -record.

59. Stengel, J. (2011). *Grow: How Ideals Power Growth and Profit at the World's Greatest Companies.* Currency.

60. Twenge, J. (2017). *iGen: Why Today's Super-Connected Kids Are Growing Up Less Rebellious, More Tolerant, Less Happy—and Completely Unprepared for Adulthood—and What That Means for the Rest of Us.* Simon & Schuster.

61. Pennebaker, J.W. (1997). *Opening Up: The Healing Power of Expressing Emotions.* Guilford Press.

62. Ibid.

63. Ibid.

64. Ibid.

65. Ramirez, G., & Beilock, S.L. (2011). Writing about testing worries boosts exam performance in the classroom. *Science, 331*(6014), 211–213.

66. Pennebaker, J.W. (1997). *Opening Up: The Healing Power of Expressing Emotions.* Guilford Press.

67. Nolen-Hoeksema, S., Wisco, B.E., & Lyubomirsky, S. (2008). Rethinking rumination. *Perspectives on Psychological Science, 3*(5), 400–424.

68. Tedeschi, R.G., & Calhoun, L. (2004). Posttraumatic growth: conceptual foundations and empirical evidence. *Psychological Inquiry 15*, 1–18.

69. Cohen, G.L., Garcia, J., Apfel, N., & Master, A. (2006). Reducing the racial achievement gap: A social-psychological intervention. *Science, 313*(5791), 1307–1310.

70. Pang, D., & Ruch, W. (2019). Fusing character strengths and mindfulness interventions: Benefits for job satisfaction and performance. *Journal of Occupational Health Psychology, 24*(1), 150–162.

71. Loveday, P.M., Lovell, G.P., & Jones, C.M. (2018). The best possible selves intervention: A review of the literature to evaluate efficacy and guide future research. *Journal of Happiness Studies, 19*(2), 607–628.

72. Yeager, D.S., Henderson, M.D., Paunesku, D., Walton, G.M., D'Mello, S., Spitzer, B.J., & Duckworth, A.L. (2014). Boring but important: A self-transcendent purpose for learning fosters academic self-regulation. *Journal of Personality and Social Psychology, 107*(4), 559–580.

73. SI Staff. (2021). Michael Phelps says he contemplated suicide in 2012. Retrieved from https://www.si.com/olympics/video/2018/01/19/michael-phelps -anxiety-depression-suicide.

74. Kaufman, S.B. (2020). *Transcend: The New Science of Self-Actualization.* TarcherPerigee.

75. Dutton, J.E., & Wrzesniewski, A. (2020). What job crafting looks like. Retrieved from https://hbr.org/2020/03/what-job-crafting-looks-like.

76. Ibid.

6. Relationships

1. Kotter, J.P. (1995). *The New Rules: How to Succeed in Today's Post-Corporate World.* Free Press Paperbacks. NY: NY.

2. Frankfurt, H.G. (2005). *On Bullshit.* Princeton University Press.

3. Rozovsky, J. (2015). The five keys to a successful Google team. Retrieved from https://rework.withgoogle.com/blog/five-keys-to-a-successful-google-team/.

4. Duhigg, C. (2016). *Smarter Faster Better: The Transformative Power of Real Productivity.* Random House.

5. Edmondson, A. (1999). Psychological safety and learning behavior in work teams. *Administrative Science Quarterly, 44*(2), 350–383.

6. Wanless, S.B. (2016). The role of psychological safety in human development. *Research in Human Development, 13*(1), 6–14.

7. Edmondson, A. (1999). Psychological safety and learning behavior in work teams. *Administrative Science Quarterly, 44*(2), 350–383.

8. Malone, C., & Fiske, S.T. (2013). *The Human Brand: How We Relate to People, Products, and Companies.* John Wiley & Sons.

9. Spencer, R., Walsh, J., Liang, B., Mousseau, A., & Lund, T. (2016). Having it all?: A qualitative examination of affluent adolescent girls' perceptions of stress and their quests for success. *Journal of Adolescent Research, 33*(1), 3–33.

10. Yeager, D.S., Purdie-Vaughns, V., Garcia, J., Apfel, N., Brzustoski, P., Master, A., Hessert, W.T., Williams, M.E., & Cohen, G.L. (2014). Breaking the

cycle of mistrust: Wise interventions to provide critical feedback across the racial divide. *Journal of Experimental Psychology: General, 143*(2), 804–824.

11. Umarji, O., Dicke, A.L., Safavian, N., Karabenick, S.A., & Eccles, J.S. (2021). Teachers caring for students and students caring for math: The development of culturally and linguistically diverse adolescents' math motivation. *Journal of School Psychology, 84,* 32–48.

12. Malone, C., & Fiske, S.T. (2013). *The Human Brand: How We Relate to People, Products, and Companies.* John Wiley & Sons.

13. Karcher, M.J. (2005). The effects of developmental mentoring and high school mentors' attendance on their younger mentees' self-esteem, social skills, and connectedness. *Psychology in the Schools, 42*(1), 65–77.

14. Spencer, R., Walsh, J., Liang, B., Mousseau, A., & Lund, T. (2016). Having it all?: A qualitative examination of affluent adolescent girls' perceptions of stress and their quests for success. *Journal of Adolescent Research, 33*(1), 3–33.

15. Liang, B., Lund, T., Mousseau, A., & Spencer, R. (2016). The mediating role of engagement in mentoring relationships and self-esteem among affluent adolescent girls. *Psychology in the Schools, 53*(8), 848–860.

16. Ibid.

17. Blattner, M.C., Liang, B., Lund, T., & Spencer, R. (2013). Searching for a sense of purpose: The role of parents and effects on self-esteem among female adolescents. *Journal of Adolescence, 36,* 839–848.

18. Liang, B., Spencer, R., West, J., & Rappaport, N. (2013). Expanding the reach of youth mentoring: Partnering with youth for personal growth and social change. *Journal of Adolescence, 36*(2), 257–267.

19. Zarrett, N., & Lerner, R.M. (2008). Ways to promote the positive development of children and youth. https://www.childtrends.org/wp-content/uploads/2014/05/2008 -11PositiveYouthDev.pdf.

20. Dunbar, R.I.M. (2017). Breaking bread: The functions of social eating. *Adaptive Human Behavior and Physiology, 3*(3), 198–211.

21. Chapple-Sokol, S. (2013). Culinary diplomacy: Breaking bread to win hearts and minds. *Hague Journal of Diplomacy, 8*(2), 161–183.

22. For more ideas, check out Pasricha, N. (2010). *The Book of Awesome.* Putnam.

7. School

1. Walker, R. (2006). The brand underground. Retrieved from https://www .nytimes.com/2006/07/30/magazine/30brand.html.

2. Smith, D., Schlaepfer, P., Major, K., Dyble, M., Page, A.E., Thompson, J., Chaudhary, N., Salali, G.D., Mace, R., Astete, L., Ngales, M., Vinicius, L., & Migliano, A.B. (2017). Cooperation and the evolution of hunter-gatherer storytelling. *Nature Communications, 8*(1), Article 1853.

3. Lakoff, G., & Johnson, M. (2008). *Metaphors We Live By.* University of Chicago Press.

4. Ibid.

5. Armstrong, A., Krasny, M., & Schuldt, J. (2018). Using metaphor and analogy in climate change communication. In A.K. Armstrong, M.E. Krasny, & J.P. Schuldt, *Communicating Climate Change: A Guide for Educators* (pp. 70–74). Cornell University Press.

6. Huang, S.C., & Aaker, J. (2019). It's the journey, not the destination: How metaphor drives growth after goal attainment. *Journal of Personality and Social Psychology, 117*(4), 697–720.

7. Ibid.

8. Hamel, H.R. (1963). Job tenure of American workers, January 1963. *Monthly Labor Review, 86,* 1145.

9. U.S. Bureau of Labor Statistics. (2020). Economic news release: Employee tenure summary. Retrieved from https://www.bls.gov/news.release/tenure.nr0.htm.

10. Viguerie, S.P., Calder, N., & Hindo, B. (2021). 2021 corporate longevity forecast: As S & P 500 lifespans continue to decline, fast-shaping "hybrid industries" create new risks and opportunities. Retrieved from https://www.innosight.com/insight/creative-destruction/.

11. Deming, D.J., & Noray, K. (2020). Earnings dynamics, changing job skills, and STEM careers. *Quarterly Journal of Economics, 135*(4), 1965–2005.

12. Ibid.

13. Fu, P., & Fox, M. (2012). *Bend Not Break: A Life in Two Worlds.* Penguin Books.

14. Lesser, E., (2020). *Cassandra Speaks: When Women Are the Storytellers, the Human Story Changes.* Harper Wave Publishing.

15. Campbell, J. (2008). *The Hero with a Thousand Faces* (3rd ed.). New World Library.

16. Wilson, T.D., Damiani, M., & Shelton, N. (2002). Improving the academic performance of college students with brief attributional interventions. In J. Aronson (Ed.), *Improving Academic Achievement: Impact of Psychological Factors on Education* (pp. 89–108). Academic Press.

17. Oyserman, D., Elmore, K., Novin, S., Fisher, O., & Smith, G.C. (2018). Guiding people to interpret their experienced difficulty as importance highlights their academic possibilities and improves their academic performance. *Frontiers in Psychology, 9,* 781.

18. Vogler, C. (1998). *The Writer's Journey.* Michael Wiese Productions.

19. Ibid.

20. Ibid.

21. Rowe, G., Hirsh, J.B., & Anderson, A.K. (2007). Positive affect increases the breadth of attentional selection. *Proceedings of the National Academy of Sciences, 104*(1), 383–388.

22. Bolte, A., Goschke, T., & Kuhl, J. (2003). Emotion and intuition: Effects of positive and negative mood on implicit judgments of semantic coherence. *Psychological Science, 14*(5), 416–421.

23. Fredrickson, B.L., Cohn, M.A., Coffey, K.A., Pek, J., & Finkel, S.M. (2008). Open hearts build lives: Positive emotions, induced through loving-kindness meditation, build consequential personal resources. *Journal of Personality and Social Psychology, 95*(5), 1045–1062.

24. Ibid.

25. Ibid.

26. Bailey, C., & Madden, A. (2016). What makes work meaningful—or meaningless. Retrieved from https://sloanreview.mit.edu/article/what-makes-work -meaningful-or-meaningless/.

27. Shanafelt, T.D., West, C.P., Sloan, J.A., Novotny, P.J., Poland, G.A., Menaker, R., Rummans, T.A., & Dyrbye, L.N. (2009). Career fit and burnout among academic faculty. *Archives of Internal Medicine, 169*(10), 990–995.

28. Koch, R. (2011). *The 80/20 Principle: The Secret to Achieving More with Less.* Hachette UK.

29. Bastian, B. (2018). *The Other Side of Happiness: Embracing a More Fearless Approach to Living.* Penguin.

30. The Official Licensing Website of Arthur Ashe. (2021). Quotes. Retrieved from http://www.cmgww.com/sports/ashe/quotes/.

8. Higher Ed

1. McGurran, B. (2021). 5 college application and enrollment trends to watch for in fall 2021. Retrieved from https://www.forbes.com/advisor/student-loans /college-application-and-enrollment-trends/.

2. Gallup. (2019). Half in U.S. now consider college education very important. Retrieved from https://www.gallup.com/education/272228/half-consider-college -education-important.aspx.

3. Barshay, J. (2021). Poll: Nearly half of parents don't want their kids to go straight to a four-year college. Retrieved from https://hechingerreport.org/poll -nearly-half-of-parents-dont-want-their-kids-to-go-to-a-four-year-college/.

4. Klebs, S., Nguyen, S., Fishman, R., & Hiler, T. (2021). One year later: COVID-19s impact on current and future college students. Retrieved from https://www.thirdway.org/memo/one-year-later-covid-19s-impact-on-current-and -future-college-students.

5. Goldstein, S. (2021). Nine out of 10 new jobs are going to those with a college degree. Retrieved from https://www.marketwatch.com/story/nine-out-of-10 -new-jobs-are-going-to-those-with-a-college-degree-2018–06–04.

6. Webber, D. (2021). Is college worth it? Going beyond averages. Retrieved from https://www.thirdway.org/report/is-college-worth-it-going-beyond-averages.

7. Carnevale, A.P., Cheah, B., & Van Der Werf, M. (2021). A first try at ROI: Ranking 4,500 colleges. Retrieved from https://cew.georgetown.edu/cew-reports /CollegeROI/.

8. Carnevale, A.P., Jayasundera, T., & Gulish, A. (2016). America's divided recovery: College haves and have-nots. Retrieved from https://cew.georgetown.edu /cew-reports/americas-divided-recovery/.

9. Ibid.

10. CEW Georgetown. (2021). Tracking COVID-19 unemployment and job losses. Retrieved from https://cew.georgetown.edu/cew-reports/jobtracker/.

11. Delbanco, A. (2012). 3 reasons college still matters. Retrieved from https:// www.bostonglobe.com/magazine/2012/03/04/reasons-college-still-matters/Dfav44 acJ8HpkU6Xu2D5CN/story.html.

12. Jaschik, S. (2018). The missing black students. Retrieved from https://www .insidehighered.com/admissions/article/2018/04/16/study-finds-undermatching -remains-major-problem-especially-black.

13. Patel, Neil. My biggest regret in life: Going to college. Retrieved from https://www.forbes.com/sites/neilpatel/2016/12/26/my-biggest-regret-in-life-going -to-college/?sh=6435afa71ac7.

14. Slide, C. (2011). 33 factors for how to choose a college. Retrieved from https://www.moneycrashers.com/factors-choose-college/.

15. Reid, K. (2018). Eduventures annual survey of admitted students examines the enrollment decisions of college-bound high school students. *Eduventures Research*. Retrieved from https://www.prweb.com/releases/2018/02 /prweb15202158.htm.

16. Saavedra, J., MacLeod, W., Riehl, E., & Urquiola, M. (2016). Why college reputation matters so much to students and employers. Retrieved from https:// healthpolicy.usc.edu/evidence-base/why-college-reputation-matters-so-much-to -students-and-employers/.

17. Rivera, L.A. (2015). *Pedigree: How Elite Students Get Elite Jobs*. Princeton University Press.

18. MacLeod, W.B., Riehl, E., Saavedra, J.E., & Urquiola, M. (2017). The big sort: College reputation and labor market outcomes. *American Economic Journal: Applied Economics 9*(3), 223–261.

19. Felten, P., & Lambert, L.M. (2020). *Relationship-Rich Education: How Human Connections Drive Success in College*. Johns Hopkins University Press.

20. Ibid.

21. Bensimon, E.M. (2007). The underestimated significance of practitioner knowledge in the scholarship on student success. *Review of Higher Education, 30*(4), 441–469.

22. Chambliss, D.F., & Takacs, C.G. (2014). *How College Works*. Harvard University Press.

23. Ibid.

24. Loury, L.D. (2006). Some contacts are more equal than others: Informal networks, job tenure, and wages. *Journal of Labor Economics, 24*(2), 299–318.

25. Gallup. (2013). State of the American workplace: Employee insights for U.S.

business leaders. Retrieved from http://www.gallup.com/strategicconsulting/163007
/state-american-workplace.aspx.

26. Ibid.

27. Ibid.

28. HERI. (2021). CIRP freshman survey. Retrieved from https://heri.ucla.edu
/cirp-freshman-survey/.

29. Gallup. (2021). The 2014 Gallup-Purdue index report. Retrieved from
https://www.gallup.com/services/176768/2014-gallup-purdue-index-report
.aspx.

30. Ibid.

31. Ibid.

32. Lambert, L.M., Husser, J., & Felten, P. (2018). Mentors play critical role
in quality of college experience, new poll suggests. Retrieved from https://thecon
versation.com/mentors-play-critical-role-in-quality-of-college-experience-new-poll
-suggests-101861.

33. Chambliss, D.F., & Takacs, C.G. (2014). *How College Works*. Harvard
University Press.

34. Fisher, J.F. (2018). *Who You Know: Unlocking Innovations That Expand
Students' Networks*. John Wiley & Sons.

35. Ibid.

36. Gallup. (2021). Forging pathways to purposeful work: The role of higher
education. Retrieved from https://www.gallup.com/education/248222/gallup-bates
-purposeful-work-2019.aspx.

37. Association of American Colleges & Universities. (2018). Employers agree:
College degrees are worth it. (2018). Retrieved from https://www.aacu.org/aacu
-news/newsletter/2018/september/facts-figures.

38. Chronicle of Higher Education. (2012). The role of higher education
in career development: Employer perceptions. Retrieved from https://chronicle
-assets.s3.amazonaws.com/5/items/biz/pdf/Employers%20Survey.pdf.

39. Bonet, G., & Walters, B.R. (2016). High impact practices: Student
engagement and retention. *College Student Journal, 50*(2), 224–235.

40. Ibid.

41. Kilgo, C.A., Sheets, J.K.E., & Pascarella, E.T. (2015). The link between
high-impact practices and student learning: Some longitudinal evidence. *Higher
Education, 69*(4), 509–525.

42. Gallup. (2019). Six college experiences linked to student confidence on
jobs. Retrieved from https://news.gallup.com/poll/246170/six-college-experiences
-linked-student-confidence-jobs.aspx.

43. Ibid.

44. Putnam, R.D. (2016). *Our Kids: The American Dream in Crisis*. Simon &
Schuster.

45. Lambert, L.M., Husser, J., & Felten, P. (2018). Mentors play critical role

in quality of college experience, new poll suggests. Retrieved from https://thecon versation.com/mentors-play-critical-role-in-quality-of-college-experience-new-poll -suggests-101861.

46. Cigna. (2021). Cigna surveys loneliness in America. Retrieved from https:// www.cigna.com/about-us/newsroom/studies-and-reports/loneliness-epidemic -america.

47. Ibid.

48. Nelson, S. (2021). *The Business of Friendship: Making the Most of Our Relationships Where We Spend Most of Our Time.* HarperCollins Leadership.

49. Holt-Lunstad, J., Smith, T.B., Baker, M., Harris, T., & Stephenson, D. (2015). Loneliness and social isolation as risk factors for mortality: A meta-analytic review. *Perspectives on Psychological Science, 10*(2), 227–237.

50. Murthy, V.H. (2021). *Together: Loneliness, Health and What Happens When We Find Connection.* Profile Books/Welcome Collection.

51. Baker, W. (2014). *United America.* Read the Spirit Books.

52. Lee, F. (2002). The social costs of seeking help. *Journal of Applied Behavioral Science, 38*(1), 17–35.

53. Brooks, A.W., Gino, F., & Schweitzer, M.E. (2015). Smart people ask for (my) advice: Seeking advice boosts perceptions of competence. *Management Science, 61*(6), 1421–1435.

54. Baker, W. (2020). *All You Have to Do Is Ask: How to Master the Most Important Skill for Success.* Bantam.

55. Ibid.

56. Ibarra, H. (2019). Lack of sponsorship is keeping women from advancing into leadership. (2019). Retrieved from https://hbr.org/2019/08/a-lack-of-sponsorship-is -keeping-women-from-advancing-into-leadership.

57. Ibid.

58. Gelman, A. (2013). The average American knows how many people? Retrieved from https://www.nytimes.com/2013/02/19/science/the-average-american-knows -how-many-people.html#:~:text=The%20average%20American%20knows%20 about%20600%20people.

59. Gonçalves, B., Perra, N., & Vespignani, A. (2011). Modeling users' activity on Twitter networks: Validation of Dunbar's number. *PLOS One, 6*(8), Article e22656.

60. Carnegie, D., & Cole, B. (2011). *How to Win Friends and Influence People in the Digital Age.* Simon & Schuster.

61. Titova, L., & Sheldon, K.M. (2020). Thwarted beneficence: Not getting to help lowers mood. *Journal of Positive Psychology.* https://doi.org/10.1080/17439760 .2020.1858339.

62. Aknin, L.B., Whillans, A.V., Norton, M.I., & Dunn, E.W. (2019). Happiness and prosocial behavior: An evaluation of the evidence. *World Happiness Report 2019.* Retrieved from https://worldhappiness.report/ed/2019/happiness -and-prosocial-behavior-an-evaluation-of-the-evidence/.

63. Toepfer, S.M., Cichy, K., & Peters, P. (2012). Letters of gratitude: Further evidence for author benefits. *Journal of Happiness Studies, 13*(1), 187–201.

64. Hutchinson, A. (2021). Twitter outlines the biggest tweet trends of 2020, including TV shows, sports, people and more. Retrieved from https://www.social mediatoday.com/news/twitter-outlines-the-biggest-tweet-trends-of-2020-including-tv -shows-spor/591773/.

9. Work (and the World)

1. Wallace, D.F. (2009). *This Is Water: Some Thoughts, Delivered on a Significant Occasion, about Living a Compassionate Life.* Hachette UK.

2. The World Bank. (2021). United States [Statistics]. Retrieved from https:// data.worldbank.org/country/united-states?view=chart.

3. Thomson Reuters Global Data. (2021). A decade of record job creation [Figure]. Retrieved from https://fingfx.thomsonreuters.com/gfx/mkt/13/873/871 /Pasted%20Image.jpg.

4. Burns, D., & Schneider, H. (2020). U.S. employment in the 2010s in five charts. Retrieved from https://www.reuters.com/article/us-usa-economy-jobs-graphic /u-s-employment-in-the-2010s-in-five-charts-idUSKBN1Z92AK.

5. Horowitz, J.M., Igielnik, R., & Kochhar, R. (2020). Trends in U.S. income and wealth inequality. Retrieved from https://www.pewresearch.org/social-trends /2020/01/09/trends-in-income-and-wealth-inequality/.

6. Desilver, D. (2018). For most Americans, real wages have barely budged for decades. Retrieved from https://www.pewresearch.org/fact-tank/2018/08/07/for -most-us-workers-real-wages-have-barely-budged-for-decades/.

7. Boyington, B., Kerr, E., & Wood, S. (2021). 20 years of tuition growth at national universities. Retrieved at https://www.usnews.com/education/best-colleges /paying-for-college/articles/2017–09–20/see-20-years-of-tuition-growth-at-national -universities.

8. Property Management. (2020). Average rent by year. Retrieved from https:// ipropertymanagement.com/research/average-rent-by-year.

9. KFF Health Affairs. (2020). Average family premiums rose 4% to $21,342 in 2020, benchmark KFF employer health benefit survey finds. Retrieved from https://www.kff.org/health-costs/press-release/average-family-premiums-rose-4-to -21342-in-2020-benchmark-kff-employer-health-benefit-survey-finds/.

10. Giridharadas, A. (2019). *Winners Take All: The Elite Charade of Changing the World.* Vintage.

11. Collins, C., & Hoxie, J. (2015). *Billionaire Bonanza: The Forbes 400 and the Rest of Us.* Institute for Policy Studies.

12. Twenge, J.M., Cooper, A.B., Joiner, T.E., Duffy, M.E., & Binau, S.G. (2019). Age, period, and cohort trends in mood disorder indicators and suicide-related outcomes in a nationally representative dataset, 2005–2017. *Journal of Abnormal Psychology, 128*(3), 185–199.

13. Coley, R.L., Sims, J., Dearing, E., & Spielvogel, B. (2018). Locating economic risks for adolescent mental and behavioral health: Poverty and affluence in families, neighborhoods, and schools. *Child Development, 89*(2), 360–369.

14. Spencer, R., Walsh, J., Liang, B., Mousseau, A., & Lund, T. (2016). Having it all?: A qualitative examination of affluent adolescent girls' perceptions of stress and their quests for success. *Journal of Adolescent Research, 33*(1), 3–33.

15. Saad, L. (2013). Americans say family of four needs nearly $60K to "get by." Retrieved from https://news.gallup.com/poll/162587/americans-say-family-four-needs-nearly-60k.aspx.

16. Howell, R.T., & Howell, C.J. (2008). The relation of economic status to subjective well-being in developing countries: A meta-analysis. *Psychological Bulletin, 134*(4), 536–560.

17. Kahneman, D., & Deaton, A. (2010). High income improves evaluation of life but not emotional well-being. *Proceedings of the National Academy of Sciences, 107*(38), 16489–16493.

18. Howell, R.T., & Howell, C.J. (2008). The relation of economic status to subjective well-being in developing countries: A meta-analysis. *Psychological Bulletin, 134*(4), 536–560.

19. Payne, K. (2017). *The Broken Ladder: How Inequality Affects the Way We Think, Live, and Die.* Viking.

20. Solnick, J.S., & Hemenway, D. (1998). Is more always better?: A survey on positional concerns. *Journal of Economic Behavior & Organization, 37*(3), 373–383.

21. Adjusted for 1997 dollars: original scenario was $25,000/$50,000 and $100,000/$200,000.

22. Luttmer, E.F.P. (2005). Neighbors as negatives: Relative earnings and well-being. *Quarterly Journal of Economics, 120*(3), 963–1002.

23. Cheung, F., & Lucas, R.E. (2016). Income inequality is associated with stronger social comparison effects: The effect of relative income on life satisfaction. *Journal of Personality and Social Psychology, 110*(2), 332–341.

24. Adler, N.E., Epel, E.S., Castellazzo, G., & Ickovics, J.R. (2000). Relationship of subjective and objective social status with psychological and physiological functioning: Preliminary data in healthy, white women. *Health Psychology, 19*(6), 586–592.

25. Kirkham, E. (2021). Most Americans can't cover a $1,000 emergency with savings. Retrieved from https://www.lendingtree.com/debt-consolidation/cant-cover-emergency-with-savings/.

26. Berbaum, J. (2020). Survey reveals spending habits during COVID-19. Retrieved from https://highlandsolutions.com/blog/survey-reveals-spending-habits-during-covid-19.

27. Access One. (2020). Facing loss of income and insurance, many Americans fear they are unable to afford medical expenses in 2021. Retrieved from https://www.accessonemedcard.com/2020/12/16/medical-expenses-patient-finance-report/.

28. Fottrell, Q. (2021). One in five American households have "zero or

negative" wealth. Retrieved from https://www.marketwatch.com/story/one-in-five
-american-households-have-zero-or-negative-wealth-2017-11-11.

29. Semega, J.L., Fontenot, K.R., & Kollar, M.A. (2017). Income and poverty
in the United States: 2016 (Current Population Reports 60–259). Retrieved from
https://www.census.gov/library/publications/2017/demo/p60-259.html.

30. Loudenbeck, T. (2021). Here's the income it takes for a family to be part
of the 1% in every state. Retrieved from https://www.businessinsider.com/personal
-finance/income-family-top-1-percent-every-state-2019-4.

31. Gold, H. (2021). Never mind the 1 percent. Let's talk about the 0.01
percent. Retrieved from https://review.chicagobooth.edu/economics/2017/article
/never-mind-1-percent-lets-talk-about-001-percent#:~:text=That's%20more%20
than%20seven%20times,annual%20income%20of%20%247%20million.

32. Schwartz, B., Ward, A., Monterosso, J., Lyubomirsky, S., White, K., &
Lehman, D.R. (2002). Maximizing versus satisficing: Happiness is a matter of
choice. *Journal of Personality and Social Psychology, 83*(5), 1178–1197.

33. Iyengar, S.S., Wells, R.E., & Schwartz, B. (2006). Doing better but feeling
worse: Looking for the "best" job undermines satisfaction. *Psychological Science,
17*(2), 143–150.

34. Schwartz, B., Ward, A., Monterosso, J., Lyubomirsky, S., White, K., &
Lehman, D.R. (2002). Maximizing versus satisficing: Happiness is a matter of
choice. *Journal of Personality and Social Psychology, 83*(5), 1178–1197.

35. Iyengar, S.S., Wells, R.E., & Schwartz, B. (2006). Doing better but feeling
worse: Looking for the "best" job undermines satisfaction. *Psychological Science,
17*(2), 143–150.

36. Crocker, J., Olivier, M.A., & Nuer, N. (2009). Self-image goals and
compassionate goals: Costs and benefits. *Self and Identity, 8*(2–3), 251–269.

37. Loyalka, P., Zakharov, A., & Kuzmina, Y. (2018). Catching the big fish
in the little pond effect: Evidence from 33 countries and regions. *Comparative
Education Review, 62*(4), 542–564.

38. McGhee, H. (2021). *The Sum of Us: What Racism Costs Everyone and How
We Can Prosper Together.* One World.

39. Zeitlin, M. (2021). Goldman Sachs is harder to get into than Harvard, Yale, or
Princeton. Retrieved from https://www.buzzfeednews.com/article/matthewzeitlin
/goldmans-analyst-program-is-harder-to-get-into-than-harvard.

40. Parker, A.M., De Bruin, W.B., & Fischhoff, B. (2007). Maximizers versus
satisfiers: Decision-making styles, competence, and outcomes. *Judgment and Decision
Making, 2*(6), 342–350.

41. Walker, S. (2017). *The Captain Class: The Hidden Force That Creates the
World's Greatest Teams.* Random House.

42. Ibid.

43. Rogers, K. Group Selection. Retrieved from https://www.britannica.com
/science/group-selection.

44. Ibid.

45. Atkins, P.W., Wilson, D.S., & Hayes, S.C. (2019). *Prosocial: Using Evolutionary Science to Build Productive, Equitable, and Collaborative Groups*. New Harbinger Publications.

46. Muir, W.M. (2013). Genetics and the behaviour of chickens: Welfare and productivity. In T. Grandin & M. Deesing (Eds.), *Genetics and the Behaviour of Domestic Animals* (2nd ed., pp. 1–30). Elsevier.

47. Mondello, M., & Maxcy, J. (2009). The impact of salary dispersion and performance bonuses in NFL organizations. *Management Decision, 47*(1), 110–123.

48. Breza, E., Kaur, S., & Shamdasani, Y. (2018). The morale effects of pay inequality. *Quarterly Journal of Economics, 133*(2), 611–663.

49. Cowherd, D.M., & Levine, D.I. (1992). Product quality and pay equity between lower-level employees and top management: An investigation of distributive justice theory. *Administrative Science Quarterly, 37*, 302–320.

50. Pfeffer, J., & Langton, N. (1993). The effect of wage dispersion on satisfaction, productivity, and working collaboratively: evidence from college and university faculty. *Administrative Science Quarterly, 38*, 382–407.

51. Walker, S. (2017). *The Captain Class: The Hidden Force That Creates the World's Greatest Teams*. Random House.

52. Cederholm, C.J., Kunze, M.D., Murota, T., & Sibatani, A. (1999). Pacific salmon carcasses: essential contributions of nutrients and energy for aquatic and terrestrial ecosystems. *Fisheries 24*(10), 6–15.

53. Duffy, R.D., Blustein, D.L., Diemer, M.A., & Autin, K.L. (2016). The psychology of working theory. *Journal of Counseling Psychology, 63*, 127–148.

54. Rudolph, C.W., Katz, I.M., Lavigne, K.N., & Zacher, H. (2017). Job crafting: A meta-analysis of relationships with individual differences, job characteristics, and work outcomes. *Journal of Vocational Behavior, 102*, 112–138.

55. Laschinger, H.K.S., Heather, K., Leiter, P.M., Day, A., Gilin-Oore, D., & Mackinnon, P.S. (2012). Building empowering work environments that foster civility and organizational trust: testing an intervention. *Nursing Research, 61*(5), 316–325.

INDEX